THE SOCIAL CONTEXT
OF CONDUCT

THE SOCIAL CONTEXT OF CONDUCT

Psychological
Writings of
Theodore Sarbin

Edited by
Vernon L. Allen
Karl E. Scheibe

PRAEGER

PRAEGER SPECIAL STUDIES • PRAEGER SCIENTIFIC

Library of Congress Cataloging in Publication Data
Main entry under title:

The Social context of conduct.

087895

    Bibliography: p.
    Includes indexes.
    1. Sarbin, Theodore R. 2. Psychology--
Philosophy. 3. Social role--Psychological aspects.
4. Psychology, Pathological--Social aspects.
5. Cognition. I. Allen, Vernon L., 1933-
II. Scheibe, Karl E., 1937-
BF38.S6   150 .1   82-473
ISBN 0-03-059716-1   AACR2

Published in 1982 by Praeger Publishers
CBS Educational and Professional Publishing
a Division of CBS Inc.
521 Fifth Avenue, New York, New York 10175 U.S.A.

© 1982 by Praeger Publishers

23456789 145 987654321

Printed in the United States of America

TO TED AND GENEVIEVE
WITH ADMIRATION AND AFFECTION

ACKNOWLEDGMENTS

The editors wish to acknowledge with gratitude the permission granted by the publishers of the following previously copyrighted articles for reprinting portions of those materials in this volume:

Self-reconstitution processes: A preliminary report. The Psychoanalytic Review, 1970-71, 57, 599-616. (copyright Human Sciences Press, 1971)

The transvaluation of social identity. In C. Bellone, Organization Theory and the New Public Administration. (copyright, Allyn and Bacon, 1980)

The present status of the mental illness concept. In A. Plog and W. Edgerton (eds.), Changing Perspectives of Mental Illness. (copyright, Holt, Rinehart and Winston, 1969)

Contextualism: The root metaphor for modern psychology. Nebraska Symposium on Motivation. (copyright, University of Nebraska Press, 1976)

Role theory. In G. Lindzey and E. Aronson (eds), Handbook of Social Psychology, 2nd edition. (copyright, Addison-Wesley Publishing Company, 1968)

On the distinction between social roles and social types, with special reference to the hippie. American Journal of Psychiatry, 1968, 125, 1024-1031. (copyright, American Psychiatric Association, 1968)

The mythic nature of anxiety. American Psychologist, 1968, 23, 411-418. (copyright, American Psychological Association, 1968)

PREFACE

The purpose of this book is to bring together in one place the most important essays and articles by Theodore R. Sarbin, formerly professor of psychology and criminology at the University of California, Berkeley, and currently Emeritus Professor of Psychology at the University of California, Santa Cruz.

Professor Sarbin's publishing career in psychology spans 40 years; his work bridges the areas of social, clinical, and cognitive psychology. From the beginning of his career, Sarbin's ideas and arguments have been highly original and challenging. Although his work is iconoclastic, it is consistently thorough and penetrating in its scholarship. His papers have been published in various sources over a long period of time, and have ranged across very diverse topic areas. A basic unity in the work is readily apparent, however, when viewed at a more basic theoretical level. We hope that this book will be the unique source for general access to the full scope of Sarbin's challenge to contemporary psychology.

This collection of conceptual papers consistently deal with issues of current and lively concern, and the discussions point to the directions that are likely to be taken by psychological thought for the remainder of this century. Professor Sarbin's list of publications contains at present about 150 items, among which are a number of truly seminal contributions on key issues in contemporary psychology. Reprinted in this book are 9 articles from this list (abridged when necessary to preclude overlap) and 6 papers that have not been previously published.

As the reader will see, the content of the book is quite broad topically. But at the conceptual level the material has a very strong coherence throughout. In an introductory chapter the editors provide some biographical material and place Sarbin's contributions in broader perspective. Introductory material is also provided by the editors for each major section; delineating central themes and referring to ancillary material should help provide continuity to the book. The selections have not been arranged in chronological order; in fact, the first chapter and the last two chapters represent Sarbin's most recent writings on two interesting areas that he has not directly addressed previously. In the first chapter on "contextualism," Sarbin consolidates his views on the major metaphysical and methodological premises on which modern psychology should be based; and to a remarkable degree the remainder of the book serves to illustrate these points in a variety of contexts.

The intended audience for this book consists primarily of psychologists—researchers, teachers, and practitioners. In addition, however, it should be of interest to social scientists generally (especially to sociologists and criminologists). The book would be appropriate for use in graduate and advanced undergraduate classes in psychology, although it is not intended primarily to be a textbook.

The editors of this volume are former graduate students of Sarbin's, and they have collaborated with him in writing and research. He has provided us with full cooperation and complete

access to material for preparing the book.   All the duties required in connection with preparing the book were shared equally
by the co-editors, and the order of editorship merely reflects
the vagaries associated with alphabetical listings.

Vernon L. Allen
Madison, Wisconsin

Karl E. Scheibe
Middletown, Connecticut

CONTENTS

THE SOCIAL CONTEXT
OF CONDUCT

INTRODUCTION: PROLOGUE, PERFORMANCE, AND APPRAISAL

I

This book of essays has the character of a visit. It is a visit to the work and thought of one man, Theodore R. Sarbin. Like most visits, some might think it too long and some too brief, depending upon the reader's point of view and the competing items on the reader's agenda. Like all visits, these essays surely must be conceded to provide a very limited sample of all that would be possible. We make scant attempt here to be representative and much less to be comprehensive. One reason is that Sarbin's work and thought continue apace; there is really no way of knowing what he will turn to next. The other reason is that his more than 150 published papers, books, and chapters in books defy synopsis because of their wide topical range. But if we have succeeded at all in conveying the intellectual flavor of Sarbin's thought, certainly the reader will find this visit to have a salutory effect.

Visits with Sarbin are fascinating because of his continual confounding of conventional expectations. The last two essays in this collection, on metaphor, are not the sort of analyses that psychologists ordinarily perform. On a recent visit to Wesleyan University, where he presented a colloquium outlining these chapters, he read to a cluster of questioners after the talk these lines from T.S. Eliot:
... And so each venture
Is a new beginning, a raid on the inarticulate
With shabby equipment always deteriorating
In the general mess of imprecision of feeling.
These borrowed words express the deep restlessness of a true teacher. As we will show, Sarbin's career has followed a zig-zag course among the provinces of psychology's subspecialties. The continuity of this course is established by his constant challenging of the traditional and the conventional within psychology. The thread of continuity for Sarbin, the psychologist and scholar, must be expressed in the delicate

1

combination of courage and humility that is captured in Eliot's lines. He has launched many new beginnings, many raids on the inarticulate. But with it all Sarbin has always had an acute sense of the precariousness of final explanations within psychology. He has shown an aversion to dogma, an awareness that the armamentarium of the psychologist is not made of hard steel but of inherently unstable language and concept. Renewals and reinterpretations are imperative, lest the psychologist be cut off from the richnesss of his subject matter by the rigidity and opaqueness of his thought. It is a point of intellectual morality to believe in the correctness of a current interpretation while at the same time recognizing that each position must in time be abandoned.

A few biographical notes will provide at least some context for enhancing the intelligibility of the intellectual moves that are described in his own essays. Ted Sarbin's life is a testimony to the possibility afforded by the United States in the 20th century for what the sociologists call upward social mobility. As a poor lad, born in Cleveland in 1911, he acquired a fascination for books. He attended a technical high school and acquired skills to make things with his hands--skills that he has continuously employed as he and his wife, Genevieve, have turned house after house into a special expression of good taste. He characterizes himself as a non-college bound youth who entered Ohio State University at the beginning of the depression because the fees were low, there were no jobs available anyway, and he had heard that one could have better job prospects with a college degree. So 1934 found Theodore R. Sarbin working as a "hasher" in a fraternity house at Ohio State to help with his expenses.

At Ohio State, Sarbin enrolled in a large introductory psychology class for which Frank Stanton, later to gain fame as the head of the Columbia Broadcasting System, was the teaching assistant. Stanton was impressed with Sarbin's informed and penetrating questions, for his fascination for books had led him to read well beyond the syllabus outline. Sarbin's precocity as an undergraduate led to his being singled out and employed as an undergraduate assistant in the psychology department. He finished the four-year course of studies in two calendar years and was elected to Phi Beta Kappa. Still, upon graduation, no job prospects beckoned, so Sarbin enrolled in an M.A. program at Western Reserve. After completing the degree work there in one year, he returned to Ohio State to enter the doctoral program in psychology.

By this time, Sarbin's appetite for psychology and for the academic life had truly been whetted. If before college he had no clear aspirations other than to find a way of earning a living in a hard world, his reading and the encouragement he received from professors for pursuing his ideas confirmed his interest in a scholarly vocation. Although his professors admired his abilities, they were cautious about his future prospects in the halls of academe, since antisemitism was a fact of life in American universities at that time. He was advised to enter an applied field of psychology, where institutional prejudices might be less limiting. Thus, he made a tentative decision to specialize in industrial psychology.

One of the major objectives of the industrial psychologist is to increase the scientific precision of personnel selection and placement through the use of psychological tests and interviews. In broad terms, this objective is also common to clinical psychologists who make prognoses and to counseling psychologists who base their advice on predictions of outcomes. Sarbin chose to examine in his doctoral dissertation the fundamental question of the ability of a psychologist to improve his predictions by the exercise of his intuitive powers, as opposed to a straightforward statistical or actuarial prediction based upon test results and biographical data. After completing the course work for the Ph.D. at Ohio State, he secured a position at the University of Minnesota counseling center, working under the guidance of E.G. Williamson. There he was able to compare the relative accuracy of predictions of grade-point averages of undergraduates using two sources of information: (1) test scores and rank in high school class combined in a regression equation and, (2) the same information plus all the other information in student files, which guidance counsellors were allowed to combine in any way they wished. Despite Sarbin's initial expectation that the clinical method would prove to be superior in prediction, the results showed no difference in the relative merits of the two procedures. Sarbin's demonstration introduced to clinical psychologists the specter of an unskilled clerk producing predictions that were demonstrably as good as the labored prognostications of the most sophisticated and highly trained theoreticians. That Sarbin's thesis struck a sensitive nerve is witnessed by the amount of controversy and subsequent research on the clinical versus actuarial prediction problem (see Gough, 1962; Kleinmutz, 1969; Meehl, 1954; Sarbin, Taft, and Bailey, 1960).

In all, Sarbin spent three years working at the University of Minnesota, returning to Ohio State in 1941 to defend his dissertation. These were very productive years, for Williamson impressed upon Sarbin the importance of publication; and by the end of 1941, Sarbin could list 21 items on his vita. Most of these publications deal with counseling methods and procedures in personnel work. A few years after completing the dissertation he published the results in the American Journal of Sociology and published a general theoretical treatment of the prediction problem in psychology in the Psychological Review. As auspicious a beginning as this may have been, however, Sarbin was not to assume a full-time academic position for almost a decade after completing his dissertation.

Before describing the beginnings of Sarbin's career as a clinical psychologist, it is necessary to note several major influences on his intellectual and professional development while he was a graduate student. His work on hypnosis, begun at Ohio State, was almost accidental. A fellow graduate student, J.W. Friedlander, asked Sarbin to assist him in a research project on hypnosis, since it was customary at the time for an observer to be present at all hypnotic sessions. This experience led Sarbin to collaborate with Friedlander in the development of an objective procedure for measuring susceptibility to hypnotic induction. The Friedlander-Sarbin scale, published in 1938, is the basis for the standard scale for hypnotic susceptibility now in general use--the Stanford Scale developed by Hilgard and Weitzenhoffer in 1963.

In terms of psychological theory, Sarbin was profoundly influenced in his graduate student days by the psychologist J.R. Kantor, then at the University of Indiana but a frequent visitor to Ohio State. Kantor's "Interbehavioral Psychology," with its twin emphasis on the emptiness of mentalistic terms in psychological theory and on the importance of interactive context in the determination of behavior, provided Sarbin with essential ingredients for developing his own thinking. The writings of the philosopher, Hans Riechenbach, provided Sarbin with a way of thinking about probabilism in psychology, and was later manifested in his cognitive theories as well as his conceptualization of the problem of psychological prediction.

Upon completion of the doctorate, Sarbin received two years of fellowship support from the Social Science Research Council (SSRC), spending a good portion of this time at the University of Chicago. It was there, in association with the Chicago school of sociologists, that Sarbin assimilated the work of George Herbert Mead, the progenitor of role theoretical ideas in American social science. Mead had been dead for ten years when Sarbin came to Chicago, but his spirit was still pervasive. This spirit was communicated to Sarbin most directly through his contact with the sociologist, Ernest Burgess. Sarbin also had a good deal of contact during this period with psychoanalysts and other psychiatrists. It is safe to say that the experience did not leave a strong positive impression about the critical intellectual performance of practicing clinicians.

In the latter part of Sarbin's SSRC fellowship, he received funds to visit several centers of clinical research and theory in the eastern part of the United States. He visited Henry Murray's clinic at Harvard and, later, J.L. Moreno's institute in New York. At Moreno's invitation, Sarbin prepared for the journal, Sociometry, his first theoretical paper on role theory. This paper, "The concept of role-taking," received a good deal of notice as an attempt to account for phenomena of hypnosis and psychopathology in role-theoretical terms (Sarbin, 1943).

At the conclusion of his fellowship period, Sarbin worked for a time at the Elgin State Hospital in Illinois, and later at a state school for mental retardates in Lincoln, Illinois. His experience at Lincoln was highly frustrating, because he received little support from the school's administrators for possible reinterpretations of psychopathology. Thus, he resigned the position at Lincoln after a few months and entered private practice as a clinical psychologist in Chicago.

His private clinical practice began in 1944, the year after the publication of an article with Julian Lewis reporting that hypnotic suggestions could cause a decrease in gastric contractions which simulated the effect of food ingestion. This article gained a good deal of public attention; it was reported by both The Readers' Digest and Life magazine. The resulting publicity was a boon to Sarbin's new clinical practice.

After little more than a year's practice in Chicago, Sarbin grew restless again and, at the suggestion of a client, moved his clinical practice to Los Angeles. Though successful, the clinical work resulted in a stronger conviction than ever that his proper vocation in psychology was in the academic world. Sarbin characterizes his period of clinical practice as a gap in his professional life. He was applying techniques (including hypnosis) that often enough produced the desired results, but which provided little satisfaction that the principles underlying either success or failure were understood. In 1947 he began to teach part-time at Long Beach State College. Satisfaction with teaching was such that he began to consider taking a full-time academic position. In May, 1948, Jean MacFarlane invited him to give a talk on role theory at the University of California at Berkeley. The talk was well received, and Sarbin was offered a one-year position at Berkeley, funded by grant money from the National Institute of Mental Health. In 1949 he was appointed Lecturer in Psychology and, in rapid succession, was promoted in rank, finally becoming Professor of Psychology in 1956.

Certainly the need to publish in the academic world was a stimulus to Sarbin's productivity. At that time it was unusual for a practicing clinical psychologist to have published more than a score of articles prior to obtaining the first academic position. The first few years at Berkeley produced a large number of significant new papers, including the Psychological Review article on hypnosis and a chapter on role theory for Lindzey's Handbook of Social Psychology.

During 20 years in the psychology department at Berkeley, Sarbin supervised more doctoral dissertations than anyone else in the department. In part, this is due to his areas of interest. Before Sarbin's appointment, the Berkeley department did not offer strong encouragement to students interested in personality, social or clinical psychology. But Sarbin's popularity as a thesis advisor and mentor can be attributed more correctly to two other characteristics: his tolerant range of interest, and his authentic concern for his students as people. Many of the dissertations he supervised had very little connection to Sarbin's own work; he never insisted that students must labor in the pits of his own mines. He was celebrated among students at Berkeley as a mensch--welcoming them to his home, celebrating their passages and triumphs by appropriate rites and ceremonies.

Several scholars with whom Sarbin had contact at Berkeley should be mentioned as having influenced the development of his ideas. In a real sense, Edward Tolman functioned for Sarbin, and also for the rest of the department, as a kind of role model until his death in 1959. Egon Brunswik also had a strong effect on Sarbin's thinking, particularly in the development of the idea of psychological ecologies. Sarbin had a close association with Erving Goffman, whose ideas on mental illness in many respects supported his own. Perhaps less conspicuous at the time was the influence of the philosopher Stephen Pepper, the distinguished authority on values. Pepper's little book, World Hypotheses, provided Sarbin with the key ideas for developing his own conception of contextualism, the result of which appears as the first essay in this collection.

In 1961-62, Sarbin spent a year at Oxford on a Guggenheim Fellowship. This period provided an opportunity for negotiating a real turning point in his own scholarly interests and writings. Sarbin's habit of reading very widely had aroused a desire to launch into new areas of research. In particular, he had read Logan Piersall Smith's History of the English Language and Gardner Murphy's analysis of the history of chivalry in his personality textbook. The year at Oxford, then, provided an opportunity for beginning what Sarbin and his students came to call Belletristic Psychology, several examples of which are included in this collection.

Sarbin was appointed Professor of Criminology and Psychology in 1966, a title that he retained until the end of his teaching career. He supervised a number of dissertations in the Berkeley School of Criminology, and became deeply involved in the theory and practice of jurisprudence. It was this work that led him to develop theoretical ideas on topics such as crime and danger.

Sarbin spent all of 1968-69 and the spring of 1974 at the Center for the Humanities at Wesleyan University. After the first period at Wesleyan, he returned to California--but not to Berkeley. He became Chairman of the Board of Studies in Psychology at the newly formed campus at Santa Cruz. He and Genevieve lived on campus, in the student dormitories; there they served as friends and counsellors to many undergraduates. Sarbin retired from his position at the University of California in 1976, very much at the height of his intellectual powers. He and Genevieve live in Carmel, California. At this writing, Sarbin's scholarly work continues unabated.

II

In this section we will attempt to identify some of the basic themes common to most of Sarbin's work. First, though, a point should be made about the nature of the selections for this book. In the interest of maintaining a fairly strong interconnection among the papers in the present volume, the selections do not represent all the areas in which Sarbin has worked. Empirical studies are also not included among the papers selected, but the reader should not leave with the erroneous conclusion that Sarbin did not engage in experimental research. On the contrary, he has always been an active empiricist as well as theorist, authoring or co-authoring a large number of experimental studies. More than one-third of the entries in his bibliographical listing are reports of empirical research. The majority of these studies focussed on issues in the substantive areas of role theory, hypnosis, and juvenile delinquency. In connection with these empirical studies several new methods and tests were devised that are worth mentioning. For instance, as a means of subtly measuring nonconformant behavior, a nonverbal instrument was devised called the "stick figures" test (Sarbin and Hardyck, 1955), which has been used in several other areas of research. Also, the "as if" test was devised to measure role-taking aptitude (Sarbin and Jones, 1956). An active involvement in problems of empirical research and methodology persists throughout Sarbin's career.

It may be useful briefly to describe the topical or substantive areas of Sarbin's work before proceeding with a more general discussion of underlying themes. Making a rigid classification of Sarbin's papers is impossible because of their overlapping membership across almost any set of categories that can be devised. By simplifying a great deal, however, the following main content areas appear to accommodate most of the work: (1) personnel selection; (2) clinical inference; (3) role theory and self; (4) hypnosis; (5) behavior pathology ("mental illness"); (6) deviant behavior and crime; (7) belletristic psychology.

As already mentioned, the earliest published papers by Sarbin dealt with personnel psychology; these were followed by reports based on his dissertation work, the clinical-statistical prediction problem. As we said earlier, the empirical findings and subsequent theoretical papers on the clinical-statistical prediction problems made an important contribution to the field. Sarbin argued that the so-called intuitive activity of the clinical psychologist was not qualitatively different from other logical methods used to arrive at conclusions. This early work constituted a strong and direct challenge to the confidence that clinical psychologists had placed in their diagnostic acumen. The questions that had been raised by Sarbin were debated widely in clinical psychology; for a number of years the clinical-statistical prediction problem was a very active one in psychology, and generated a great deal of controversy. Sarbin published his latest thinking on the topic of clinical versus actuarial prediction in the form of a book, Clinical Inference and Cognitive Theory, in 1960 (Sarbin, Taft, and Bailey, 1960). Sarbin's raw empirical work on the problem of clinical inference culminated in a very general theoretical treatment of the psychology of cognition. It was a treatment, so we may say, for which the world was not quite ready, for psychology had not yet entered the modern cognitive era.

The contributions made by Sarbin to a third topic, role theory, are very well known by social scientists. He was one of the first persons to import the idea of social roles to the domain of psychology and to use the theory effectively in research. Numerous experimental studies served to demonstrate to critics the utility of the role-theoretical approach to psychological problems. In addition to primacy in the application of role theory to psychological problems, Sarbin made important direct contributions to the theory in other ways. First, he systematized role theory and clarified its conceptual structure for psychologists. In Sarbin's (1943) first paper on role theory, he identified several factors that were hypothesized to determine the quality of role enactment (viewed as the outcome or dependent variable). In later publications these factors were further refined and supplemented by new ones. Introducing the dimension of self-role involvement greatly enhanced the usefulness and scope of role theory. The important concept of the self system was incorporated as an integral component of role theory by positing self-role congruence as one of the factors determining the quality of role enactment. Furthermore, a detailed theoretical analysis of stages of growth of self (the "epistemogenic" theory of self) was an important basic contribution to self theory in the tradition of Baldwin and Cooley (Sarbin, 1952).

Another topic area, hypnosis, is a problem with a long and fascinating history in psychology; it has attracted the attention of persons of the scientific stature of Wundt, Charcot, Braid, Freud, Binet, and Hull. Sarbin's name will certainly be added to this illustrious list of scientists in any future historical account of the development of ideas concerning the nature of hypnosis. If we may oversimplify somewhat by dichotomizing the position of current theorists about the nature of hypnosis into those who are "true believers" versus those who are "skeptics," then Sarbin would clearly belong in the latter camp. From his earliest writings, Sarbin has maintained that hypnosis can be explained without resorting to mysterious and mystical entities such as the "trance state." He has promoted the alternative view that normal psychological processes are sufficient to explain the phenomena occurring during hypnosis (which he sometimes calls "influence communication"). The alleged demonstration of "age regression" under hypnosis was disputed in one study (Sarbin, 1950b); and other research showed that findings of previous investigators were artifactual due to lack of appropriate controls (Sarbin and Andersen, 1963). One paper having important implications was a chapter in which Sarbin attempted to develop a satisfactory account of the effect of hypnosis on physiological responses (Sarbin, 1956). The most general theoretical contribution was, of course, the application of role theory to the analysis of "hypnosis." Sarbin argued that hypnosis could be considered to be a special case of role enactment; in numerous experiments it was shown convincingly that the variables that affected role enactment in general also affected hypnotic behavior--or enactment of the hypnotic role in the same way. Therefore, it is not necessary to appeal to mysterious concepts such as a "trance state" to account adequately for the behavior of an individual during "hypnosis." This view of the nature of hypnosis has been very influential, and has stimulated a great deal of research that supports Sarbin's point of view (Barber, 1969; Orne, 1959).

Various phenomena that can be subsumed under the rubric of "mental illness" form the focus for a considerable number of Sarbin's papers. Most of his work in this area consists of critical analyses of the general concept of "mental illness," and also of various subsidiary concepts such as "schizophrenia," "hallucination," "anxiety," and the like. For a long time the disease or medical model has been used to discuss deviant behavior. So thoroughly and unquestioningly was the disease model accepted, that its underlying assumptions were never laid bare. To Sarbin belongs a great deal of the credit in the struggle to move away from the medical model as a way of thinking about behavior. Although others sometimes offered broad critiques (Szasz, 1961) and interesting observational data (Goffman, 1961a), Sarbin exposed clearly to a critical examination the theoretical assumptions and historical origins of the medical model of behavior. Using the technique of historico-linguistic analysis with great effectiveness, he revealed in a series of scholarly and stimulating papers that several key concepts had their origin in metaphor--and were later reified. Published in a variety of books and journals, this wide-ranging attack upon entrenched thought models used in the diagnosis and treatment of behaviors labelled "mental illness" continues to exert a very significant impact on other workers in the field.

A large number of empirical studies have been conducted by Sarbin and collaborators on the substantive problem of juvenile delinquency, though none of these papers is included in this volume. Research in this area was stimulated by Sarbin's analysis of stages of the self, and the hypothesis that the self-system of delinquents was fixated at a primitive stage. This research later gave way in Sarbin's thinking to a more complex conceptualization of deviant behavior, in which explanatory variables were sought in the social or interactional context rather than exclusively in the internal dynamics of the self-organization. His interest in deviant behavior was further developed in the course of writings dealing with issues in criminology such as a criticism of the chromosomal explanation of crime (Sarbin and Miller, 1970) and the critical analysis of the notion of the criminal type (Sarbin, 1969).

Looking back over the total corpus of Sarbin's scholarly effort indicates that he has successfully surmounted the artificial barriers that are often erected between subspecialties: His intellectual forays have ranged widely across several subfields within psychology and have even extended into other disciplines as well. In spite of the range and diversity of this performance, perhaps it is still possible to detect some underlying motifs that appear to characterize the work as a whole. Identifying the recurrent themes may disclose that at a deeper level there are distinct strands that give coherence and continuity to the fabric as a whole.

One of the basic motifs that seems to animate Sarbin's work across several heterogeneous content areas is a general approach or frame of mind which for want of a better term might be called "informed skepticism." That is, he usually adopts a very critical stance toward a problem. As we noted earlier, Sarbin was influenced by the critical approach to psychology espoused by J.R. Kantor. Time and again in Sarbin's own work we see him attacking prevailing beliefs by taking the unpopular or anti-traditional--perhaps we should say "radical"--point of view. In a word, Sarbin has usually taken the iconoclastic rather than the conformist position. This was true, for example, with his position on the clinical-statistical prediction problem, hypnosis, and behavior pathology ("mental illness"), to mention some prominent examples. It cannot be said, however, that he, like Don Quixote, was merely tilting at windmills in the false belief that they were dragons; in the case of his targets the dragons were indeed only too real. Thus, his numerous critiques were always scholarly, analytic, and substantive in their thrusts, rather than simply offering criticism for criticism's sake. Moreover, alternative models or explanations for the phenomena or concepts being criticized were usually offered, along with some implications for research and reinterpretation of findings. Another way of characterizing this motif in Sarbin's work is to say that throughout his career he has been engaged in a campaign to "demythicize" psychology. Cited in one of Sarbin's publications is the following quotation from W.B. Yeats that expresses succinctly this sentiment: "Science is the critique of myths."

To continue the discussion of thematic elements at the level of theory, it is apparent that cognitive theory was a pervasive influence in Sarbin's work long before it became popular throughout psychology. Its most obvious presence is in the work on clinical inference and the subsequent comprehensive cognitive theory that was developed to deal more adequately with this problem. A direct excursion into cognitive theory is represented by the long scholarly essay that evaluated the "immediacy postulate" in philosophy (Sarbin and Bailey, 1966). To test the philosophic postulate of sensory immediacy the authors developed a cognitive model which was adapted from Brunswik's lens model. Use was also made of cognitive theory in several other areas as well. For instance, central to the theory of deviant behavior developed by Sarbin was the concept of cognitive strain and the associated adaptive mechanisms. Sarbin's version of role theory also possessed a strong measure of cognitive processes and concepts. In several other publications, it is obvious that the richness of thought and analysis owes a great deal to Sarbin's acceptance of a broad cognitive theoretical perspective to psychological phenomena.

Turning now to a more substantive level, another motif in Sarbin's work is the creative application of role theoretical concepts to a wide variety of behavioral phenomena. It seems that the perspective provided by role theory has served, in Sarbin's hands, as a particularly effective heuristic device for thinking about a variety of problems. The analysis of hypnosis shows the successful use of role theory very clearly, but it also has found application in research on imagination, critiques of mental illness, and elsewhere. The social identity model, which has been applied to several areas, was also an outgrowth of role theory. Other instances could be cited as well. Furthermore, the creative use of role theoretical concepts extends to empirical research as well. More recently Sarbin has called for a new "world-view" or metatheoretical position ("contextualism") which grows out of the dramaturgic perspective. In fact, it can be maintained that much of Sarbin's thought has proceeded from the "contextualist" world view, which he apparently possessed before he knew he did. Certainly he did not have the label for it until recently in his career. It is noteworthy that in the application of the role theoretical perspective to new areas the theory has often been expanded and enriched in the process. In Sarbin's hand the theory has not remained static, but has constantly undergone revision and reconceptualization.

Another motif that can be identified in Sarbin's work is a concern with problems of psychological change. Several papers have been addressed directly to the analysis of processes of change in social identity and in overt behavior. The paper on self-reconstitution processes (Sarbin and Adler, 1971) provided a detailed theoretical interpretation of the dramatic changes that frequently occur in situations such as religious conversions. A theoretical paper on the transformation of social identity,one on hypnosis (Sarbin, 1956), and one on social roles (Sarbin, 1964) also explicitly addressed the issue of producing change in self or in behavior. Less explicitly, the problem of change in self and behavior as well as in the social system were also discussed in several other publications. Thus, a concern with psychological change appears to be a recurrent theme that cuts across several different content areas.

Another theme can be detected in several papers that cluster naturally together around a set of interrelated concerns and techniques; this work represents a substantive area that can be given the sobriquet "belletristic psychology," alluding, of course, to "belles lettres" or literature. The major objective of this work is focussed on the level of language and concept. Skillful use has been made by Sarbin of the technique of etymological analysis in the critiques of outworn metaphors that still obscure problems in psychology. Going beyond the use of linguistic analysis to clarify concepts (e.g., "mental illness"), Sarbin has turned his attention more directly to substantive problems in belletristic psychology. Resulting from this new interest are the chapters on metaphors of death and psychology of metaphor which appear in this volume. The creative use of "belles lettres" for the purposes of psychology is represented in an essay expounding the implications of the "Quixotic Principle" for explaining imagination and social behavior. We can agree with Sarbin's comment in one of the papers in this belletristic group when he said that if the answers produced were not always convincing, at least it was certain that the right questions were being asked.

A theme that we would like to stress in Sarbin's work is his strong commitment to humanistic values. Throughout his work are reflected strong scientific and rational values, which can be seen in his rejecting mysterious explanations and criticisms of ambiguous concepts. His commitment has been to the values of science, however, not merely to scientism or to the trappings of science. And it must be the goal of science to increase the arena of our understanding; frequently he has aptly stated that the purpose of an essay was to "illuminate the dark corners" of a particular subject at hand. Furthermore, in many published papers he takes pains to point out the consequences of our current thinking and acceptance of the status quo in psychology for the people whose lives are being affected. If we had to characterize the basic assumption that he seems to hold about "human nature," it would be close to the contextualistic position, to wit, the belief that an individual's behavior is strongly influenced by the matrix of social forces in which he or she is enmeshed--a strong environmentalist position. The following statement appearing in a discussion of crime in one of his papers seems to reflect this point of view: "The solution to one of the most acute problems in contemporary society ... will be found in efforts to break up the systemic bonds whose origins are in historical processes, not in human nature " (Sarbin, 1969, p. 28).

A final characteristic of much of Sarbin's work is worth noting--that is, his ideas have often been ahead of their time. It would seem fair to make this statement in the case of the writings on clinical inference, hypnosis, and critique of mental illness. His present work on contextualism challenges the current assumptions of psychological theory in the area of human social behavior, and offers an alternative world view with associated implications for new methods and explanations. Perhaps this latest challenge to the status quo is also a harbinger of future paths that will be taken in the endless quest to increase our understanding of that "strange and wonderful" creature, homo sapiens.

We would like to conclude this introductory chapter on a personal note. Earlier, we mentioned some of the characteristics of Sarbin--the scientist and the person--that elicited enthusiasm, respect, and affection from his students. One of the most important characteristics was his ability to become excited about ideas, which in turn stimulated intellectual excitement in others. The importance of his delightful sense of humor in establishing an atmosphere of warmth and support cannot be overemphasized. But the credit for the collegial and friendly relationship established with his students--and that often persisted long after their departure--cannot be claimed by Ted alone. His wife, Genevieve, gained the affection of all the students with her unflagging cheerfulness and concern for their welfare. Her many acts of kindness will not be forgotten by former students. Both of them--Ted and Genevieve--have served for many of us as role models in science as well as in joie de vivre.

PART I
Contextualism

      This first section includes a single paper that was published originally in the 1976 Nebraska Symposium on Motivation. The paper served as the keynote address for that symposium, which was actually held in mid-1975. The theme for the symposium was the personal construct theory of George Kelly. In the part of the paper concerning Kelly's theory, it is argued that Kelly had approached but never quite achieved the contextualist world-view that Sarbin regards as most appropriate for modern psychology. While Sarbin's commentary on Kelly's theory is itself of interest, the most significant part of the paper consists of an elaboration of the meaning of the contextualist position for psychology as well as a spirited argument that this position demands a rejection of the formist and mechanistic world-views which have dominated scientific psychology in the 20th century. (In the abridgement of the paper, the Kelly material has been deleted.)

      Two comments are in order concerning the significance of this chapter in relation to the course of Sarbin's writing and research. First, Sarbin's early work is subject to the same criticism that he makes of Kelly--namely, an implicit adherence to the mechanistic world-view of science. Throughout the major portion of Sarbin's published work, one may identify the values and standards of science as supreme. This is evident in his efforts to defeat psychological interpretations that were based on mentalistic notions or upon mystical or formist metaphors. But the second point is that, like Kelly, Sarbin has been working toward the articulation of the contextualist position throughout his career, having already accepted it in a partial way. Sarbin's early importation of role-theory to psychology was an attempt, after the fashion of G. H. Mead, to make psychology more complete as a science of the person in society. But with the articulation of the contextualist position in psychology, Sarbin's work has taken on a much more challenging, even revolutionary character. Sarbin argues in this paper that the fundamental unit of analysis for psychology is "the historical event." The restoration of historical context is meant to achieve intelligibility for the psychological processes that have been artificially isolated by the demands of mechanistic science. But the placing of "the historical event" at the center of the psychologist's attention compromises dramatically the claim for the continuity of psychology with the natural sciences. Since the validation of this claim has been the major preoccupation of 20th century psychology, Sarbin's position represents a sharp break with an orthodoxy of which his own early work seemed to be a part.

The triggering event for the full development of the contextualist position by Sarbin was provided by a little book written in 1942 by the philosopher, Stephen Pepper. Pepper's contact with Sarbin occurred in the mid-1950's, when they shared some office space at Berkeley. This fortuitous encounter provided Sarbin with something like a road-map for territory that he had been exploring without such clarifying aid. It was some time, however, before the heretical consequences of this metaphorical map would become clear. The paper that follows is the result of that clarification. The result is a statement that appropriately stands at the forefront of Sarbin's contributions to psychology.

1

CONTEXTUALISM: A WORLD VIEW FOR MODERN PSYCHOLOGY [1]

The framework for this essay is drawn from a contribution to the history of metaphysics, the late Stephen Pepper's seminal work, World Hypotheses. Published in 1942, it has gone through many printings and has already achieved the status of a classic. Pepper employed a method of analysis called the root-metaphor method. In brief, he allocated the world views of philosophers to one of six classes: animism, mysticism, formism, mechanism, contextualism, and organicism. (The first two, animism and mysticism, he rejected as not having sufficient scope or communicable categories.) Each of the classes of world hypotheses is derived from a basic or root metaphor. The root metaphor operates to provide a frame for the analysis and understanding of occurrences in the natural and man-made worlds. The frame constrains the kinds of philosophical or scientific models to be applied either to the task of observation and experiment or to the hermeneutic task. The categories of analysis and the kinds of questions to be asked are similarly constrained by the choice of root metaphor.

Root metaphors reflect a common achievement of human beings: metaphor making. When a person is faced with an occurrence for which he has no ready-made category or class, the occurrence remains uninstantiated (unclassified, unassimilated, unidentified) until a class, category, or dimension is located. The recognition of similarity on some dimension (construct) provides the basis for analogy, and if linguistic translation is necessary, the partial similarity is expressed as metaphor. To say that the ruler of a state is a puppet of one of the superpowers communicates the analogy of political power. Once the metaphor is expressed by a speaker and decoded by a listener, the world of puppetry provides auxiliary metaphors, such as pulling strings, manipulating characters, the puppet stage, the script writer, and so on. Freud, as we all know, was a prolific metaphor maker. One of his analogies, that the human mind is like a hydraulic system, has enriched our vocabulary with such terms as repression and tension-discharge and has given a kind of scientific legitimacy to many of the presenting complaints recorded in psychological clinic files, such as "I feel like I'm about to burst with overwhelming anxiety," "If I don't get relief from this tension, I'll blow my stack," "My repressed anger is discharged in migraine headaches."

One feature of our facility in metaphor making needs special emphasis. As long as the metaphor is marked by clear context, emphasis, or the use of auxiliary modifiers, such as in the sentence "it is as if the psyche is a municipal water system," the interpreter of the human condition is free to create and use other metaphors. He may notice similarities between the occurrence of interest and familiar events other than those that supplied the vehicle for the initial metaphor. For example, the psyche (itself a metaphor-turned-myth) is a many-layered geological system; a tree with roots, trunk, and branches; a multi-stranded rope; a glazed pot; a computer; and so on.

For reasons that can be identified (Chun and Sarbin, 1970; Sarbin, 1968a), once a metaphor has done its job of making sense of an occurrence, the metaphoric quality tends to become submerged. In time, the metaphor takes on the characteristics of an entity, it becomes literalized, reified. One description of the reification of metaphor is provided by C.S. Lewis (1939):

> On the one hand, there is the metaphor we invent to teach by, on the other, the metaphor from which we learn. They might be called the 'master's metaphor' and the 'pupil's metaphor.' The first is freely chosen. It is one among many possible modes of expression, it does not at all hinder, and slightly helps, the thought of its maker. The second is not chosen at all; it is the unique expression of a meaning that we cannot have on any other terms; it dominates completely the thought of the recipient; his truth cannot rise above the truth of the original metaphor.

When a curious man or woman turns attention to cosmological questions, such as, "What is the substance of the world?", or, "What is the essence of creation?", or, "What is humankind?", he has no choice but to construct or invent a metaphor. In so doing he employs a master's metaphor and at the same time is on the way to a cosmological theory.

Anthropological and historical sources make clear that human beings create problems for themselves by asking cosmological questions. Pepper tells the story of Thales, the Milesian philosopher of the sixth century B.C., who puzzled about the nature of the world. He was not satisfied with current mYthological explanations. He made note of a "common-sense fact," water. As a resident of a maritime city, he was bombarded with the importance of water and entertained the hypothesis that water was the key to unlocking the secrets of all objects and events. After all, water covers large areas of the known world, it has multiple forms such as mist, clouds, fog and rain. It evaporates and condenses. Water is necessary to sustain life and its absence is equivalent to death.

Thales provided the master's metaphor. It was picked up and further developed by a series of pupils--water remaining the core of the pupillary metaphor. Pepper (1942) points out that the successor to Thales, Anaximander, regarded as incomplete the postulate "All things are water." "The substance of all things, metaphysical water, was not after all common water" (p. 92). The substance of all things was not only water, as usually perceived, but also all the phases, qualities, and forms of water.

The master's metaphor "The world is water" becomes the basis for a world view, a world hypothesis, a metaphysical system. Pepper employed root metaphor as a term to mark the master's metaphors for world views. Pepper summarized the root-metaphor method as follows:

A man desiring to understand the world looks about for a clue to its comprehension. He pitches upon some area of common sense fact and tries to understand other areas in terms of this one. This original area becomes his basic analogy or root metaphor. He describes as best he can the characteristics of this area, or, if you will, discriminates its structure. A list of its structural characteristics (categories) becomes his basic concepts of explanation and description . . . In terms of these categories he proceeds to study all other areas of fact . . . He undertakes to interpret all facts in terms of these categories. As a result of the impact of these other facts upon his categories, he may qualify and readjust . . . them so that a set of categories commonly changes and develops (over time). (P. 91)

The following is a brief abstract of the four root metaphors identified as relatively adequate by Pepper.

Formism is the term applied to views that stress the organization of the world on the basis of similarities and differences among entities. The formist concentrates on describing events by classifying. This world view is associated with Plato, Aristotle, and the Scholastics, among others.

The common-sense root metaphor of formism is derived from two sources: the activities of the artisan in fashioning different things on the same plan, such as a baker baking loaves of bread or a chandler making candles, and the observation of natural objects whose appearance follows the same plan, such as redwood trees, poodle dogs, ears of corn. Take a dozen loaves of bread. The baker has an ideal form or plan for the loaves. The plan is the implicit norm which the baker employs to shape each loaf. The norm may never be precisely fulfilled--but the loaves come out recognizably similar. The similarity is accounted for by the identity of plan. It is important to note that the norm is not fully revealed in the loaves, but transcends them. Norms exist in nature.

Exemplars of psychological theories flowing from the formist root metaphor are the turn-of-the-century structuralists and contemporary personality trait theorists. The first posited structures or dimensions of the mind; the second, structures or dimensions of the personality. I am indebted to White (1972) for pointing out the connection of the formist root metaphor to the underlying structure of the idiographic method. Gordon Allport (1937) gave currency to the term in his argument that the idiographic method provided a more valid portrait of the individual than the nomothetic method. Allport leaned on the historiographer Windelband (1921), who argued that the nomothetic, or rule-seeking, method was the appropriate method for Naturwissenschaften, the idiographic, or descriptive, method for Geisteswissenschaften, such as history and biography. In the following pages, I use formism and idiography interchangably.

Mechanism is the dominant world view in modern western civilization. The root metaphor is the machine. The kind of machine used as the underlying image may be a simple lever, a clock, a dynamo, a computer. Mechanism is the name given by some to a world view associated with such figures as Democritus, Lucretius, Galileo, Descartes, Berkeley, and Hume. The mechanist world view regards events in nature in terms of the transmittal of forces; modern science has been dominated by this world view, a view that supports the scientist's endless quest for causes. Cause and effect, sometimes rendered as antecedent and consequent or efficient causality, is the stock in trade of the scientist working with one or another paradigm within the world view of mechanism. Behaviorism in its many forms exemplifies the commitment to the mechanistic world view.

Contextualism, according to Pepper, might as easily be termed pragmatism. The world view is connected to the writings of C.S. Pierce, William James, John Dewey, and G.H. Mead. While formism and mechanism are analytic types of theories, contextualism is a synthetic type. The root metaphor for contextualism is the historical event. Not necessarily an event in the past, the event is alive and in the present. In this sense, history is an attempt to re-present events, to bring them to life again. The historic event, the event in actuality, is the dynamic dramatic act.

One would run the least risk of being misunderstood if one spoke only with present participles to illustrate the root metaphor of contextualism. Reference may be made to incidents in the plot of a drama or a novel--persuading a crowd, solving a mystery, performing a role, or diagnosing a disease.

Contextualism at first appears chaotic to those who have been schooled to use the idiographic or the mechanist world views. The categorical statements of contextualism assert change and novelty. Events are in constant flux; the very integration of the conditions of an event will alter the context of a future event which appears to have a similarity to a preceding event. The texture of an event, argues the contextualist, can be understood by noting the integration of the conditions of the event within the context of the event.

Piaget's theories of psychological functioning illustrate the use of a contextualist paradigm. Piaget (1954) has constructed category statements which attempt to define the cognitive activity of the person. These statements embody a conception of persistent change. In describing a psychological event, Piaget expounds a basic principle that any incorporation of the stimulus situation into a person's cognitive structures implies adjustments (accommodations). These adjustments alter the conditions that enter the context of seemingly similar future events.

Organicism is often referred to as absolute or objective idealism. It is associated with Hegel, Bradley, and Royce, among other philosophers. Organicism views the world as an organism rather than a machine. The philosopher or psychologist committed to organicism is concerned with understanding parts within wholes. The familiar cliche' "The whole is greater than the sum of its parts" is an organistic notion. To the organicist, every actual event is a more or less concealed organic process. Organicism directs us to engage in careful examination of an event in order to determine its organic structure - that is, in noting step-by-step growth and in recognizing the ultimately achieved organic structure. There is an ideal structure to be attained somewhere at the end of the progressive steps or stages.

Exemplars of this view among recent and contemporary psychologists would include Maslow (self-actualization), Rogers (personal growth), K. Goldstein (the organism), and several developmental psychologists who depend on the notion of stages of maturation.

Clearly, this has been a very rough sketch. In the analysis to follow, I shall make little use of the last-named world view. Although the root metaphor of the organism has not been completely neglected, its categories have been less widely used by personality psychologists than the categories of the other three world views.(2)

Dramaturgical Model and Emplotment

The historical event as the root metaphor of contextualism requires some further explication. The imagery called out by the historical event metaphor is that of an ongoing texture of multiply elaborated episodes, each leading to others, each being influenced by collateral episodes, and by the efforts of multiple actors who perform actions in order to satisfy their needs and meet their obligations. Contained in the metaphor is the idea of constant change in the structure of situations and in the positions occupied by the actors. Linearity is not intended.

In social psychology, at least two models have been constructed which can be cited as exemplars of the contextualist root metaphor: the field theory of Kurt Lewin (1935) and the dramaturgical model attributed to G.H. Mead (1934), and elaborated by Goffman (1959), among others.

Lewin's field theory influenced the development of one wing of modern social psychology. The language of physics--valences, forces, barriers, permeability--however, gave the model a mechanistic cast, especially with its quasi-mathematical equations. However, Lewin did bring into the purview of psychology the proposition that contexts such as group membership had to be included in the texture of an event. The group dynamics movement is one outgrowth of Lewin's field theory, a movement whose practitioners dropped the language of physics and willingly sacrificed precision for scope. The incongruity of the language of physics for describing ongoing social events no doubt contributed to the loss of interest in field theory. The physical science metaphors, providing mechanistic overtones to the theory, probably helped to influence some social psychologists of the 1940s and 1950s to seek general laws by taking their problems to the laboratory. As we know now from bitter experience, the yield from laboratory studies has been disappointing. The laboratory warranty of objectivity--of making experimental subjects into manipulable objects--could not be ratified. Only recently have social psychologists recognized that the meanings attributed to the laboratory situation are an important part of the context of the subject's performances. (See, for example, Orne, 1962.)

The dramaturgical model has acquired a large circle of adherents in the sociological wing of social psychology. George Herbert Mead, especially during the 1920s, influenced the prestigious University of Chicago social scientists. Large numbers of scholars employed the concepts of the drama as vehicles for understanding social behavior. Mead's concept of role-taking as the central unit of his system has continued to win adherents. The drama as a model of human action has face validity, at least, especially when we recognize that the drama is a vehicle for illuminating the recurring problems of human beings trying to make their way in imperfectly organized and changing social worlds. Central to Mead's system is the concept "taking the role of the other." This concept is patently contextual. Not only must the person take into account the role of the other in formulating his own actions; the role performances and the judgments made about such performances serve as building blocks for construing the self.(3)

The principal characteristics of the dramaturgical model may be listed as follows:

1. The dramaturgical model is a guide to the study of "meaningful" conduct. The meaning itself arises through interaction among participants; meaning must therefore be social.

2. The self, self-identity, the self of continuity, the recognition of individuality and of separateness of others, etc., does not arise sui generis but is constructed in social interactions.

3. Also, the dramaturgical perspective regards the participants in social interaction as actors. It is important to note that actors not only respond to situations but also mold and create them. In this respect the model is clearly not a mechanistically determined one--its propositions have a future reference.

4. The operations of a hypothesized Cartesian mind have no place in the definition of the situation. The units are not individuals, not organisms, not assemblages of traits, but interacting persons.

5. As episodes begin and end, human beings continually construct and reconstruct meanings to make sense of their observations of the performances of others and of self (Turner,1974).

This is not the place to present a detailed account of one form of dramaturgical model: role theory (see Sarbin and Allen, 1968). Suffice it to say that the observation of central interest is role enactment. It is appropriate to look for the strands that contribute to a particular role enactment. Among these strands are the actions of various reciprocal role players and of audiences.

In any drama a particular action of one actor can influence the actions of other actors. The influence is of course mediated by a plot, the features of which are constantly reconstructed as the result of the changing social identity of each actor. Rather than look for the causal connections between antecedent and concurrent events as demanded by mechanistic models, or for immanent causality as in formistic models, the contextualist looks for the method of emplotment.

In employing the metaphor of emplotment (the construction and elaboration of dramatistic plots) we are reminded of the as if quality of the drama. The theater-goer, as well as the participant in any social interaction, must be able to place an arbitrary frame around a given episode or scene to separate it from other episodes or scenes (Bateson, 1972; Goffman, 1974). (It was Kurt Lewin who popularized the expression "frame of reference" for psychologists.) In the theater, the framing is carried out by artifacts such as curtains, programs, costumes, makeup, seating, lights, and bells, and by conventions acquired by both actors and audiences. The construction of the frame supports the stage actor's role-taking, "It is as if I am King Lear," and the audience's complementary role-taking, acting toward the staged drama as if it were as credible as events in the commonplace world. In everyday behavior, frames have to be constructed, also for purposes of emplotment, in order to make sense of the complex of happenings of nature and the doings of persons. A clear-cut example of constructing a frame for social behavior is the shift from serious goal-directed activity to play. The message "This is play," no matter how delivered, whether by word, gesture, facial expression, or contextual marker, frames one scene from another. The communication "This is play" signals a particular context, the condition for special kinds of role enactment (Bateson, 1972; Miller, 1973).

How can we describe complex role enactments and the implied context in ways that would make sense to social scientists? So accustomed are we to thinking in terms of cause and effect that the mere suggestion of an alternate form of description invokes puzzlement, if not incredulity. The psychologist's image of a world bereft of causality is, to say the least, upsetting. Consider that the science of psychology was born into a world molded by the Newtonian laws of motion, weaned on Cartesian dualism, schooled in the transferral of forces implicit in motivational concepts, and confirmed by advocates of stimulus-response mechanics.

It would serve our purposes briefly to inquire into the concept of causality. In everyday speech and in the lexicon of science, causality is a taken-for-granted category. In dealing with the relatively stable world of objects, we have become accustomed to describing happenings in terms of antecedent happenings. Our familiar clockwork universe is a metaphoric description employing levers, wheels, screws, inclined planes, forces, and so on. Observations are replicable, and causal (functional) relations are discovered and confirmed. The utility of the root metaphor of the machine has given a broad warrant to the concept of causality. That the efforts of scientific psychology have been addressed to the uncovering of causality needs no documentation here. Since Helmholtz and Fechner, and probably before, scientific psychologists have sought to emulate the physical sciences in providing functional relations of the form: given stimulus condition A, response B is the inevitable consequence. Save in trivial situations, such functional relations in psychology have not been firmly established. An error term, usually large, remains. The error is assumed to be a reflection of the crudity of mensuration devices or sampling, and that with more attention to refinement of the variables under study the error terms would decrease, ultimately to zero.

Error is only one way of looking at discrepancies from prediction. There is another way of looking upon such events: situations are variable. Stimulus A is a condition for response B if conditions 1,2, . . . n obtain. Although multivariate design can in principle take into account such interactions, the fact of novelty and change induced by the interaction of the components in a behavioral formula renders such efforts futile.

Must we despair? Is there no alternate way of describing human actions? Perhaps we are at a historical junction not unlike the period when idiographic descriptions were challenged by the apparently more powerful mechanistic descriptions. I have already alluded to an alternate approach to describing human events, an approach that follows from the root metaphor of contextualism: the historical event. Human beings carry on their commerce with each other and with the natural and man-made worlds episodically. The episode, or to be more dramaturgical, the scene, is, to be sure, a multivariate scene, but in addition, a changing scene. The root metaphor of science--the machine--is feebly inappropriate as a trope to convey the complexity of human episodes and the effect of a constantly changing milieu. But episodes, scenes, acts--even lives--are describable without recourse to the immanent causality of forms or the transferral-of-force causality of the machine. I have already suggested that contextual description requires attention to actors engaged in reciprocal actions and that their developing actions can be epitomized as plots. In place of causality as the ultimate description of human action, let us look at emplotment. It is an alternate way of attaining a systematic description of episodes or scenes that has the warrant of long usage, if not the seal of science. The notion of emplotment provides us with at least minimal assurance that we can explore other possibilities before we surrender to chaos.

Is it possible to classify plots? Yes, if we work from the premise that the classification has limited purposes, such as understanding a relatively circumscribed event involving a limited number of actors. Such a modest aim will obviate one scholar establishing a presumably exhaustive list of plots and another scholar compiling a different list. With out modest aim, we are not likely to repeat the futile history of the hormic psychologists, each of whom advocated a different list of instincts as the ultimate explicanda of human action.

I have no firm catalog of plots to offer. The dramaturgic literature contains a suggestion for studying emplotment. Polti (1916) made a claim that there are no more than 36 dramatic plots. He supported his claim by analyzing the dramatic situation in 1,200 literary works, 1,000 from dramatic literature, 200 from other literary genres. The sample includes works from the Orient and the Occident, from the classical period, the Middle Ages, the Renaissance, the romantic revival, and modern times. Polti believed that the classification was useful beyond literature; "this investigation can and should be pursued in human nature, in courts of justice, and in daily life" (p. 11).

The metaphor employed by Polti is that of "emotions."
> There are in life but 36 emotions . . . there we have the unceasing ebb and flow which fills human history like tides of the sea; which is, indeed the very substance of humanity itself . . . 36 situations, 36 emotions, and no more. It is then comprehensible that in viewing on the stage the ceaseless mingling of these 36 emotions, a race or nation arrives at the beginning of its definite self-consciousness; the Greeks, indeed, began their towns by laying the foundations of a theatre. (P.9)

To illustrate Polti's method, I list a few of the plots.
> I. Supplication (dramatis personae: a persescutor, a supplicant, a power in authority whose decision is doubtful).
> II. Deliverance (dramatis personae: an unfortunate, a threatener, and a rescuer).
> IX. Daring enterprise (dramatis personae: a bold leader and an adversary, and a desired object).
> XX. Self-sacrificing for an ideal (dramatis personae: the hero and the "creditor" or the person or thing sacrificed, and the ideal).
> XXII. All sacrificed for a passion (dramatis personae: the lover, the object of the fatal passion, and the person or thing sacrificed).

To be sure, another cataloger of dramatic situations could compile a different list, one suggested by a metaphor other than emotions. My present objective is only to show that plots are, in principle, subject to taxonomic sorting.

Besides dramatistic literature, the classifier of plots may get some help from the folklorists. For well over a century, scholars of the folk tale have been engaged in taxonomic efforts. Aarne and Thompson (1964) and Thompson (1946) are the most frequently cited sources. Their efforts at classifying the world's folktales have been fruitful--at least, folklorists can communicate with each other through the use of a well-developed classification. If we assume that folk tales are not casual, capricious, or meaningless, but rather reflect episodes in the lives of human beings, then the modern psychologist's study of emplotment might be illuminated by the efforts of the folklorists. After all, we are interested in answering the same questions about the human condition as the folklorist: our raw materials are drawn from the actions of men and women trying to make their way in imperfectly organized and changing worlds; the folklorist's raw materials are the folk tales about men and women (or their symbolic equivalents) trying to accommodate to the same kinds of worlds. Shared by the actions of actors in folk tales and actors in contemporary real-life drama is the notion of plot.

Thompson (1946), in considering the numerous forms of oral narrative, such as fairy tales, legends, Marchen, novellas, household tales, sagas, and the like, remarks:

> We shall find these forms not so rigid as the theoretician might wish, for they will be blending into each other with amazing facility. Fairy tales become myths, or animal tales, or local legends. As stories transcend differences of age or of place and move from the ancient world to ours, or from ours to a primitive society, they often undergo protean transformations in style and narrative purpose. For the plot structure of the tale is much more stable and more persistent than its form. (P. 10)

In his systematic classification, Thompson employs type and motif. The type is a traditional narrative that "has an independent existence" (p. 415). That is, it requires no support from other tales in order to understand its plot. A motif is the smallest element in a story, an element that provides the conditions for persistence, must have something unique, striking, and unusual. Thompson says that most motifs can be sorted with a threefold classification: (a) actors, such as gods, witches, ogres, and conventionalized human social types like the cruel stepmother, the firstborn son, the favorite youngest child; (b) background items, such as magic objects, strange beliefs, and unusual customs; (c) single incidents. The third class of motifs can, of course, have an independent existence and become coterminous with a type.

Reference to the work on folk tales is only for the purpose of illustrating my claim that complex material, not unlike the accounts of everyday dramatic episodes, has been subject to systematic analysis. It remains to be seen whether we are creative enough to describe, for example, the functions of dramatis personae in everyday episodes as usefully as Propp's (1968) analysis of the functions of the dramatis personae in fairy tales.(4)

I point to another effort that may be helpful in constructing a taxonomy of plots. The late Eric Berne

(1964), operating from a contextualist stance, identified a number of "games people play" in their efforts to solve their problems. His choice of the language of games reflects the dramatistic, performing, acting features of human social conduct rather than the "exchange" features often associated with mathematical game theories.

The context for Berne's sorting was the psychotherapeutic transaction--but his descriptions of plots go beyond traditional psychopathological formulations. That Berne recognized "change and novelty," the central features of the historic-event root metaphor, is noted in the following quotation:

> The collection (of games) is complete to date (1962), but new games are continually being discovered. Sometimes what appears to be another example of a known game turns out, on more careful study, to be an entirely new one . . . The individual items of the analyses are also subject to change as new knowledge accumulates, for example, where there are several possible choices in describing dynamics, the statement given may turn out later not to have been the most cogent one. (P. 69)

He systematically employed a set of analytical categories, among them title, thesis, aim, roles, dynamics, examples, paradigm, moves, and advantages. His plot analyses drew their main descriptors from the run of attention of the actors, rather than from remote psychological or psychiatric theories. He coined colloquialisms to identify games, a word or a phrase that identified the plot structure. His classification includes life games, such as "Alcoholic," "Kick me," "See what you made me do"; marital games, such as "If it weren't for you," "Look how hard I've tried"; Party games; sexual games; underworld games; consulting games; consulting room games; good games. Each game is described in terms of the analytical categories, the composite description carrying most of the meaning of emplotment. Linear causality is eschewed in favor of looking upon human social actions as embedded in historical contexts.

Selected Illustrations of the Use of Contextual

At this juncture, I shall consider selected subject-matter areas to show how models developed from idiographic, mechanistic, and contextual root metaphors account for observations. Studies of schizophrenia, hypnosis, and imagination lend themselves to comparative formulations.

Before embarking on a discussion of these substantive areas, a word is in order about the propriety of comparing research models constructed from different world views. Pepper has argued that it is inappropriate to use the catagories of the root metaphor to evaluate the adequacy of another. Since the four world views are all reasonably adequate in terms of such criteria as scope and precision, the metaphysician need not concern himself with making comparisons, save to reject world views that have inadequate scope or precision. However, one may be interested in comparing the effectiveness of different models in acounting for processed data. Pepper would have been the first to point out that "data," that is, that which is given, may be differentially construed by the users of different modes. Most of us, recognizably influenced by the materialist or mechanistic paradigm, can in principle agree on the criteria for establishing what are data. In this connection, Pepper's position calls for "rational clarity in theory and reasonable eclecticism in practice." For intellectual clarity, he goes on, "we want our theories pure and not eclectic."

With a few notable exceptions, most of the work done on schizophrenia takes its point of departure from the root metaphor of the machine. In its simplest form, the disease "schizophrenia" is the consequent; the antecedent is biochemical abnormalities, neurological defects, genetic lacks, perceptual disorders, cognitive slippage, schizophrenogenic mothers, the double bind, inability to respond to censure, inability to hold a segmental set, or loss of the abstract attitude. If schizophrenia could be diagnosed in the same way as, say, pneumonia, then the carefully executed research of the past 60 years would have identified at least one causal agent. But--and this may surprise you--not one dependent measure has been identified that would allow a professional diagnostician to make a reliable diagnosis, in the ordinary sense of the term.

James Mancuso and I reviewed 300 research articles on schizophrenia published in the Journal of Abnormal Psychology and its predecessor, the Journal of Abnormal and Social Psychology (1958-1974). We selected this publication outlet because of its high standards. The usual experiment followed a simple model. The experimenter (usually a Ph.D. candidate) selected 30 to 50 schizophrenics residing in a mental hospital (usually a Veterans Administration hospital). The diagnosis was made by "two psychiatrists," "a psychiatrist and a psychologist," "diagnostic staff consensus," etc. For control subjects, he would enlist 30 to 50 hospital staff members, relatives, nonschizophrenic patients, and sometimes college students. Sometimes, but not always, he would try to match on demographic variables.

Then, drawing upon a theory derived from an apparently mechanistic metaphor, he would propose a hypothesis: the schizophrenics will do poorly on my experimental task when compared with the normals. The experimental task can be anything from guessing colors to solving syllogisms to operating a pursuit-rotor. Making use of his skills in experimental inference, the experimenter analyzes the data and, more often than not, discovers that the means of the schizophrenics represent poorer performance when compared with the means of the controls. In general, the mean differences are small. The experimenter concludes that schizophrenia is caused by whatever it is that is assessed by his experimental task. The purpose of all this work is to find an objective means of diagnosing schizophrenia; therefore, the experimental task should in principle be substitutable for the subjective judgments of the psychiatrists. But this is not what happens!

The overlap in distributions is so great that the use of the experimental variable produces an inordinate number of false positives and false negatives. A review of the distributions leads to the conclusion that most schizophrenics are like most nonschizophrenics.

The failure of the schizophrenia model is not difficult to locate, given the root-metaphor method. The experimenters begin at the wrong place, selecting subjects who have been through various bureaucratic, legal, medical, and nursing routines. The subjects have been removed from their communities for the alleged violation of propriety norms. The prepatient conduct may lead significant and powerful others to invoke the formistic concept "badness." A person who engages in "bad" conduct (residual deviance) finds his way to a mental hospital, where the moralistic label "bad" is illicitly converted to the scientific sounding label "schizophrenic." As mentioned before, eclecticism, combining the categories of formism and mechanism, leads to confusion. All the scientific apparatus of neurology, psychology, genetics, and the like cannot identify the implied immanent causality of forms, in this case the form of "badness."

Is it any wonder that, to date, not one hard scientific fact can be uttered about schizophrenia? The independent variable schizophrenia-nonschizophrenia is a moral judgment, and the dependent variable is a performance; the moral judgment requires the actions of another person. To focus only on the object of moral judgment, and not on the person making the judgment, speciously reduces the data for analysis.

Because we argue that schizophrenia is a myth, we are not ignoring the fact that human beings--all of us--sometimes violate propriety norms. We have become accustomed to speaking of deviant conduct. But the underlying metaphor is the historical event: the target person's actions and the moral judgments of relevant (usually powerful) others are both regarded as strands in the texture of the event. The case of the dissident Soviet scientist who is incarcerated in a psychiatric hospital makes our own "diagnostic" procedures more clear.

The contextualist takes as his unit, not schizophrenia, not improper conduct, not the rules of society, but as much of the total context as he can assimilate. His minimal unit of study would be the man who acted as if he believed he could travel unaided through space and the person or persons who passed judgment on such claims. Elsewhere I have spoken of the power of the ideological premises held by jurists and physicians who have the legitimate power to assign labels such as madness, psychosis, insanity, and schizophrenia (Sarbin, 1974).

In sum, the traditional mechanistic science of deviance has failed because its practitioners overlooked the fact that they were participating in a moral, not a scientific, enterprise (Sarbin and Mancuso, 1970).

The history of attempts to understand the conduct subsumed under the label hypnosis lends itself nicely to a discussion of the place of root metaphors. Since the scientific study of hypnotism goes back about 200 years, we would expect to find theories predicated on the root metaphor of the machine. Mesmer, for example, made use of animal magnetism, borrowing from the known properties of mineral magnetism. He posited the transmittal for forces via a subtle fluid to account for the counterexpectational conduct of his patients. Like many other theorists who followed, he made an eclectic slip by admitting formist categories. The "magnetic force" was a form, a natural gift, that was given to him and perhaps a few others. The "magnetic force" could not be accounted for by mechanical principles.

Theorists in the 18th and 19th centuries employed various eclectic combinations of formist categories and mechanical transmission. The claims of the 19th-century Nancy School were primarily concerned with antecedent-consequent causality and employed "suggestions" as the mechanical force. Their pronouncements made no claims for esoteric forms, preferring naturalistic common-sense explanations. Suggestibility, however, was not clearly defined. Not subject to categorization as a scientific, mechanical concept, suggestibility took on the character or a form.

At the same time, Charcot, in Paris, developed a theory of hypnosis using neuropathology as a model. Although working during a period of rapidly expanding neurological knowledge, knowledge that made the nervous system a medium for the mechanical transmittal of force, Charcot's theory of hypnosis was primarily formist. For him, it was in the nature of neuropathological patients to exhibit unusual behavior, and hypnosis was an artificially induced neuropathology.

Most contemporary theories of hypnosis continue the metaphysical eclecticism. Because of individual differences in response to hypnotic induction, a form, a trait, "hypnotizability," was posited. The record shows that the 50-year search for a psychometric test for hypnotizability has been futile. However, the methods of psychological science--the control experiment, sampling of subject populations, and so on--have been widely employed. The older mechanistic notion that "the hypnotic induction" was a prerequisite to the counter-expectational conduct is no longer viable. The same kinds of conduct can be produced by subjects who are "motivated," asked to imagine, or asked to simulate. Barber (1969), among others, has shown the influence of settings on role performance.

Until recently, the underlying notion of the hypnotic subject was that of a passive organism, a biological machine, so to speak. Contributing to the belief was the apparent automaticity of the subject's actions. Today, we know that the automaticity is apparent only -- that the subject performs in ways that meet the expectations of the role. The older descriptions made use either of immanent causality or of mechanical causality: this practice was implied as a consequence of regarding the behavior of the subject or client as a happening. Popular literature depicting mechanical puppetlike responses in passive women, the strings manipulated by a sinister Svengali, helped to fix the belief of hypnosis as a happening.

I invoked the dramaturgical model in the early 1940s and emphasized hypnosis as a doing rather than a happening. The conduct of the hypnotic subject can be seen as the enactment of a role. Anyone who has witnessed a clinical or experimental demonstration is aware of the dramaturgical possibilities. The most recent work takes into account not only the actions of the role-performer, but also the actions of the audience, including the hypnotist. It came as a surprise to some "scientists" that the conduct of a person reflects the subtle characteristics of his audiences (see Rotenberg and Sarbin, 1971).

Current research underscores the worth of the dramaturgical perspective. For example, the dramatistic possibilities of the laboratory, of the clinic, and of the nightclub are quite different one from the other. The performances of all the actors--subjects, hypnotists, and audiences--are influenced by the differential contexts. Hearkening back to my discussion of emplotment, it becomes apparent that different plot structures are represented when the dramatis personae interact with stage settings designed for ostensibly different purposes: scientific experiments, healing, and entertainment.

In a series of papers (Sarbin, 1967a, 1972; Sarbin and Juhasz, 1966, 1967, 1970, 1975; Sarbin, Juhasz and Todd, 1971) I laid the groundwork for an understanding of "hallucination." Historical-linguistic analysis, laboratory experiments, and clinical observation all converged on the conclusion that no determinant logical or psychological tests could differentiate one imagining from another so that one might be labeled hallucination.

The traditional views, based on formist and mechanist notions, was that hallucination was a product of a disordered mind, or the end result of biochemical, neurological, or psychic forces. Our research led us to the conclusion: hallucination is a term for which the definition is not content-free. The problem for the student of imaginings is not, What are the causes of a person's imaginings? but rather, What are the contexts that (a) encourage a person to report his imaginings, and (b) influence another person to regard a particular imagining as pejorative, hence, hallucination?

In the late 1930s and 1940s several attempts were made to apply stimulus-response models to the study of imagining. This was a blind alley. The claim that an "image" is a conditioned response has received no empirical or logical support. It was not until imagining was treated as actions, as doings, of actors that we could write a psychology of imagination. Here the dramaturgical perspective proved helpful. The actor can engage in conduct at various levels or "hypotheticalness." He can pretend, can engage in "as if" behavior, can play one part and then its reciprocal part, and so on. Not only can he engage in as if conduct overtly, but he can play his parts convertly. He can mute his actions. His hypothetical conduct can be enacted against a backdrop of hypothetical persons and stage props. The skill to operate at different levels of hypotheticalness frees the person from domination by the immediate environment and allows for action at a distance, not only in space but in time.

In order to illustrate the formist, mechanist, and contextualist approaches to imaginings, I cite several reference cases that would be called instances of imagining by most psychologists.

A three year-old child engages in animated play with a fictitious rabbit. She is said to have an imaginary playmate.

A novelist describes his work habits as having conversations with imaginary characters. This is often called creative activity.

A Plains Indian, after suitable preparation, ventures into the unknown and returns with tales of the supernatural. He is said to have had a vision.

Descriptions drawn from a mentalist (formist) model would approximate the following: the three-year-old plays with a rabbit, a replica of which is in her mind; the novelist listens to the conversation of his characters with his mind's ear (parallel to his mind's eye); the Plains Indian is hallucinating, is having a unreal or absurd or distorted image in his mind.

Descriptions drawn from a mechanistic model would be something like the following: the three-year-old has been conditioned to have a sensation of seeing a rabbit under precisely these circumstances, and to say that she is seeing it; the novelist has been conditioned to hear voices of his characters under precisely these conditions, and to say that he hears them, the Plains Indian has been conditioned to say under precisely these circumstances, "The Spirit of the Mountain spoke to me and said . . ."

Descriptions drawn from a contextual-dramaturgical model would approximate the following: the three-year-old child entertains the hypothesis that she is playing with a rabbit (the casual observer, on the contrary, might say she is playing with nothing); the novelist constructs hypothetical occurrences about his fictional characters; the Plains Indian solves an existential problem by forming the hypothesis that the Spirit of the Mountain is present, that he "sees," "hears," and "speaks to" the Spirit.

The serial descriptions of the reference cases contain the basis for continued dissatisfaction with the formist-mentalist and the mechanistic formulations of imagining. The descriptions in the language of hypotheticals appear to be most continuous with the data as seen from a common-sense point of view.

I have sketchily presented three areas of study with which I have been intimately involved. Like most of my contemporaries, I began long ago from a mechanistic metaphysic. I have discovered, sometimes unhappily, that the search for knowledge about people and their actions is unsatisfying when the starting premise is that man is a machine, subject to study the same as other objects that fit the machine metaphor.

Coda

Mine is not a lonely voice crying in the wilderness. I have plenty of company. More and more, contemporary psychologists are recognizing that the causal models of 18th- and 19th- century science are not fruitful. To illustrate, I point to papers by

Jenkins (1974), Cronbach (1975), and Gergen (1973).

Under the unforgettable title "Remember That Old Theory of Memory? Well, Forget It!," Jenkins (1974) has demonstrated how associationism, the principal category of the mechanistic world view, guided the work of experimental psychologists. In relation to learning and memory, the findings of numerous experiments are found wanting because of a failure to take into account the context. In fact, Jenkins reviews the data collected under the guidance of the associationist doctrine and concludes that the contextual view better accounts for the data than traditional associationism. This is not the place to review Jenkins' exciting paper--one sentence will communicate the thrust of his review: "what memory is depends on context" (p. 786). His contrast of associationism with contextualism is worth repeating. "Association (mechanism) asserts that there is one correct and final analysis of any psychological event in terms of a set of basic units and their basic relations. When you have reduced an event to these terms, you are through . . . The contextualist takes the much less comfortable position that a "complete" or "final" analysis is a myth, that analyses mean something only in terms of their utilities for some purposes. This means that being a psychologist is going to be much more difficult than we used to think it to be" (p. 789).

Cronbach (1975), for example, in updating his influential 1957 paper that identified "the two disciplines of psychology," had argued that research in psychology had been held back because of a historical schism between experimental psychology and the study of individual differences. The experimentalists manipulated variables, the observers of individual differences correlated variables. He recommended a crossbreeding, the issue of which would be a science of "Aptitude x Treatment Interactions" (ATIs). In his more recent essay, addressing inconsistencies in instructional research, he says: "Important as ATIs are proving to be, the line of investigation I advocated in 1957 no longer seems sufficient. Interactions are not confined to the first order; the dimensions of the situation and of the person enter into complex interactions. This complexity forces us to ask once again, should social science aspire to reduce behavior to laws?"

He documents the fact that, all too often, inconsistency is evidence of unidentified interactions. "Once we attend to interactions, we enter a hall of mirrors that extends to infinity. However far we carry our analysis--to third order or fifth order or any other--untested interactions of a still higher order can be envisioned" (p. 119).

Although his diagnosis of the plight of contemporary psychology is abundantly documented, he only hints at a solution. He recognizes that an untenable premise has served as the foundation of our research strategy: that psychological processes are perduring and can be isolated one from the other. From this premise, formal questions can be raised, to be answered by scientific experiments or by systematic observation to fill the cells of a correlation matrix. "Intensive local observation," Cronbach asserts, "goes beyond discipline to an open-eyed, open-minded appreciation of the surprises nature deposits in the investigative net. This kind of interpretation is historical rather than scientific. I suspect that if the psychologist were to read more widely in history, ethnology, and the centuries of humanistic writings on man and society, he would be better prepared for this part of his work" (p. 125).

In a concisely written article, "Social Psychology as History," Gergen (1973) arrives at a conclusion that would be congenial to Cronbach's position, quoted above. The thrust of Gergen's argument is that theories of social behavior that guide the search for antecedent-consequent causality are primarily reflections of contemporary history. The scientific search for the authoritarian personality, for example, was a response to a historically engendered interest in the personal attributes of fascists. Gergen points to the interaction of historically generated research and actions taken by people in response to that research. People who are "psychologically enlightened" may react to promulgated scientific findings by intentionally engaging in conduct that would contradict, ignore, or conform to such findings. Making public the results of scientific research introduces "change and novelty," a condition with which mechanistic science cannot cope.

Gergen concludes that social scientists are essentially engaged in a systematic account of contemporary affairs, not in the search for the ultimate dimensions for a social science. He offers a prescription for a historical science of social behavior in the form of five alterations to present practice. When examined and distilled, the contents of the paragraphs that describe these alterations--in the language of the present paper--are critical of those operations that flow from the mechanistic world view. Gergen's arguments fit nicely into the proposition: the root metaphor of the historical event is likely to engender models for a more complete understanding of concrete contemporary human and social problems.

Models that flow from the root metaphor of contextualism may appear to reflect chaos--especially to the mechanistically inclined. The latter tries to avoid chaos by simplifying the object of study, by fragmentation, by ecological impoverishment, and by striving for replicability. But chaos is a relative term. Episodes in a drama might appear chaotic to a scientist who looks at the blurred actors through an out-of-focus high-powered microscope. But the human condition must be lived in episodes that are not arbitrarily simplified, fragmented, ecologically impoverished, or replicable.

As I said before, continual change and novelty are fundamental aspects of the dramaturgical model. From my perspective, continual change and novelty are fundamental to the set of facts that need to be ordered into descriptions of human conduct.

Are we compelled to adopt the historical event as the root metaphor for making sense of the world? Are we ready to heed the contextualist's overriding emphasis on novelty and change? William James once argued that "Each step (that persons or collectivities) make brings unforeseen chances into sight, and shuts out older vistas, and the specifications of the general purpose have to be daily changed." Here is a nicely phrased statement that points to the "novelty and change" feature of the contextualist world view. No documentation is required to support the fact that the success of a purposive action only churns up new sources of strain, new conflicts to be dissolved.(5)

In their efforts to construct actions to serve their values, men and women alter their contexts and find themselves in worlds that are ever renewing. Earlier dramatists invoked the formistic concept of fate to explain the observation that the intentions of human beings result in unforeseen and unwanted outcomes, in unintended consequences. Although useful to the Greek playwrights, fate is not likely to be restored as a model of causality in the contemporary world. More recently developed psychological models based on the root metaphor of the machine are not designed to deal with novelty and change. It is my belief that no aesthetically satisfying account of the human condition can be constructed without taking into account the continually changing texture of events. Our job now is to find a way of satisfying our need to describe how people live their lives. Since neither fate nor mechanical causality are convincing descriptions, we are directed to seeking other ways of describing contexts. As a start I suggest we seek enlightenment from the efforts of dramatists, novelists, and other observers who view life as theater. Their success as portrayers of the human condition lies in their ability to construct plots, narratives that hang together. The magnitude of the task may be greater than our resources: but I see no place for psychology in the modern world unless we turn our attention and our creative talents to the study of emplotment. Our goals should be modest. The gigantic scientific feats of Newton, Linnaeus, and Mendeleev should be put aside as models to be emulated. Instead, let us deal with the human condition as we find it: in ever changing, ever renewing drama.

Footnotes

1. Abridged from The Nebrska Symposium on Motivation, 1977, 1-41. The notes for this paper were originally prepared during my tenure as a visiting fellow of the Center for the Humanities, Wesleyan University, Spring, 1975.
2. J.D. Laird and M. Bethel (1974) of Clark University have constructed a personality assessment scale based on Pepper's four relatively adequate metaphysical systems. Individuals are given scores in terms of their preferences for explanations of everyday events. Preliminary data seem to suggest that such metaphysical preferences are relatively firm. Laird and Bethel are also presently investigating demographic and other correlates of world hypotheses preferences.
3. Lyman and Scott, in The Drama of Social Reality (1975), compare Freud, Mead, and Goffman, all of whom employed dramatistic metaphors. They point out that Freud's dramas are peopled by such allegorical characters as id, ego, and

superego, and the actions are carried out on a psychic stage. In short, an individual is de-composed into psychic components, and these become the dramatis personae for a "monodrama." Freud's use of dramatistic metaphors is compared with Mead's and Goffman's. In comparing Freud to Mead, Lyman and Scott hold that Mead conceived of psychological acts in a more complex way: "generalized monodrama and specific naturalistic dramas." The monodrama has but two actors, the well-known "I" and "me". The naturalistic dramas are essentially rehearsals and recollections of actual performances in social life. Lyman and Scott comment on these rehearsals, "they stand in relation to an actual performance as a pre-text stands to a text. They are models of and for action" (p. 103).

Goffman's dramaturgy is different in that the performances are not in people's heads but in public places. His analysis (1959) suggests that people, not mental objects, entertain the dramaturgical perspective in their efforts to solve everyday problems arising from the demands of social life.

A complete psychology, of course, would find all three dramatistic perspectives useful in uncovering the plot structure of an episode.

4. Colby (1970) has enlisted the aid of computers to investigate regularities in narrative patterns. By identifying frequencies of occurrences of selected classes of words, he was able to point to cultural differences in narrative patterns. Contributions of this type may suggest additional approaches to the study of emplotment.

5. At another time, I hope to amplify this proposition, incorporating additional arguments based on dialectical theory. Burke (1945) and Riegel (1975), among others, offer penetrating dialectical analyses. Another helpful source is Turner (1974), who sees social dramas as arising in conflict situations. He identifies four phases of public action in such social dramas: (a) breach of norm-regulated social relations; (b) crisis; (c) redressive action; and (d) reintegration. The fact of reintegration does not imply statis, nor even a value judgment about societal equilibrium. Borrowing from W.H. Auden, Turner advises us "to learn to think of societies as continually 'flowing' as a 'dangerous tide . . . that never stops or dies . . . And held one moment burns the hand'" (p. 37).

PART II
Modern
Role Theory

    This section consists of two papers that are representative of Sarbin's contributions to the conceptual development and the practical application of the theory of social roles. Sarbin's interest in social roles was first aroused when he was a Social Science Research Council postdoctoral fellow at the University of Chicago, where the intellectual legacy of G.H. Mead still exerted a powerful influence. Sarbin's first paper on role theory was published in Sociometry in 1943, in response to an invitation from J.L. Moreno. In this paper an attempt was made to identify in a systematic manner some of the important variables that influence the enactment of a social role. That the variables discussed in that seminal paper are of crucial importance is demonstrated by their successful use in later empirical and theoretical work.

    The theory of social roles employs the metaphor of the drama to represent the complexities of social behavior in everyday life. Role theory is a very promising orientation for interpreting complex social behavior, since it uses concepts taken from the cultural, societal, and the individual levels. In Sarbin's hands role theory has been developed in an impressively rich and variegated way, yet always in conjunction with relevant empirical studies that were inspired by theoretical advances.

    In 1954 Sarbin integrated his theoretical ideas and empirical research in a chapter published in the Handbook of Social Psychology. The chapter was revised in 1968, and appears in abridged form as the first article in this section. Role enactment is focussed upon as the social behavior of primary theoretical interest; the dimensions along which role enactment may vary are discussed, with particular attention being devoted to the dimension of organismic involvement. Six major variables are posited as determining the effectiveness of role enactment: role expectations, role location, role demands, role skills, self-role congruence, and the audience.

The second selection in this section illustrates the fruitfulness with which Sarbin has applied role theory to other problem areas. In this paper a distinction is made between social roles and social (or folk) types, the latter developing from stylistic variations in the behavior of persons who occupy undifferentiated positions in a society. The concept of social types affords a conceptual bridge between the individual and society by providing a pool of recruits which are needed when new positions appear. Thus, the concept of social types can be used as a linkage between role theory and social change. In illustrating the utility of these concepts, Sarbin notes that the folk type "hippie" enables certain individuals to establish a social identity, and he speculates about the ultimate historical fate of this social type.

It will be obvious to the reader of this book that the theory of social roles has served as an important intellectual resource to draw upon in Sarbin's work in other areas such as hypnosis, social identity, and deviant conduct. As indicated by the two selections in this section, he has enriched the theory of social roles and has applied the basic orientation most creatively and fruitfully to a wide range of problems.

2

ROLE THEORY [1]

Role, a term borrowed directly from the theater, is a metaphor intended to denote that conduct adheres to certain "parts" (or positions) rather than to the players who read or recite them. In the semantics of the word "role" there is a historical continuity not usually found associated with words in psychological vocabularies. The current term developed out of several earlier forms, roll, rolle, and rowle, the reference for which was a sheet of parchment turned around a small wooden roller (Lat. rotula) for convenience of handling. The sheet of parchment carried the written script or "part" from which the actor recited. The antecedent to the writing, and later reciting and acting, of such parts was (and is) the conduct of real-life men and women struggling to make their way in imperfectly organized societies. Thus the metaphorical continuity is from real life to drama, and from drama to a psychological theory about people enacting real-life dramas.

One of the meanings sometimes attributed to the dramaturgical model is that the conduct of an actor in a dramatic role is divorced from "reality," that he is merely play acting. Because the audience knows that in fact the actor is not Hamlet, but is only playing the role of Hamlet, his performance is assigned to a class of action called "playing a role." There is an equivocation here that centers around two meanings of the word "play." Sometimes the word carries the meaning of "sham" as in games of "let's pretend," in which one acts without self-involvement, or acts for the purpose of deceiving the audience. However, it is illicit to assimilate to this meaning all the uses of the word "play" which denote some role enactment. This equivocation comes about through inventing two categories to account for conduct: play and work. The latter is seen as genuine, serious, and self-involving, the former as sham, without serious intent, and nonself-involving. Not infrequently, too, play is seen as having pejorative connotations, particularly when implicitly contrasted with work. This suggests a false dichotomy. Play of any kind can be highly self-involving and may represent work, as in the case of a virtuoso playing the violin or a professional football quarterback playing in a championship game. To avoid the overgeneralization and equivocation that role playing is akin to sham behavior, we use the term "role enactment."

A note regarding the meaning of the word "theory" in the term role theory: We understand it to denote a set of propositions employing a consistent idiom that guides the search for facts. The test of a scientific theory, of course, is not whether it is "true" but whether it is useful. We begin by noting the fact of resemblance between the conduct of social man and the conduct of characters who pass before us on the stage. Shakespeare was also impressed with this resemblance: "All the world's a stage, and all the men and women merely players. . ."

Role Enactment

To the social psychologist whose observations are guided by role concepts, the object of study is the role enactment of persons in social settings. To codify conduct as role enactment immediately places constraints on the methods of observation and analysis, and on the consideration of both antecedent and concurrent conditions of individual variation in enactment. The focus of attention is on overt social conduct. Concern with role enactment immediately occasions such questions as: What are the positions of the others with whom the actor is performing? How effective is the actor in validating the occupancy of his status? What is the contribution of the others to the enactment--do they provide reinforcements, do they provide discriminative cues which lead the actor to select another role performance? Unlike some psychological theories, role theory, with its focus on role enactment, bridges the gap between the individual and the group, between personal history and social organization.

Study of the isolated individual per se has no place in role theory. The stimulus-response model that has served psychology so well for several decades is of little help to the analyst of social psychological behavior. In the typical case, the behavior scientist controls the stimulus events, observes the subject's response, then categorizes the response as correct or incorrect. For example, in the maze learning situation, the binary choices permit simple inferences on the part of the observer (or recording machine) as to correctness or incorrectness. This model has little utility for the analyst of social interaction. Where the object of observation is a person enacting a social role, the observer can rarely apply a simple correct-incorrect criterion; rather, he must make inferences as to the appropriateness, propriety, and convincingness of the enactment. The questions that guide one's observations of social behavior and consequent inferences are of this kind:

1. Is the conduct appropriate to the social position granted to or attained by the actor? That is, do his performances indicate that the actor has taken into account the ecological context in which the behavior occurs? In short, has he selected the correct role?

2. Is the enactment proper? That is, does the overt behavior meet the normative standards which serve as valuational criteria for the observer? Is the performance to be evaluated as good or bad?

3. Is the enactment convincing? That is, does the enactment lead the observer to declare unequivocally that the incumbent is legitimately occupying the position?

The answers to such questions, by and large, can be achieved only through the activation of human judgmental processes.

By remaining aloof from the necessity for judgment, psychologists dependent on the stimulus-response model have tried to emulate the objectivity of the nineteenth century physicists. The search for truth, in this view, is to objectify observations so that the observer's norms and expectations cannot produce error. Save for trivial instances, however, the analyst of social psychological conduct cannot be free of expectations in making his inferences. To determine whether a man's conduct is that of hero, villain, or fool, one must attend to multiple cues and apply criteria that allow statements about appropriateness, propriety, and convincingness of the role enactment.

Contained in the process of judging the effectiveness of a role enactment is the implicit operation of probabilistic inference. The audience's judgments about the appropriateness, propriety, and convincingness of an actor's performance are made on the basis of samplings of the ecological texture--that is, samplings of the overt conduct of the actor, of complementary actors, and of the settings, including symbols and artifacts. Samplings cannot produce deterministic conclusions, only probabilistic ones. The probabilistic assessment of another's role enactment, then, cannot be entirely free of error. Since audiences provide both discriminative cues and reinforcement cues, the actor must maintain a semblance of flexibility and be ready to take into account the probabilistic nature of interaction. The recognition of this fact renders role theory continuous with an interactional and functionalistic framework. This is contrary to the unwarranted belief that role theorists regard human beings as operating on the basis of a pseudo-homeostatic principle, seeking a perfect fit between role expectations and enactment. This stereotype has been perpetuated in part by the illustrative use of the graphic table of organization applied to formal organizations. Such a graphic table merely exemplifies the formal structure of a society; it does not pretend to show the variability in role expectations or the limits of tolerance for role enactments. The table of organization shown in handbooks of business management must be regarded at best as a useful fiction. Although the fiction may approach the reality in small closed societies, for example, in a cloister of nuns, there are no instances where it can be seen as an accurate representation of the actual happenings within social organizations.

In keeping with our preference for interpreting conduct with the help of dramaturgic metaphors, we are interested in specifying the major components of role enactment. Overt conduct, that is, what the person does and says in a particular setting, is the first specification of role enactment. From time to time, suggestions have been made that performances be dimensionalized according to such characteristics as style, tempo, motility, and duration. Such suggestions have had little effect, in all probability because of the equivalence of several acts in satisfying the expectations in a given setting. The range of behaviors from which an actor may choose is great indeed, for which reason we are compelled to depend on ratings, judgments, and global assessments of human observers.

Among the dimensions of role enactment that appear to have conceptual or practical utility are (1) number of roles, (2) organismic involvement (effort), (3) preemptiveness (time).

Number of Roles

It is obvious that the more roles in an actor's repertoire, the better prepared he is to meet the exigencies of social life. In principle, the problem of counting the number of roles presents no insurmountable difficulties. Representativeness and generality could be obtained by an observer's keeping a constant surveillance on a particular actor and noting all his behaviors, particularly with reference to the occupants of complementary positions. Among his observations, he might note the time spent by the actor in particular roles and the degree of engrossment or involvement in the enactment. This type of naturalistic field study is commonly practiced by anthropologists, for example, by Ford (1941) and by Talayesva (1947). The ultimate work in establishing ecological generality is provided in One Boy's Day by Barker and Wright (1951).

The small group is a useful setting for studying the number of roles that emerge and are distributed among its members. The names applied to the roles that become differentiated will flow, of course, from the vocabulary used by the observer to categorize the dependent variables. Such roles as the opinion giver, the orienter, the clown, the expert, and the director have appeared in reports of observations of discussion groups (Benne and Sheats, 1948).

Organismic Involvement Dimension

Even the casual observer can identify characteristics of role enactment along an intensity dimension. Goffman (1961b) has used the label engrossment to refer to enactments at high intensities; Sarbin (1954, 1956) has denoted this variable as organismic involvement. At the low end of this continuum one finds enactments with minimal degrees of effort and visceral participation. The role of ticket seller in a neighborhood cinema during a slow period of business may be regarded as an exemplar of a role enactment with minimal involvement. The performance requires listening to the patron's request for number of tickets, pressing the appropriate button, and, if necessary, making change. Interaction is minimal. From self-reports, one could determine that the involvement of self is also minimal. At the high end of the continuum one finds enactments which involve great degrees of effort, that is, muscular exertion or participation of the viscera through autonomic nervous system activation, or both. The role of a quarterback during a championship football game, of a paratrooper in combat, of a woman in love, of a surgeon at work--these exemplify role enactment at the end of the continuum.

In everyday affairs, roles tend to be enacted with a minimum degree of organismic involvement. Efficiency of conduct would be reduced if all roles were enacted with maximum effort. All cultures are organized in such a way that there are few demands for maximally intense role enactments. In addition, autonomic safeguards limit the time span of role enactments that call for large mobilizations of energy. The complexities of roles make it difficult to construct an interval rating scale for assessing the degree of organismic involvement. At the present time, we must use a variant of the ordinal rating scale, employing reference cases as exemplars of regions on the dimension. We identify eight levels, the accompanying figure (Figure 1) indicating overlapping bands.

Level Zero: Noninvolvement. The lowest degree of involvement is characterized by the enactment of such roles as lapsed membership in a club or secretary of a high school class that has not met for 30 years. Merely occupying a status is a static kind of affair; there are no expectations for action. However, should the need arise, role enactments may be selected. This noninvolvement does have predictive properties, as we shall discuss later in the section on the transformation of identity.

Level I: Casual role enactment. Examples of roles with minimal involvement, that is, minimal effort and minimal affect, are the casual roles of patron in a post office, customer in a supermarket, and assembly line worker during rest periods. Role enactments of this type can be performed at the motoric level in semiautomatic fashion, while at the same time the individual vicariously enacts in fantasy other roles that may be unrelated to the public role. Ordinarily, there is little involvement of self in role at this level.

Level II: Ritual acting. This level of organismic involvement has as its point of reference the stage actor who performs the motoric actions necessary for the portrayal of the role assigned to him. This type of acting is frequently alluded to as mechanical acting, or push-button acting. On cue, the actor "pushes the button" to depict anger, lust, vanity, or whatever is called for. On self-examination, the actor will report some involvement of self in the assigned role. He must maintain a certain degree of consistency in the role enactment, which engages more of the self than in casual roles. Archer's classic study (1889) contained self-reports of competent stage actors who reported that under some conditions the actor does not get involved but maintains his identity, giving service to

Zero. Noninvolvement

I. Casual role enactment

II. Ritual acting

III. Engrossed acting

IV. Classical hypnotic role taking

V. Histrionic neurosis

VI. Ecstasy

VII. Object of sorcery and
witchcraft (sometimes
irreversible)

Role and self differentiated
Zero involvement
Few organic systems
No effort

Role and self undifferentiated
Maximal involvement
Entire organism
Much effort

Figure 1. Scale representing dimension of organismic involvement.

the stage role only through stylized gestures, intoned sentences, and sham affect.This low degree of involvement is seen in many everyday encounters--the waitress who "puts on a big smile" for the customer; the bank teller who asks, "Is it hot enough for you?"; the employee who puts up a front of busy-ness to impress his employer.

Level III: Engrossed acting . Frequently called "heated" acting, this level of involvement is noted in the stage actor who "takes the role" literally. He throws himself into the action, temporarily separating himself from his own identity and taking on the identity of the character. The successful stage actor who engages in engrossed acting does not surrender his entire identity to the part. In order to change his tempo, intensity, and amplitude commensurately with changing and unforeseen conditions, he must maintain some contact with his role as actor. The observer may note motoric as well as expressive (affective) features of the involvement. To reach the optimum degree of organismic involvement for a role calling for angry denunciation, an actor may work up a sham rage by violently shaking a sandbag or a piece of furniture.

Level IV: Classical hypnotic role taking . The role of the hypnotic subject as reported in the literature since the time of Mesmer is one that is enacted with relatively high degrees of organismic involvement. The classical behaviors of the hypnotic subject include catalepsies, compulsive posthypnotic behaviors, sensory and motoric changes, etc. Modern hypnotic theory accounts for these changes in terms of role demands and the side effects of organismic involvement. The mediating psychological mechanism is the engagement in "as if" behavior. The convincing subject behaves as if he is blind, in pain, analgesic, etc. The effects of organismic involvement can be monitored by various measurement devices, including galvanic skin response (GSR), sphygmomanometer, and gastric manometer (Sarbin, 1956). The overlap with Level III is great--the involvement in heated acting is frequently as great as the involvement in hypnotic acting. The self is engaged to a high degree, as can be inferred from retrospective accounts (Hilgard, 1965; Sarbin, 1956).

Level V: Histrionic neurosis . Psychiatric clinics continue to report the admission of patients who behave as they were afflicted with some organic dysfunction in the absence of pathology. Although the term conversion hysteria is still widely used, Ziegler, Imboden, and Rodgers (1963) have presented data and argument to justify the label histrionic neurosis for at least some of the patients. The range of involvement covered by this reference class overlaps considerably the previous two classes. The organismic involvements in histrionic neurosis are less self-limiting and more prolonged than in the enactment of the classical hypnotic role.

In the same range of involvement is the couvade. In this custom the husband lies in; the essence of the custom is the husband's taking the role of the pregnant wife. "As soon as birth approaches, the husband puts his wife's clothes upon himself, makes the woman's mark upon his forehead and lies-in. He is treated as a mother during the whole period of 'uncleanness'" (Crawley, 1902, p. 186). The role taker reports and acts as if he were in pain and agony. The degree of engagement of self and role is high indeed; effort and affect are of a high order.

Level VI: Ecstasy . At this level of involvement, there is usually a suspension of voluntary action. (It is interesting to note that the word ecstasy was used as a diagnostic label by practitioners of Galenic medicine less than 300 years ago.) Role enactments of this intensity are not ordinarily encountered in everyday transactions. Such states cannot be prolonged over time without damage to the functioning of the body. The reference cases that show this high degree of involvement are drawn for the most part from ethnographers' accounts of trance experiences, possession, and mystical unions. The same order of involvement is noted in religious conversions, in the "swooning" behavior of female teenage Beatle fans, discotheque dancing, and similar activities where there is relatively prolonged skeletal activity together with excitement, dread, awe, or other cognitive-affective dispositions. All these activities are terminated through institutionalized rituals, fatigue and exhaustion, the regulatory powers of the biological systems, or some combination of these.

Level VII: Bewitchment . The ultimate level of the involvement dimension extends beyond the range of experiences denoted by ecstasy. The term bewitchment is meant to cover the conduct of persons who believe themselves to be the objects of sorcery, witchcraft, and magic. The social and physiological controls that limit the somatic and social effects of lesser stages of organismic involvement may cease to operate; the effects may be irreversible and the bewitched may die. A number of cases of voodoo deaths have been reported in the literature. The descriptions suggest that the bewitched person takes the role of a moribund person. Furthermore, the community participates in this belief and provides the cues to support the role. Devereux (1939), in a study of the Mohave Indians, reported that when a person discovers that he has violated the incest taboo, he takes the role of the moribund. Rivers (1924) wrote of similar beliefs and practices among the Papuans and Melanesians: men who have offended one whom they believe to have magical powers sicken and die, as the direct result of their belief; and if the process has not gone too far they will recover if they can be convinced that the spell has been removed.

This rather extensive treatment of the organismic involvement dimension will be employed in a later section. Suffice it to say here that for every role enactment, the observer has a set of expectations of the proper range of involvement. If the involvement appears too much or too little, the enactment may be judged as unconvincing, and may be declared negatively valued.

Preemptiveness of Role

A third dimension of role enactment is simply the amount of time a person spends in one role relative to the amount of time he spends in other roles. The variability in time spent is applicable primarily to roles that have an achieved aspect. A person can move into and out of the position of, let us say, musician. He may spend 14 hours a day in the enactment of the role of musician, or he may alternate with teacher, citizen, friend, and other roles. Choice of amount of time spent is not applicable to roles that have a large ascribed component. Being in the position of male, adult, mother, etc., usually means being in the role all the time. In the vernacular of the theater, one would say that some positions require that the actor be "on" nearly all the time (Messinger, Sampson, and Towne, 1962). The implications of this variation in role enactment will be discussed in a later section.

A word about the plan of this chapter: Our first objective has been an exposition of the major dependent variable, role enactment. This is followed by the specification of several independent variables which have proved useful: role expectations, role location, role demands, role skills, self-role congruence, and audience effects. We handle these variables as though they were conceptually independent one from the other. Continuing and future research will dictate whether some of these should be telescoped, further differentiated, or abandoned.

Role Expectation

The conceptual bridge between social structure and role behavior is the concept of role expectations. This is a cognitive concept, the content of which consists of beliefs, expectancies, subjective probabilities, and so on. The units of social structure are positions or statuses (in specialized contexts, jobs and offices). These units are defined in terms of actions and qualities expected of the person who at any time occupies the position.

Role expectations are comprised of the rights and privileges, the duties and obligations, of any occupant of a social position in relation to persons occupying other positions in the social structure. The position of college president is filled over a number of years, even centuries, by different persons. The conduct expected of the occupant of the position, the exercise of rights and privileges and the fulfillment of duties and obligations, applies to the person who at any time is assigned this role. This is not to say that the content of the expectations does not vary from one time to another. Historical processes bring about changes in role expectations no less than in other beliefs or cognitive systems.

It is important again to stress the interbehavioral nature of the concept of social role. Following Kantor (1929), we hold that the occupant of one social position interbehaves with the occupant of complementary social positions. Thus a person's conduct takes into account the role behaviors of occupants of other positions, the specific nature of the conduct varying with the position held by the other interactant. The role expectations of the college president are reciprocal to such complementary roles as faculty member, student, regent, and dean. A person in any social position is confronted with several other persons occupying complementary positions in interaction with him. In all these interactional contexts, the person occupying the social position of college president remains in the position of president and enacts his role accordingly. Yet he behaves somewhat differently in interaction with each one of the complementary roles in the system of which his position is a unit. The totality of complementary roles related to a given role has been called a role set (Merton, 1957).

The terms appropriateness and propriety were used earlier in our discussion of the criteria for evaluation of role enactment. This terminology reflects the fact that role expectations have a normative or evaluative character. The occupant of a social position ought to do particular things in specified ways, and ought to hold certain beliefs instead of others. In role enactment an individual is "expected to behave in particular ways" in the sense that the behavior is predictable; more important, however, he is "expected to behave in particular ways" in the sense that others believe he ought to do so. The ought aspect of role expectations implies that approval or disapproval by other people is contingent on the nature and quality of one's role enactment. Role expectations can be said to define the limits or range of tolerated behavior. In short, role expectations are specifications for adherence to group norms. In cases of chronic failure to conform to role expectations the person may be removed from the position, particularly if it is an achieved one.

Although in general people do seem to conform to role expectations, we should again emphasize that role behavior does not consist of the rigid following of specific directives. Most role expectations require only that some end result be accomplished, within some limits. This allows the actor considerable freedom in the specific types of acts he can employ to accomplish the end. In other cases, the stylistic or ritual qualities of role behavior are important, permitting little variation from role expectations. Even in the most formal roles, however, stylistic variations unique to the individual may be permitted or even encouraged. Spontaneity occurs more often, and is approved more often, in the course of valid role enactment than one might at first assume.

Role Location

In order to survive as a member of a society, the individual must be able accurately to locate himself in the social structure. From his repertory of roles, he must select one that is appropriate to the situation. How is this accomplished? Since roles are enacted in interactional settings, the position of others must be taken into account if he is to locate himself accurately. Locating the position of self and other is a reciprocal, alternating, interactive affair. It is the first part of the social act, and it consists of the (usually) silent or tacit naming of the position of the other on the basis of observed cues and inferred qualities. At the same time, the individual makes a decision regarding his own role. It is as if the interactant is guided by the question, "Who are you?" (or "Who is he?"), the answers to which constrain tacit replies to the reflexive question, "Who am I?"

The answers to these questions are normally phrased in substantive terms such as teacher, daughter, friend, foe, officer, buffoon, old man, etc. Each term implies a complementary position calling for a counter-role: for teacher, students; for daughter, parents; etc. If placement of the other and, coordinately, of self is incorrect, then the choice of role and resulting role enactment is likely to be inappropriate, improper, or unconvincing.

Locating oneself in the role system may best be described as a cognitive process. Although the process can be subsumed under the term role perception, we prefer the spatial metaphor of locating one's role on social dimensions; it is more continuous with other components of role theory.

The time elapsing between the beginning of a social act and role enactment may be infinitesimal, so that observers overlook the cognitive phase. In infants, of course, the locating of an object and motoric discharge are continuous processes. With the development of language, gestural and speech activities (such as pointing and naming) occur between the appearance of ecological events and resulting respondent behavior. With the muting of speech, the locating and naming processes become silent and tacit.

The cues to locating the position of another person, of course, are his acts and appearances. These may be further characterized as everything publicly exhibited by the other in deed or in contour. A catalog of such cues would include gross skeletal movements, verbal acts, physique, stature, clothing, facial expression, posture, gait, carriage, accent, pitch, intonation, adornments, visible emblems and badges of office, tattoo marks, and so on. The wearing of a uniform and silver badge, for example, is part of the role of the policeman. The recognition of these objects on a person leads to predictable role behavior on the part of the actor (provided the role expectations, that is , the major premises, of the actor are known). The choice of role follows from the location of self in the social structure, such location being determined conjointly with locating the position of the other. And locating the position of the other becomes a matter of attending to inputs, separating relevant inputs (that is, forming cues), and aligning these cues with acquired role expectations to construct a proposition of the type "X occupies position Y." This cognitive process has been spelled out in detail elsewhere (Sarbin, Taft, and Bailey, 1960). A brief summary is presented here.

For effective participation in a culture, man must locate himself efficiently in a number of distal ecological systems. These ecological systems represent specific differentiations of the all-encompassing concept of environment, and they may be seen as convenient ways of portioning the world of occurrences which give rise to sensory events, some of which may function as inputs. We can identify five distal systems, each of which provides the occurrences that the actor must instantiate (make sense of). He must locate himself in the self-maintenance system, in the space-time system, in the social system, in the normative system, and in the transcendental system. Although placement in all these systems has relevance for role theory, our focus is on placement in the social system, in the structure of society. The social ecology, then, is that part of the world of occurrences that generates inputs which lead to inferences about what position a person is occupying, what role he is enacting. The inputs stem from the overt behaviors of other persons, from social symbols, and from artifacts that have social implications.

Locating oneself in any system is an inferential process of which the syllogism may be taken as the typical form. Major premises in the form of role expectations are acquired through socialization and enculturation experiences. In fact, socialization and enculturation are heavily weighted with the acquisition of major premises that link behaviors, symbols, and artifacts with specific positions. These major premises stand ready to instantiate inputs arising in the context of action. In schematic form, the inferential process could be described in the following series:

1. Major premise: A proposition that asserts what cues go with what positions (for example, uniform, silver badge, gesturing to motorists, standing in middle of traffic, etc., go with the position of traffic control officer).

2. Minor premise: A proposition that links current inputs with an individual (for example, that person wears a uniform, badge, etc.).

3. Conclusion: A proposition that connects the subject of the minor premise with the predicate of the major premise (for example, that person is a traffic control officer).

4. Implication: that the observer should then adopt the complementary role behavior (operating his motor vehicle according to the orders of the trafic control officer).

The inputs form the minor premise only if there has been a learning experience in which the cues were correlated with the position. In the absence of such prior learning, the actor can easily make a faux pas, be accused of a misdemeanor, or even make a fatal mistake.

To be sure, the actor does not go about the process of locating the other and the self in such deliberate fashion. In the typical interaction situation, the actor and the other make multiple inferences, frequently tentative, matching emerging inputs with role expectations until they reach a satisfactory conclusion.

Under ordinary conditions the location of the other in the social ecology occurs without deliberate reflection, partly because much social behavior is ritualized, partly because badges of office are more or less obvious. Occasions arise where the more obvious cues do not provide sufficient information for correctly locating the position of the other. In such cases, the actor must scrutinize or probe the subsurface ecology in order to make inferences about covert behavior of the other. In short, he must make shrewd guesses regarding the feelings, affects, expectancies, attitudes, prejudices, etc., of the occupant of the reciprocal position. The actor constructs inferences about such covert characteristics by attending to such cues as posture, diction, linguistic forms, gesture, and facial expression. A case in point is placement of persons in social class categories in England through nuances of diction (Pear, 1957; Shaw, 1963).

Role Demands

Once an interactant accurately locates the position of other interactants on the basis of behavioral, symbolic, or artifactual cues, the range of possible role behaviors is reduced from near infinity to a small number. For example, to a person entering a school building, the number of possible positions he will consider for any person he encounters is reduced from the thousands of positions known to him to four or five. The positions of any persons encountered will be student, teacher, principal, secretary, or custodian. The locations will be compounded by age and sex characteristics, such as young female teacher, male student, and old male principal. This reduction in role alternatives follows from a more or less static view of social interaction. In ritualized programs or in the enactment of casual roles, no further constraints need be considered. However, the conduct of the other will provide cues that may place further constraints on the actor. The behavior of the other guides the location of the specific position of the other and from this the actor selects the appropriate role. Potentially more coercive constraints on the choice of role are introduced when some additional features of the situation are taken into account. These may be called role demands, that is, demands for a specific role enactment. Under ordinary conditions role demands are implicit.

A series of experiments by Orne (1959) supports the conclusion that the role-demand variable is one of the most important features of steh experimental situation. In his first study, Orne demonstrated that the role enactment of the subject intent upon simulating the role of the hypnotic subject could not be differentiated from the role enactment of the subject whose performance followed traditional hypnotic induction procedures. In short, he was able to approximate the role demands contained in the standard induction procedures by experimentally manipulating instructions to the simulators. His simulators were instructed by an associate to pretend to be hypnotized and to engage in performances designed to deceive the experimenter. This study, together with others reported over the past two decades (see, for example, Barber, 1965; Sarbin, 1950; Sarbin and Andersen, 1963, 1967), lends support to the assertion that hypnotic behavior is role enactment and that the manipulated demand for a specific set of performances is, to a large degree, an important antecedent variable.

Role demands, especially if regarded as a conceptual extension of folkways and mores, are generally silent and subtle. This tacit or hidden character is probably responsible for the neglect of this variable not only by psychological experimenters but, more generally, in efforts to account for human conduct. A notable exception is to be found in the practical experience of social survey experts who have learned that the form of the question, the race of the interviewer, and so on, may have overriding demand characteristics.

Our view is that the sophisticated analyst of social behavior must be alert to the operation of role demands. Any situation that departs from the conventional, the predictable, and the familiar is likely to activate role demands of the type described here. In a hypothetical static, closed, and perfect society there would be no need for the role-demand variable--the role expectation variable would be sufficient. Under such conditions conduct would be completely ritualized, the behaviors of one person signaling the ceremonial behavior of another. Social groups, however, are in fact imperfectly organized, and propriety norms stand ready to demand specific role performances designed to maintain social balance and welfare.

The express recognition of role demands makes explicit the declaration that role theory is more than a variant of conformity theory (Turner, 1962). To be sure, in describing the main components of role theory, the requirements of exposition force the writers into presenting an oversimplified model. Our version of role theory takes its departure from the view that man is an interacting organism, that he is almost constantly active, that his performances must be accommodated to or assimilated within an ever-changing natural and social ecology. The role-demand variable ensures that the actor (and his complementary actors) will not be locked into formalized Alphonse-and-Gaston rituals.

Role Skills

A person enacting a role may be viewed as facing a task, the task being to fulfill as well as possible the expectations of the role. How well the person performs the task depends on the relevant skills at his disposal. With other variables such as role expectations, role location, role demands, and self-role congruence held constant, some of the remaining variance in role enactment may be accounted for by differential role skill.

A skill can be defined as a physical and psychological readiness to perform some task to some given level of competence. Role skills, then, refer to those characteristics possessed by the individual which result in effective and convincing role enactment: aptitude, appropriate experience, and specific training. Most role skills are probably learned. Because all roles include some content from early socialization experiences, the learning conditions of early life are important for the acquisition of such skills, though one can enhance role skills, within limits, through appropriate training in later life.

In this discussion, we shall consider the concept of role skill as an analog to the concept of skill or aptitude employed by the personnel and industrial psychologist. In fact, we shall take as our model for role skills the domain of perceptual-motor skills, since the important components of skill in role enactment appear to be the general perceptual-cognitive and the motoric skills. Implied in our conceptualization of role skills is the assumption that persons differ in basic attributes, in past experience, and in relevant training, all of which interact to influence role enactment.

Just as any skill may consist of a number of distinguishable components, so too do role skills seem to involve several factors which influence the convincingness of role enactment. The components of role skills may be broadly divided into cognitive and motoric skills. Each of these components may, in turn, be divided into general skills and role-specific skills.

We turn our attention first to the two general components of role skills. The cognitive component consists of those general cognitive skills which facilitate role enactment. These include the ability to infer validly from available cues the social position of the other, and of the self, and to infer appropriate role expectations for the positon. Ability to analyze a social situation and accurately infer the role of the other is a necessary prerequisite for accurate role enactment. These include the ability to infer validly from available cues the social position of the other, and of the self, and to infer appropriate role expectations for the position. Ability to analyze a social situation and accurately infer the role of the other is a necessary prerequisite for accurate role enactment. General intellectual ability may be, but is not necessarily, related to such general cognitive skill.

One aspect of cognitive role skill has received most theoretical interest and empirical examination. This is the aspect of role skill covered by the terms role taking, empathy, social sensitivity, identification, and (broadly) social perception. These concepts have somewhat different specific meanings, but refer in general to cognitive and affective responses made in reference to another person as social object. Several writers have discussed role taking, or, more accurately, taking the role of the other. The importance of taking the role of the other has been emphasized by G.H. Mead (1934) and others, who have analyzed social behavior from the interactionist's point of view. Taking the role of the other is a (covert) cognitive process, the ability symbolically to put oneself in the place of the other.

The second general component in role skills is the motoric. Enactment of any role requires appropriate posture, movements, facial expression, and tone of voice. Motoric responses include movements of body parts, highly differentiated muscular responses, and certain types of vocal responses. Rather precise control and flexibility are necessary for successfully executed social behavior. It is immediately apparent that some roles require the individual to have greater skill in controlling vocal and physiognomic behaviors than do others.

The expressive function is a particularly important aspect of the motoric component of role skills. Expressive actions reveal the involvement of the person while he is performing certain roles, and in many roles the expression of a particular "emotion" is the most important characteristic of the role. Certain expressive reactions are appropriate, for example, to attending a party, to comforting a sick friend, to attending a funeral. Facial expressions, gestures, bodily comportment, and vocal intonation are used to express these fine nuances of meaning.

We have just discussed the general and motoric components

of role skills which influence the enactment of a number of
roles. Other skills are less general, and are required for the
effective enactment of a particular role but not for others.
Such role-specific skills may be either cognitive or motoric.
The enactment of the role of surgeon, for instance, requires
particular cognitive and motoric skills. A specific motor skill,
eye-hand coordination, and a role-specific cognitive skill,
tension handling, are required of the surgeon.

We shall begin our disscussion of the relation of role
aptitude to role enactment with a review of Coe and Sarbin's
(1966) study of the contribution of aptitude to enactment of the
hypnotic role. They chose two groups of subjects who were
thought to represent extreme points on the continuum of role
aptitude--undergraduate drama students and undergraduate science
students. The results of the Coe and Sarbin study showed that of
the several variables tested in relation to enactment of the
hypnotic role, by far the best predictor was the role-aptitude
variable. Furthermore, within the sample of drama students,
intention of making acting a career was related to hypnotic
responsiveness.

To the degree to which lack of role skill is due to absence
of appropriate experience and training rather than lack of
aptitude, role skill can be improved by instruction and
practice. Argyle (1964) has initiated a research program
directed toward analyzing social skills, their acquisition and
transfer. And results of a study by Mattis (reported in Davitz,
1964) suggest that individuals may increase their emotional
sensitivity by specific training.

Self-Role Congruence

An important concept in role theory, the self, can be seen
as coordinate with role. Social roles are perceived and enacted
against the background of the self. The interrelation of self
and role has been assumed throughout our presentation. As a
central concept in role theory, the self must be taken into
account as a factor in determining the quality of role
enactment. The term "self" refers to the inferences the person
makes about the referent for "I." It is a cognitive structure
and derives from past experience with other persons and with
objects. We define the self as the experience of identity
arising from a person's interbehaving with things, body parts,
and other persons.

Before discussing self-role congruence as an independent
variable affecting role enactment, some time must be devoted to
the concept of self and its place in role theory. Social
interaction as the basis of development of self was the subject
of extensive and profound analysis by G. H. Mead (1934). He
assumed the self to arise as a result of the response of others
toward the person, and of one's own ability to respond toward
himself as object, that is, to take the role of the other toward
the self.

Two parallel series of events are responsible for the

residue of experience which is the self: the maturational series and the personal-social series. The self, of course, is not observable, but inferences can be made about its nature on the basis of acts and self-report. Whereas inferences about the roles a person may play in his personal-social experience have reference to his acts, inferences about the self have reference in general to qualities. The formation of qualities begins early--every person has experiences of crucial importance to the development of the self prior to his development of the use of language--and although the organization of the qualities which compose the self cannot at first be verbalized, language later becomes an extremely important factor in the development of the self. There is no denying the importance of social interaction, the responses of others, and the acquisition of the ability to place oneself in the role of the other and to respond to oneself in the way another person does; and all of these depend on language. The origin and structure of the self have been presented in detail elsewhere (Allport, 1943; Murphy, 1947; Sarbin, 1952); at this time only a brief survey of the stages of its development will be given.

The foci of cognitive organization, empirical selves, result from past experience. The first focus, the somatic self, arises from experiences that take place in the first few weeks of life. This initial cognitive structure is the basis for later differentiation of the self from nonself, but at this period the infant's own body is not differentiated from the external world. The primary differentiation made by the organism at this time is between the qualities of tension and quiescence. Later in the maturational sequence, a second focus of self is organized around the receptor and effector processes. At this time the self is still quite undifferentiated. Beginning at about six months of age a third focus of development can be identified, the primitive construed self. At this level of development of self the child begins to recognize differences between objects instrumental in tension reduction and agents instrumental in tension reduction. With further maturation and additional social experience, the child can associate gestures with things and with persons. Cognitive structure at the fourth stage, the introjecting-extrojecting self, sets the stage for the development of the socius. At this stage, during the fourth quarter of the first year, the child anticipates in play and other "pretend" activities, and words are differentiated and imitated. The fifth focus of development, the social self, differentiates persons in terms of social roles. The child begins to show some skill in taking the role of the other at this stage, and through language ability can assign qualities to the self ("good," "bad," "stupid").

In sum, then, self refers to a cognitive organization of qualities. These qualities reflect the participation of the various empirical selves. The qualities of the self may be assessed by the use of "I" statements; for example, an overdeveloped somatic self may be reported in a proposition of the form "I am rugged." "I am honest," "I am trustworthy," and "I am uncontrolled" are "I" statements the origin of which may be located in earlier interactions with objects, feeding schedules, and the like. Such propositions are not necessarily expressed in the conventional syntax. A more formal method of assessing qualities of the self is through the use of the adjective checklist (Sarbin and Rosenberg, 1955), where the first-person pronoun is implicit. Another method of assessing self characteristics is the "Who are you" technique (Bugenthal and Zelen, 1950). Requirements of the role, that is, role expectations, can be assessed in similar ways. Degree of overlap between qualities of self and requirements of the role can then be determined.

Having sketched an outline of the self, we turn to the interrelation between self and role, particularly the effect of self-role congruence on role enactment. We assert that, other things being equal, when self characteristics are congruent with role requirements, role enactment is more effective, proper, and appropriate than when role and self are incongruent. By self-role congruence we mean the degree of overlap or fittingness that exists between requirements of the role and qualities of the self, as measured by techniques such as those mentioned above. Self-role congruence is reflected in observations that the person seems to like the role, is involved in it, and is committed to it. In everyday language self-role incongruence is indicated by saying that a person is not well suited to a particular role, that the job does not fit his personality, or that he is a square peg in a round hole. Sometimes enacting a role requires that a person behave in a manner which violates his self conception or values. The role may require behavior which is regarded as wrong, improper, immoral, or unbecoming to one's self system. Such extreme incongruence between values or beliefs about self and role expectations creates severe psychological effects on the individual, recognizable through somatic dysfunction, lack of concentration, and the like. If the value involved in self-role incongruence is a salient one, then role enactment will be unconvincing or perhaps break down completely.

Under conditions where self conception is congruent with role requirements, an individual may describe the role as one which he likes, to which he is attached, or in which he is involved. This assertion is in part supported by recent research in hypnosis that has focused on discovering the self characteristics congruent with enacting the role of hypnotic subject (Sarbin and Andersen, 1967). Facility in enacting the hypnotic role is greater in the case of persons having dispositional characteristics that agree with the requirements of the hypnotic subject role.

The Audience

Though the dyad is usually considered to be the unit of analysis of role theory--a role and its complementary role--more refined analysis would suggest a triad. Use of a triad would give explicit recognition to the importance of the audience in the formulation of the ongoing role-enactment process. The triad of interest in any role enactment would consist of (1) the role performer, (2) the person in the complementary role, and (3) a third member who observes the process of social interaction. This conceptualization does not necessarily mean that three or more persons are physically present during role enactment; the physical presence of the observer is not required; furthermore, the function of observer may be an extension of the functions of one of the role performers.

Borrowing terminology from the theater, we shall use the term audience to designate observers who are present during role enactment. "Audience" is customarily employed in a restricted way to denote a rather large group of relatively passive observers of other's behavior. A somewhat broader usage is intended in the present context than is usually understood by the dramatic meaning of the word. The audience was an important topic in early social psychology, paralleling the concern of the social interactionists with "the other," and "the generalized other" (Mead, 1934).

Role enactment is sometimes directed toward an audience which is only cognitively present but which is nevertheless important. Such special kinds of symbolic audiences used to evaluate and compare role performance are called reference groups. This term designates a group which a person values. It is often used to explain behavior oriented toward audiences not physically present. A reference group may be a membership or nonmembership group, a single other person, a group, a category of people, or even nonexistent groups or categories of people--for example, the future generation, God, ancestors, and the nonexistent pseudocommunity of paranoids described by Cameron (1943). The "generalized other" and the "significant other" of Mead (1934) are cognitive representations of audiences having special importance in directing and controlling a person's role behavior.

A recent skillful use of the concept of audience in the analysis of social behavior appears in Goffman's (1959) dramaturgic model of interaction. Numerous accounts are given of the relation between a role performer and his audience. For example, protective devices are often used by the audience to help the role players in their "show," for example, tactfully not seeing a slip. Audiences stay away from regions where they have not been invited, entry into which might invalidate the role enactment in some way. Stratagems on the part of the role performer also help maintain his role enactment. Thus, changing audiences prevents the actor from becoming too sympathetically attached to the audience. Excluding from an audience members of prior audiences protects the performer from being caught in inconsistencies. Goffman showed convincingly the extent to which our social behavior is "staged" in order to produce the desired impression on others, and the subtle and continuous interaction that occurs between a role performer and his face-to-face audiences.

Perhaps this section on the audience should conclude with an attempt to analyze the functions of the audience in role enactment. First, we should mention the contribution of the audience in establishing consensual reality for the role. By accepting role enactment as appropriate, the audience provides validation for the enactment and serves as public confirmation of the reality of the role. Observers create social reality for the role by their presence and attendance during the role enactment, and by accepting the role enactment as interpreted by the performer.

The cue property of the audience is its second function. This term refers to discriminative responses that guide the performer's role enactment. For example, quizzical expressions from an audience provide a cue indicating that the role behavior is ambiguous. Similarly, cues from the audience can pace the speed or intensity of role enactment. The audience in many cases may "cue in" the actor to the most desired or effective course of behavior. Imagined audiences provide a similar cue function by serving as a basis for comparison of one's behavior.

A third function of the audience is social reinforcement. An audience has many methods of demonstrating approval and acceptance, or disapproval and rejection, of role behavior. Public praise or censure can be given, for example, by applause or jeers from an audience at a stage performance. More subtle techniques of expressing approval or disapproval are even more commonly employed.

A last important function of the audience is to contribute to the maintenance of role behavior over time. Role behavior appears to be fairly constant over time and at different times and places. Role enactment over a long period of time without major deviation from expectations may be due in part to the fact that the audience continually observes the enactment. In fact, a person desiring to change his role behavior drastically usually finds it difficult if not impossible without a geographical change. To change behavior he must escape the previous audiences which helped maintain and sustain role enactment. One other facet of the maintenance function of the audience should be mentioned. An audience which observes one's enactment of several different roles can discriminate among them and therefore ensure that differentiation and a certain degree of distinctness be obtained among roles.

Complex Role Phenomena

The discussion of role theory so far has been concerned primarily with a single role, or a single role and its complementary role. Such a description of social behavior is greatly oversimplified, of course, to facilitate presentation of the basic concepts of role theory. Of necessity a theory must be simple and analytic, yet it should provide a model that fits observations from social life. The ideal and oversimplified theory presented thus far leaves something to be desired as an accurate reflection of social behavior. In real life, role behavior is seldom enacted one role at a time, nor does role performance occur in simple social ecologies. Individuals are thrust into situations where they are required to choose among alternative roles, and where multiple role obligations impinge simultaneously on the role performer. With the realization that within a short period of time an individual enacts a variety of diverse roles successively and perhaps simultaneously, the role-theoretical analysis of behavior becomes more complex than is suggested by the single-role model presented so far. Shifting from one role to another, transition among types of roles over time, allocating time and effort among various roles, conflict among roles--all these more complex role phenomena are necessary to any sophisticated analysis of social behavior.

Footnotes

1. Reprinted (in abridged form) from the chapter by T.R. Sarbin and V.L. Allen in G. Lindzey and E. Aronson (Eds.), Handbook of Social Psychology (revised edit.). Cambridge, Mass.: Addison-Wesley, 1968. Pp. 488-567.

3

ON THE DISTINCTION BETWEEN
SOCIAL ROLES AND SOCIAL TYPES,
WITH SPECIAL REFERENCE TO THE HIPPIE[1]

The concept of role has often been regarded as the bridge between personality and social structure, the connection between the individual and society. The concept connotes a set of actions performed by an individual to make good the positions he occupies in the social structure. The standards of performance are in the form of role expections held by relevant others.

Variations in the quality of role enactment may be assessed along dimensions of appropriateness, propriety, and convincingness. Such observed variations in role enactment, it has been demonstrated, may be accounted for in terms of six relatively independent antecedent conditions. These are: (1) the validity of the actor's role expectations, determined by the degree of match with the role expectations of relevant others; (2) the accuracy with which the actor locates himself in the social structure through attending to appropriate ecological cues; (3) the lack of incongruity between the requirements of the role and characteristics of the self; (4) sensitivity of role demands generated by situational conditions; (5) the quality of the actor's general and specific role-taking skills; and (6) the readiness to perceive guiding and reinforcing responses from the actor's audience (Sarbin, 1964; Sarbin and Allen, 1968).

The utility of role theory needs no defense here. Its variables are demonstrably more continuous with social conduct than, for example, the variables of psychodynamic theories. Further, predictions of behavior--the ultimate test of credibility of a proposition--are more likely to be confirmed when roles and positions are incorporated into the propositional structure.

The explanatory power of the theory of social roles, however, has its limits. It is one thing to predict the day-to-day behavior of a man if we know his roles: physician, psychoanalyst, golfer, father, president of the local school board. It is another thing to predict the variations in behavior of a person who occupies a relatively undifferentiated social position such as a recruit in a boot camp, prison inmate, college student, department store clerk, slum dweller, etc. Since large numbers of persons enact such undifferentiated roles, stylistic variations in performance--although accountable in role theory terms--are not codified through the use of labels that ordinarily denote roles.

Social Typing

It is at this point that we find a second bridge between the individual and society, the concept of social types or better, folk types. It is axiomatic that whenever a large number of persons are concurrently enacting the role behavior called for through the occupancy of an undifferentiated position, stylistic variations in performance will occur. Whatever the antecedents of such performance styles, they provide a basis for other members of the collectivity to differentiate persons, to recognize "characters."

Social types provide models of conduct that may be used to enculturate the young. Klapp (1962) has taken this approach in his analysis of social types. He was able successfully to classify most social types as heroes, villains, or fools. I acknowledge the importance of social typing for this purpose. My interest, however, is focused on another aspect of social typing: namely, that social types provide the pool of recruits for filling new positions created in a constantly changing society. The social type is constructed out of the observed variations in role enactment. Those observations that are related to the "run of attention" of the community are singled out and given a name.

The folk type is constructed out of exaggerations in expected conduct. The exaggeration, if it relates to value orientations in the collectivity, serves as the focus for socal typing.

Since variations in role performance are almost universal and since members of a collectivity cannot escape their values (or axes of life, a felicitous term coined by Strong 1943), social typing or folk typing is likely to be engaged in by nearly everyone.

Thus, any collectivity will contain a number of folk types. Strong's (1943, 1944) studies of social types in Chicago's Negro community in the late 1930s turned up a number of differentiated types that were easily recognized by the participants in the community: for example, the "white man's nigger," the "mammy," the "big shot," the "uppity," the "muck-t-muck," the "flunky," and the "cat." Schrag's (1944) study of a prison population turned up such types as "right guy," "the outlaw," "the politician," and "the square john." A recent effort to study social types on a college campus yielded such social types as the "sallie," the "freddie," the "jock," the "head," the "wimp," and the "wheeler-dealer" (Sarbin, 1968d).

Under conditions of crisis and social change, newly created positions are filled, not by change, but by recruitment from social types —- when the public features of the type have some face validity for the emerging role. To illustrate from a recent social change: When banks were subject to pressures to computerize their operations, an individual had to be appointed to install and program the computers. How was such a person selected? As in any other collectivity, informal social typing had occurred as a result of variations in the enactment of management roles. Among the types recognized were "public relation types," "scholarly types," "social climbers," and "mathematical types." When the need arose for creating a new position, a person who had already been categorized as a "mathematical type" was recruited. Thus, the introduction of computer systems led to the creation of a new status, and the first occupant of the status was a person identified as a mathematical type. A social type became, under the press of social change, the core of a social role.

Such illustrations could be multiplied ad infinitum. Perhaps the most striking demonstration of this sequence is to ask the reader to think of instances where he participated in selecting a recruit for a new role in a hospital, office, or school. It is probable that his nominee was a person who, in his system of categorizing persons, belonged to a certain type, and that type presumably had the properties called for by the new position.

Psychological Typing

Of typing and typology a great deal has been written, most of it from the view point of scholars trying to simplify the nature of man by constructing types to which all men could be allocated. Every era has had its psychological type constructs for ordering persons: the Greeks had the sanguine, melancholic, choleric, and phlegmatic types based on the humoral theory of Galen. Renaissance medicine resurrected the Galenic typology, which persisted into the 19th century. Philosophers and physicians of the 19th century introduced psychological types based on body build and on psychiatric nosology. The beginning of the 20th century witnessed the development of such systems as Freud's oral, anal, phallic, and genital types, Jung's introversive and extroversive types, Jaensch's integrate and disintegrate types, and many more. More recently psychologists have used type constructs to illuminate cognitive types such as sharpeners and levelers (Allport and Postman, 1948), perceptual defenders and perceptual sensitizers (Stein, 1953), field-dependent and field-independent (Witkin, Dyk, Paterson, Goodenough, and Karp, 1962).

The vast literature on psychological types is relatively sterile in providing a basis for understanding the phenomenon of social typing. A part of this sterility may be attributed to the fact that the social typologist is generally the man-in-the-street, a person whose epistemological background, need for cognitive clarity, and communicative skills are not congruent with those of the psychological typologists.

Psychological typing is to social typing much as a theorem is to an axiom. One requires chains of inference, the other is "given." When one contemporary college student asks a friend about another student, "What sort of a person is Smith?" the reply is ordinarily given as a type, such as "Smith is a grind" "Smith is a jock," or "Smith is a wimp." To the members of the collectivity who construct and use such folk types, the terms are informing in that their meanings contain exemplars of public conduct. On the other hand, if answers to such questions were to be given in the language of psychological types, such as "Smith is introverted" or "Smith is cerebrotonic," the meanings contain no unambiguous exemplars of public conduct but have to be worked out through measurement or chains of inference.

Several important differences between the two kinds of typing may be noted. First, the purpose of psychological typing is to locate through a series of inferences all persons in an a prioristic linear dimensional scheme; the purpose of social typing is to place a particular person into a formed figural category with certain easily recognizable properties. Second, the underlying model of psychological typologies is a set of universal constructs or genotypes, such as "neuropsychic dispositions" or "mental traits." The model for folk typing is a grouping of observable particulars of phenotypes, such as performance styles. Third, the data for placing a person in one psychological type category rather than another are the selected attributes called for by the underlying theory and may involve esoteric assessments and complicated measurements. The data for placing a person in a folk type, on the other hand, are the visible behaviors that are relevant to the value orientations of the members of the collectivity.

Fourth, it follows from the differentiae already mentioned that the inferences of the psychological typologist are essentially deductive, while the inferences of the folk typologist are primarily inductive. Fifth, the process of labeling types is different, too. The labels of psychological typologists conform to the old scholastic practice of coining Greco-Latin names for scientific and quasi-scientific concepts: e.g., introversive, recipathic, cerebrotonic, and resurgent. The labeling of folk types makes use of common speech vernacular and slang. The labeling is more continuous with the salient features of the conduct for which the type name is struck: e.g., the "striver," the "bitch," the "righteous man," the "right guy," the "grind," the "wolf," the "allrightnick." Finally, the psychological type implies a causal relationship between the type and behavior. Folk types bespeak no causality.

It is not ordained that the two approaches to typology may not converge. The late Robert C. Tryon recognized the value of constructing psychological types for the scientific purpose of predicting behavior (Tryon,, 1967). He developed a sophisticated method for constructing psychological types, cluster analysis, which is not dependent on the cultural thought model for a small set of common dimensions or traits into which all persons must be classified. His method makes use of the notion of a configuration of characteristics that support a general motif--the origins of which may be in dispositional characteristics or in social characteristics.

Parenthetically, using Tyron's method, we have succeeded in constructing a psychological typology for a large number of urban youths (Sarbin and Stein, 1967). Three of the types had been processed through juvenile courts, six of the types had had no serious encounters with the police, and one type was indeterminate as far as adjudicated delinquency was concerned. Among our next steps is an effort to determine if there are any systematic relations between constructed psychological types and folk types generated in the youth subculture. Among the folk types so far identified are the "punk," the "beanie," the "rice-eater," the "dude," and the "cold-blood."

The relationship of the concept social type to the concept stereotype should be mentioned. Bogardus (1949), preferring the term sociotypes, distinguished the two forms of typing. His major requirement for sociotypes is that they be scientifically constructed without reference to the value parameters and based on careful observation, representative sampling, and attention to the canons of logic. Stereotypes, on the other hand, are constructed unscientifically through activating the prejudices, values, and sets of the typologist.

The force of this distinction is lost because of the description of sociotypes as based on analytical procedures. When one constructs a type on the bases of social conduct, it is well-nigh impossible to cut out one's guiding postulates, including value orientations, from the cognitive process. In fact, social types, being social, cannot exist outside of the observer's concern for conduct that deviates from expectations. Bogardus' sociotypes most nearly correspond to the class psychological types as used in this paper. Stereotypes, then, are a subclass of folk types. That over-inclusion may occur and that ethical and moral dilemmas may be involved in the construction and use of folk types is not denied.

Historical Folk Types

The study of social types is by no means a new enterprise. Many of the literary characterologists, beginning with Theophrastus (372-287 B.C.), made generous use of folk types. In fact, the characterology of Theophrastus nicely fits our criteria for constructing folk types. The character, like the folk type, arises out of noting exaggerations in conduct. When the form of the conduct is related to the value system, a label is coined. Thus, Theophrastus introduced the folk type "Loquacious Man" by defining loquacity as incontinence of talk. His introductory sentence contains the dispositional term "loquacity" to note the public conduct that stands out; it also contains--by implication from the phrase "incontinence of talk"--the value placed upon the control and modulation of one's utterances. The folk type "Penurious Man" is introduced by the sentence "Penuriousness is too strict attention to profit and loss" (Jebb, 1909). The negative valuation declared on extreme behavior is connoted in the definition. The exaggerated conduct is labeled with the dispositonal term "penuriousness" and leads to the substantive labeling of the type.

The character writing that flourished in the 17th and 18th centuries resembles our present conception of folk typing. For example, John Earle (1601-1665) wrote a number of character descriptions that also fit the criteria of social types. Among his types were the young raw preacher, the grave divine, the downright scholar, the mere dull physician. Excerpts from the latter are informative of the dimensions upon which the folk type was constructed.

> His practice is some business at bedsides, and his speculation an urinal: he is distinguished from an empiric, by a round velvet cap and doctor's gown, yet no man takes degrees more superfluously, for he is doctor howsoever. He is sworn to Galen and Hippocrates, as university men to their statutes, though they never saw him. . . The best cure he has done, is upon his own purse, which from a lean sickliness he hath made lusty, and in flesh. His learning consists much in reckoning up the hard names of diseases and the superscriptions of gally-pots in his apothecary's shop, which are ranked in his shelves and the doctor's memory. He is, indeed, only languaged in diseases, and speaks Greek many times, when he knows not. If he had been but a bystander at some desperate recovery, he is slandered withit though he be guiltless; and this breeds his reputation and that his practice, for his skill is merely opinion. . .If he sees you himself, his presence is the worst visitation: for if he cannot heal your sickness, he will be sure to help it. He translates his apothecary's shop into your chamber and the very windows and benches must take physic. He tells you your malady in Greek, though it be but a cold, or head-ache; which by good endeavour and diligence he may bring to some moment indeed (Aldington, 1924).

Chaucer, Shakespeare, Dickens and many others found it useful for their literary purposes to single out social types, configurations of observed behaviors with at least one central guiding motif. Recent entries have enriched our vocabulary with such social types as Babbitt, Eliza Doolittle, Sadie Thompson, and Willy Loman.

The systematic study of folk types, however, was not opened up by social scientists until the present century. Perhaps influenced by Weber's notion of ideal types, such social scientists as Park and Miller (1921), Wirth (1928), Strong (1943), Schrag (1944), Sykes (1958), and Klapp (1962) turned their attention to the types generated by persons in their efforts to meaningfully differentiate others. Their efforts have given new directions to the study of the varieties of human conduct, and equally important, to the social and cognitive antecedents of such variation.

Folk Typing as a Cognitive Process

Folk typing, like any other classificatory behavior, may best be understood as a cognitive process. Two conditions are required for folk typing: (1) the noting of individual differences in the public performance of roles, and (2) the recognition that a particular performance style is relevant to the values intrinsic to the life of the collectivity. Many stylistic variations in conduct go unnoticed and unnamed--they are irrelevant to the "run of attention" of the group.

The cognitive process is no different from that involved when neutral sensory inputs are converted to cues, i.e., given meaning (Sarbin, Taft, and Bailey, 1960). Input per se remains noninforming until it makes cognitive contact with the matrix of beliefs and values--the residue of prior experience. The beliefs and values that have high access-ordering in one's cognitive organization stand ready, as it were, to instantiate, to make sense of any input.

Thus, an increase in the tempo of a man's performance in an occupational role would be noticed and named if the observer's values were concerned with uncontrolled competitiveness and its dysfunctional effects. The exaggerated behavior or performance style would at first be characterized by an attempt to isolate its qualitative characteristics--in our illustration the increase in tempo might be labeled "striving" or "eagerness." However, the identification of the performance style is not isolated from the actor who is the exemplar of the noticed variation in performance. Holding together the actor and the action leads quite naturally to the construction and use of type names. When the action term is transformed into a substantive one, the folk type is formed. The motif striving or eagerness would be captured in such colloquial type names as the "striver" or the "eager beaver" or the "rate-buster."

The Hippie

Having suggested how the difference between social roles and folk types may be studied, I turn to a more detailed analysis of a current folk type--the hippie. By our usual definitions the hippie is not enacting a social role. There are no complementary roles, no recognized social structures containing a position designated "hippie," no system of rights and duties that center on a status called "hippie." Rather, the hippie is a social or folk type.

As an occupant of the undifferentiated youth status in contemporary society, his performance style is readily recognized by others. The cues that lead an observer to infer that a particular person is an exemplar of the folk type "hippie" are variations in dress, manner, demeanor, health and sanitation habits, content of speech, art preferences, and conduct presumably related to drug usage. To be sure, other variations in performance style may be noted. But it is important to raise the questions: Why have these variations been noticed rather than others? And by whom? Applying the language used earlier, what are the elements in the belief-value matrix of the observers that give cue-value (meaning) to the observed stylistic variations in conduct? I submit that the sensory input generated by the performance style makes contact with that part of the cognitive system of the nonhippie world that centers on the value of conformity, on the belief that extreme differences in performance styles may lead ultimately to disastrous societal or personal consequences.

It would be instructive to examine the origins of performance styles that serve as the focal dimension for the hippie folk type. Taking into account a number of observations, it is plausible to assume that the performance style is a way of communicating the belief that existing social organizations provide little or no means for establishing a social identity. Elsewhere I have presented a detailed account of social identity as the placement of self in a social structure through responding to the valuations of relevant others to one's role enactments. If one holds no membership in a social structure, then there are no role performances to be evaluated by relevant others, and no social identity.

To some members of our society, the contradictions inherent in a rapidly changing social order render invalid the enactment of roles in conventional society. Focusing on such contradictions, the potential hippie asks, "Who am I?" Answers to such a question tend to be in the form of labels for customary social roles or their derivatives. When he examines his actual and latent statuses he discovers that the roles available to him are not congruent with his belief system. A transvaluation of social identity occurs: his answers to the who am I question make no sense. He "drops out" of established social institutions, thereby giving up the most readily available opportunities for achieving a social identity.

As I said before, the argument can be made that for some individuals, contradictions in values--inevitable in a rapidly changing social and world organization--render difficult the search for answers to the who am I questions. That is to say, the quest for an acceptable social identity leads only to dead ends.

However, the habit of asking and answering questions of the ecology is not lost. In the search for answers to existential questions, the questioner may shift the form of the question from who am I to what am I. Although the question is seldom asked in such simple terms, it is reasonable to infer that the complex behavior of the questing youth is an attempt to locate himself with reference to the cosmos. The inputs that he had sought to help construct a social identity are noninforming (irrelevant) in his new efforts to establish an existential or, if you will, a cosmological identity.

His search now is not for signs and symbols that have social meanings but rather for inputs that help him differentiate self from nonself. Such inputs are derived from stimulation of a sensate kind--visual, auditory, tactile, and somatic excitations. Such excitations may be in the form of externally generated colors, lights, sounds, noises, and touches, or in the form of motorically induced or drug-induced stimuli in the several modalities. Commerce with such happenings helps a person locate himself with reference to the world of "raw experience," a world presumably undeformed by social constraints. Whatever its side effects, the deployment of attention to the world of proximal stimulus inputs provides assurance that one has a place in the cosmos, even if he has no place in the social order.

This sketchy analysis of the antecedents to performances that are noticed and named and ultimately formed into the hippie type must suffice for our present purposes. Some additional speculations are pertinent, however, following upon my earlier remarks about folk types providing a pool of differentiated persons for recruitment into emerging social roles.

In a recent paper, Adler (1968) has argued that the hippie as a current manifestation of a type that arises under conditions of political crisis and prolonged societal strain. Going back to the third century, he has noted the similarities in conduct of persons who were disenfranchised when the social order changed. Such persons tend to deny the validity of concurrent moral law and engage in conduct that is non-conventional and anticonforming. Borrowing the theological metaphor, Adler refers to this type as the antinomian character.

A prominent feature of antinomian movements is the rejection of the approved modes of acquiring knowledge in favor of revelation, magic, and other gnostic forms. A direct parallel is evident in the belief of early gnostic sects that they possessed esoteric spiritual knowledge and in the belief of the hippies that they, too, are "in the know" in that they have special avenues to other kinds of esoteric knowledge. In this connection, it is interesting to point to the probable derivation of the word "hippie." It is the diminutive of "hip" which in turn is derived from "hep," as in "hepcat," a term used by jazz musicians,to mean "with it," to know the beat and the score, etc. The jazz musician, however, intended no allusion to extra-empirical or unconventional forms of knowing. The current meaning of "hip" is still "to be with it," but in addition it carries some of the same connotations as in the beliefs of early Christian sects who claimed a form of wisdom superior to that of the established churchmen.

Let us return to our earlier assertion that in the natural history of folk types a pool of recruits is provided for emerging statuses. Are there signs that the hippie type is ready to step into some new position created by political and technological change? At the present time, the hippie type appears not to have the properties needed to balance any strains in the system.

Perhaps we can acquire a clue as to the fate of this folk type from the study of earlier gnostic sects and other antinomian movements. Under some conditions, the type dies out--it has no survival value. The individual "drops in" to straight society. Among undifferentiated youth, where there is no social organization, replacement is likely to be haphazard, and "dropins" may exceed "dropouts." Under other conditions, the type merges into roles that are specialized units of viable subcultures--usually religious or quasi-religious organizations. As soon as one moves from being an exemplar of a folk type enacting only undifferentiated roles to being the occupant of a status in a religious institution, he is on the way to a new social identity. The new social organization provides opportunities for differentiated role enactments and also for valuations to be declared on performances. A second possible outcome is membership in utopian or millennial organizations. Again membership confers a role, and the distinguishing features of the folk type are blurred. A third possible outcome is to acquire membership in a political organization. It is said that in the 1930s, German adolescents struggling to find acceptable social identities--a social type not dissimilar from the current hippies--found new identities in roles offered by membership in Hitler Youth organizations.

Summary

This paper is intended to clarify the notion of social typing--as differentiated from psychological typing — — as a second bridge between the individual and society. The concept supplements the role theoretical explanations of human conduct. Among the uses of social types is the provision of recruits for newly emerging roles.

The hippie as a folk type was discussed as a modern version of gnosticism. Some of the antecedents of the exaggerated role enactments were examined and related to the transvaluation of social identity. Following from the proposition that folk types supply recruits for emerging social organizations, I advanced some speculations about the ultimate destiny of the hippie folk type: renewal of membership in straight society or acquiring acceptable social identities through taking out membership in religious and quasi-religious organizations, through participating in utopian organizations, or through joining political organizations.

Footnotes

1. Reprinted from American Journal of Psychiatry, 1969, 125, 1024-1031.

PART III
The Nature
of Hypnosis

Since the late 1950s hypnosis has enjoyed a resurgence of interest as a popular topic for psychological research. It is safe to say that the renewal of serious interest in hypnosis is in large measure due to Sarbin's methodological and theoretical contributions to the topic.

In 1938 Sarbin published (with J.W. Friedlander) a psychometric scale for measuring hypnotizability. It consisted of a graded set of standard hypnotic suggestions or tasks to be given subsequent to a standard hypnotic induction. This provided the basis for the two most widely used instruments in modern hypnosis research, the Stanford Scale of Hypnotic Susceptibility and its variant, the Harvard Group Scale of Hypnotic Susceptibility.

After his initial research with hypnosis, Sarbin used hypnosis as a technique in his clinical practice from 1943 to 1949. Since Sarbin had published his first article on role theory in 1943, it is not surprising that a thoroughgoing role-theoretical interpretation of hypnosis was forthcoming. Given the solidness of Sarbin's background in hypnosis, both in research and in clinical practice, the article that emerged in 1950 carried special authority. It is reprinted as the first selection in this section, with very slight abridgements and modifications.

In basic form, Sarbin's skeptical view of hypnotic phenomena has remained unaltered since the publication of the 1950 article. However, the amount of research that has been produced to buttress his position has grown impressively in the intervening period. A considerable portion of this research has been performed by Sarbin's own students at Berkeley.

It is important to emphasize the illustrative character of hypnosis as a topic in the course of Sarbin's theoretical work. Hypnosis provides a case in point for the utility of the contextualist and dramaturgic perspective. This connection is made quite explicit in the second selection for this section. The effect of Sarbin's methodological and theoretical work on hypnosis is to render the topic continuous with or comparable to other social psychological phenomena. Sarbin has shown that hypnosis has become part of the theatre of everyday life, and as such does not require the invocation of special terms such as "trance" for its illumination.

4

CONTRIBUTIONS TO ROLE-TAKING THEORY: I. HYPNOTIC BEHAVIOR[1]

This paper attempts to construct from a social psychological standpoint a workable theory of hypnosis. Briefly stated, it essays to demonstrate that hypnosis is one form of a more general kind of social psychological behavior, namely, role-taking.

That a theory based on social psychological considerations is necessary arises from the obvious social psychological nature of the hypnotic situation. The patent dependency of hypnosis on interpersonal relations calls for a theory which is more continuous with social psychological formulations than with outworn physiological speculations (Kubie and Margolin, 1944) or revived mentalistic entities (Young, 1940). Moreover, the search for shorter and more efficient psychotherapeutic measures (together with the former widespread use of hypnosis in the treatment of the hysterias) suggests a reconsideration of hypnosis in the treatment of certain behavior disorders. Such treatment will be less abused if it rests on a more substantial theoretical framework than formerly. In addition, the potential value of hypnosis as a tool for social science and medical research demands a careful evaluation of the nature of hypnosis. Thus appropriate allowances will be made for the perturbations in the experimental field introduced by the use of hypnosis as a research instrument.

Observations Which Must Be Accounted For

A theory of hypnosis must account for many phenomena subsumed under a single label. These phenomena and the conditions which elicit them may be grouped for our purposes into these four classes: (1) the apparent discontinuity or dissociation of behavior; (2) the apparent automaticity of response; (3) the disjunction between the magnitude of the response and the procedure which instigates the response; and (4) individual differences in responsiveness to hypnotic induction procedures. These four types of observations are briefly elaborated below.

Apparent Discontinuity . In hypnosis the subject appears to be in a state which is discontinuous from events prior to the initiation of the hypnotic induction procedure. From introspective accounts and from observers' protocols it seems that stimuli are perceived by a markedly altered organism and that the responses are quantitatively and qualitatively different from those in the pre- and post-hypnotic periods. Some of the more dramatic items of conduct which lead to the acceptance of the inference that the subject's behavior is discontinuous (dissociated) are: anesthesia, amnesia, post-hypnotic compulsive behavior, hyperamnesia and various somatic effects such as the inhibition of gastric contractions. To those who are content only with a superficial examination of hypnotic phenomena it appears that hypnotic subjects can perform acts which violate the limits of everyday behavior. When the data are inspected more closely, however, we find that the changes in behavior which do occur involve chiefly the skeletal musculature--i.e., voluntary responses. Responses which are involuntary, such as PGR, blood pressure shifts, and pupillary reflexes are less amenable to verbal instructions, and the limits are extended not too far from the limits of waking behavior (White, 1941). Later we shall show that those responses involving the skeletal musculature require no further explanation than that the subject is taking the role of the hypnotic subject as understood by him as a result of his previous interactions with similar social psychological situations. The extension of the limits of behavior involving the autonomic functions is understood in terms of the conception of the organism as a whole--a conception which is now generally accepted in sophisticated psychological theory.

Apparent Automaticity . Most of the early theorists were thrown off the trail of a really workable theory of hypnosis by the manner in which acts are carried out under hypnotic stimulation. The word "trance" has been used to express this meaning. In most instances the subject appears to act like an automaton. There is an apparent absence of volitional activity. The experimenter throws out commands which seem to be accepted by the subject without critical consideration. He is often slow, stuporous, and seems to be exerting a great deal of effort to perform simple acts. Retrospective accounts reveal a distinction between obedience as found in everyday behavior and the automatic acceptance of commands without the subjective experience of intent. In addition to accounting for this apparent automaticity, a workable hypnotic theory must account for many acts which are added spontaneously by the subject without the benefit of instruction from the experimenter. Unlike physiologically--oriented theories, the role-taking theory considers these observations under the concepts of role enactment and role perception.

The Disjunction Between the Magnitude of the Responses and The Procedure Which Instigates the Response . This aspect of hypnosis is probably responsible for the popular association of hypnosis with magic. The experimenter (or therapist) merely talks to the subject. How, then, can such marked changes in behavior occur merely as a result of verbal instructions? The need for explaining this observation would be less urgent if the stimuli were of the same order of magnitude as are found in extreme stress, fatigue, toxicosis, narcosis, or febrile conditions. In a later section we shall point out how verbal instructions may help the subject focus on and enact a role which may have markedly altered somatic components.

Individual Differences in Responses to Hypnotic Induction Procedures. The observation which has received the least attention from the theorists and experimenters is (at least to this writer) the most obvious one, viz., individual subjects respond differently to the same hypnotic procedures. As is well known, many subjects cannot be hypnotized at all, some will exhibit mild cataleptic reactions, and still others will exhibit all the classical responses of hypnosis. Furthermore there is a great deal of variation in the manner in which directions are accepted (or rejected) by subjects who are apparently hypnotized to the same degree. As anyone who has taken the role of a hypnotist knows, and as Brenman (1947) has concluded from her analysis of various induction procedures, little or no relationship exists between the subject's performance and the specific innovations which are introduced into the hypnotic instructions. Since the induction procedure per se cannot account for the differential responsiveness of subjects, this leaves the subject as a person as the more fruitful focus of study.

These four types of observations may be combined into a question, the answer to which will provide us with a more definite theory of hypnosis: What are the characteristics of those individuals who, in response to hypnotic induction procedures, exhibit conduct which is apparently discontinuous and apparently automatic?

Some Concurrent Theories

It is unnecessary to take time out to flog the dead horse of dissociation theory. Numerous experiments and sophisticated observations have led to the unmistakable conclusion that the hypnotized subject is simply not composed of various psychophysiological systems that can be dissociated one from the other. White and Shevach (1937) have written a thoroughgoing analysis of the concept of dissociation and have concluded that the natural cleavages in the nervous system postulated by Janet are nonexistent.

A number of writers cling to the conditioned response theory to explain hypnosis. Historically the conditioned response theory stems from this simple explanation: The word is the conditioned stimulus and acts as an efficient stimulus. This is no more than a streamlining of the old ideomotor hypothesis. In 1933 Hull stated it this way: " . . . the withdrawal of the subject's symbolic activities would naturally leave his muscles relatively susceptible to the symbolic stimulation emanating continuously from the experimenter . . ." (Hull, 1933, p. 397). From such a conclusion (which seems naively to regard the subject as a spinal animal) Welch has presented an hypothesis and an experiment which purport to give credence to the conditioning theory (Corn-Becker, Welch, and Fisichelli, 1949; Welch, 1947). Taking as his point of departure the most commonly used induction procedure, Welch says:

> If the subject analyzed himself in some naive fashion, he might say, 'When the hypnotist said I felt A, I felt A; when he said I felt B, I felt B; and now he says I feel X, I feel X.' At this point the generalization has extended to the point that whatever the hypnotist says the subject feels, he, within limits, actually feels (Welch, 1947, p. 361).

On the basis of his hypothesis that hypnosis is a kind of generalized conditioning, Welch and his co-workers performed a learning experiment (in which, incidentally, none of the subjects was hypnotized) based on this experimental analogue. ". . .a word flashed on a screen was used as analogous to the spoken word of the hypnotist, and followed by the phenomenon for which the word was a symbol. Thus the word 'music' was followed by the playing of music. After a certain number of trials the word 'electric shock' was flashed on the screen and was not re-inforced." His findings were summarized thus: ". . .in a group of 15 subjects, 11, or 73 percent gave a (PGR) response greater than to any other stimuli."

That Welch has demonstrated a type of abstract conditioning is not to be denied. But he has not shown that this type of conditioning is the important feature of hypnosis. In the first place, many subjects can be hypnotized without using the analogous procedure. If a subject comes into a hypnotic experiment with certain self-perceptions and role-taking skills, it is possible for him to become hypnotized without the usual monotonous delivery and so-called reinforcement. The present author has shown that some subjects can be hypnotized with these instructions: "Make yourself comfortable in this easy chair. I'll step out of the room for a few minutes so you can relax. When I come back I will count to ten, you will close your eyes and go into a hypnotic sleep." Even if we could accept the analogy between the Welch experiment and hypnosis, there is no answer to the question: Why did the other 27 percent not condition? If Welch could show that a correlation existed between "abstract condition-ability" and hypnotizability, we should still have to fit this correlation into a more comprehensive framework based on an understanding of the antecedents of these individual differences.

Eysenck and Furneaux (Eysenck, 1943; Eysenck and Furneaux, 1945; Furneaux, 1946) have also reported some studies which are related to the ideomotor principle. Using a factorial approach, they isolated three factors from a series of psychomotor and other tests. The first, primary suggestibility, is highly correlated with hypnotizability and is best measured by the postural sway test. The second factor, secondary suggestibility, is unrelated to hypnotizability. The third factor, unrelated to the previous two, also predicts susceptibility to hypnosis, and is measured by a test of heat illusion. They conclude that susceptibility to hypnosis is an innate characteristic (presumably on the grounds that psychomotor traits are inborn). This writer would declare this conclusion a non sequitur. That hypnotizability and certain traits are shown to be related is an acceptable conclusion, but to posit that this relationship is based on inherited factors is not continuous with the data. Below we try to fit these data into our conceptual framework.

Perhaps the most widely accepted hypothesis at the present time is a conative one which places the phenomena of hypnosis at a high integrative level. A number of writers have contributed evidence to support such a theory, notably Dorcus (Dorcus, Bretnall, and Case, 1941), Lundholm (1928), Rosenow (1928), Pattie (1941), White (1941), and Sarbin (Sarbin and Madow, 1942). The most systematic presentation of this hypothesis has been offered by White. He defines hypnosis as "meaningful, goal-directed striving, its most general goal being to behave like a hypnotized person as this is continuously defined by the operator and understood by the subject." This approach purports to look upon the hypnotic subject as a functionally intact human organism who is very much in contact with stimulus objects and events, trying to conduct himself in certain meaningful ways rather than in the manner of a spinal animal.

White's theory deals with three of the previously identified four sets of observations. It looks first upon the apparent automaticity as a form of striving: the subject tries to behave in an organized manner, following instructions as he understands them. The apparent discontinuity is treated in terms of measurable extensions of the boundaries of volitional control. How the goal-directed striving makes possible this extension of the limits is subject to speculation in terms of "disinhibition of the higher centers." The importance of the procedure for inducing hypnosis is analyzed in terms of relaxation, reduction of sensory input, drowsiness, and a contracted frame of reference. This procedure produces an altered state of the organism which makes possible the success achieved by the striving. The theory fails to provide an explanation for differential susceptibility beyond that due to motivational factors, such as need for submissiveness and deference.

This analysis places the striving in a context beginning with the experiment itself. It fails to recognize explicitly that the subject comes into the hypnotic situation with certain pre-conceptions about the experiment, the experimenter, and even about such items as the place in which the experiment is being conducted. It does not make clear that the subject also comes into the hypnotic setting with certain self-perceptions, and that these self-perceptions will operate toward the subject's being successful or not in his striving to behave "in ways defined by the operator." White's analysis would be more tenable if there were no individual differences in responding to the

operator's instructions. Relaxation, drowsiness, and reduction
of sensory input--time-consuming processes--obviously would not
be involved with those subjects who responded immediately to the
command: "Go into a hypnotic sleep." The observable differences
in individuals, not only in the depth of hypnosis, but also in
the kind and quality of spontaneous additions to the operator's
directions, suggest that we look into the reactional biography
of the subject and into the evolution of the stimulus setting
for clues as to the nature of hypnosis.

The Role-Taking Hypothesis

To fill the gap in White's goal-striving theory, another
hypothesis is herewith introduced. Hypnosis is a form of a more
general kind of social psychological behavior known as
role-taking. In the hypnotic experiment the subject strives to
take the role of the hypnotized person; the success of his
striving is a function of favorable motivation, role-perception,
and role-taking aptitude. This orientation breaks completely
with the tradition of looking on hypnosis as some strange
phenomenon for which it is necessary to invent
psychophysiological conceptions.

To adopt a frame of reference that departs from dependence
on traditional formulations, and to provide a logical link
between the observations and theory, we point to another area of
conduct which is apparently automatic, apparently discontinuous,
elicited by relatively simple verbal instructions, and
characterized by individual differences in performance: to wit,
the drama. Introspective accounts and observers' reports of
stage actors taking roles reveal a kind of behavior which may be
characterized in much the same way as hypnosis. The apparent
discontinuity, for example, has been established as an important
factor in dramatic role-taking. The actor's stage behavior
appears to be dissociated or discontinuous from his "normal
personality." In Archer's (1889) classical study of acting some
actors report losing themselves completely in certain roles so
that they are relatively unaware of the audience or of other
physical or social objects. The role may even carry over to
offstage statuses. The introspective accounts of actors taking
roles are often undifferentiated from the accounts of hypnotic
subjects.

Allen (1935) cites Oesterreich who collected a number of
observations on this point. One such observation is reproduced
here: "Martersteig compares the personality of the theatrical
character to a self suggested to the actor by hypnotism, and
states that the waking remainder of the actor's consciousness
(Bewusstseinsrest) can observe the actions of the hypnotic self,
as though it were another person, at one time feeling anxiety
with regard to them, at another time allowing them to have full
play" (Allen, 1935, p. 123).

It appears that the stage director stands in the same
relationship to the actor as the hypnotist does to the subject.
The statuses or positions are defined beforehand, the specific
role-behaviors are dictated by the attempts of each participant

to validate his status (Linton, 1947). In short, the participants interbehave with each other in ways that are appropriate to each position--provided, of course, that such interbehavior can be incorporated by each participant in his self-concept. Because acting has not been burdened with the incubus of dissociation or ideomotor theory, we are not amazed at the frequent marked changes in skeletal and visceral behavior which occur merely because the director tells the actor what to do. The analyst of dramatic acting does not seem to be concerned with such pseudoproblems as the search for a one-to-one constancy relationship between the magnitude of the stimulus (the director's verbal instructions) and the magnitude of the response (the complicated verbal, motor, and visceral reactions of the actor).

From this preliminary description we submit that the role-taking of the stage actor and the role-taking of the hypnotic subject embody the same characteristics: (a) Favorable motivation--the actor's self-concept and his perception of the part to which he is assigned must be congruent; if it is not, then his performance is unconvincing or he pays a terrific psychological price. (b) Role-perception--the actor must first perceive the role he is to play--this is achieved partly by the actor's own experiences with similar stage or real-life roles, partly by the director's definition of the role. (c) Role-taking aptitude--needless to say, some actors can take a role more completely than others. Compare, for example, the performance of Barrymore as Hamlet with the efforts of a high school senior.

Young (1940) has criticized such conceptions of hypnosis by saying that the subject is playing a game with himself and with the experimenter. This criticism is invalid because it does not consider an important dimension. In the two types of role-playing there is a quantitative difference along a continuum which we may here characterize as the "conscious-unconscious" dimension. We may ask how conscious is the actor of his surroundings, of stimulus-objects, and of himself as compared with the hypnotized subject? Or, to put it in terms more continuous with the present study, what is the relative degree of participation of the self in the role (or in Mead's terms, of the "I" in the "me")? Some actors and some hypnotic subjects become so involved in the role that perception becomes over-focalized and many self-other observations are by-passed. From those studies of acting which have come to this writer's attention, it would seem that there is a great deal of overlap with hypnotic role-taking in this dimension, but there would be, on the average, less participation of the self in the role of actors as compared with hypnotic subjects.

In the last few paragraphs we have tried to orient the reader away from the necessity of physiologizing about hypnosis by showing the similarity of hypnosis as being continuous with other social psychological events. At this time we submit certain observations to lend support to the central hypothesis, viz., hypnotic role-taking is dependent on at least three factors--favorable motivation, role-perception, and role-taking aptitude.

Favorable Motivation. The most complete paper on this topic has been contributed by White (1941). He reviews the studies which have attempted to demonstrate the relationship between hypnotizability and motivational variables. The obtained correlations have for the most part not been significantly different from zero. In his own study White finds a small but positive correlation between hypnotizability and the need for deference (.42), and also a small but negative correlation with the need for autonomy (-.42). "...there is a great deal of individual variation in the tendencies which are awakened, so that manifest needs like passivity, exhibitionism, sex, or aggression may sometimes occupy the foreground ...There is (also) reason to believe that three latent infantile needs sometimes function as motivating forces favorable to hypnosis: the need for love,...the tendency for passive compliance,...and the wish to participate in omnipotence..." He concludes with this significant statement. "It is doubtful whether the analysis of motivational factors can be pushed further except by the intensive study of the subjects as individuals" (White, 1941, p. 161).

In terms which are more continuous with those of contemporary social psychology, White's conclusion may be restated as follows: If the subject's perception of the role (here, the role of the hypnotized subject) are not disjunctive or incongruent, then he may be said to be favorably motivated.

One example is herewith presented to facilitate understanding of this formulation. The author gave a lecture and demonstration of hypnosis to a group of undergraduates. The class instructor had previously pointed out (to the author) several students whom he thought would make good subjects. One of these was a young woman of 21 whom he characterized as being dominated by the need for exhibitionism. She had volunteered, along with several others, to be a subject. She responded to the usual signs of hypnosis, catalepsy, rigidity, hallucinations, post-hypnotic compulsive behavior, amnesia, age-regression (to a period when she could only understand and speak another language), etc. At the end of the meeting those subjects who had passed the usual hypnotic tests were asked if they would participate in an experiment in the author's laboratory. She volunteered along with the others. An appointment was made for a week later. She came with some friends at the appointed hour. But instead of being the easily-hypnotized subject of the week before, she was extremely resistant and showed external signs of anxiety and conflict. After about 30 minutes the experiment was terminated. In an interview which followed, the subject said, "I could not understand why, but every time you said my eyes were getting heavier, I would try harder to keep them open. When you said I would cooperate, I seemed to say to myself, 'I mustn't do this.'" Further questioning revealed that when she had discussed the demonstration with her parents, her father had expressed vehement disapproval of her submitting herself to such indignities, and had instructed her not to participate again. At the time, she thought she gave his instructions little attention, but as the time drew near for keeping the appointment, she became more and more anxious. "You know, I always try to please my father."

In this instance we can say that for the first experiment the subject was favorably motivated. Her self-concept (dominated by the need for exhibitionism, if the instructor's appraisal was correct) and the perception of the role of the hypnotized subject were not disjunctive. In the second experiment the self-concept carried another characteristic--of greater valence than the need for exhibition--the maintenance of her father's approval. The role of the hypnotized subject was incongruent with her self-perception, which perception had been modified by interaction with her father. Although she had demonstrated before that she could perceive the role of the hypnotic subject, and could enact it with great fidelity, she could not focus on the role because of her changed self perception.

In clinical experience this writer has found that as a patient achieves a set of self-perceptions which make dependency ego-alien, resistance to hypnosis as a therapeutic aid increases. One patient, near the termination of therapy, was faced with blocking involving her school work. This same symptom had cleared up earlier after a few hypnotic sessions. When it was suggested that hypnosis be used as an auxiliary therapeutic technique, she was resistant to the idea. She said: "I know it worked before, but I would rather work this through on a more mature basis." Janet (1907) long ago made the same observation, but related it to different concepts.

Role-Perception. This concept was first introduced by G. H. Mead (1934) and later by Moreno (1946) in his studies of the psychodrama. In order to enact a dramatic or psychodramatic role, it is necessary for the subject to have a perception of the role. (The words "image" and "preconception" are used by other writers to express the same idea (Ichheiser, 1949)). Through various media of communication, such as parental instruction, motion pictures, novels, comic strips, radio stories, rumors and folktales, role perceptions are built up. The role of the father, the role of the teacher, the role of the policeman, etc., are built up from interaction with others in the social environment. When the subject enters the hypnotic situation, then, he comes not only with various self perceptions, but also with various role-perceptions, among them the role of the hypnotic subject. The announcement of the experiment and the directions of the operator serve as stimuli which elicit the perception of the role. The validity of this conception is suggested by at least three kinds of observations: (1) trance states of certain primitive and religious groups, (2) the role playing of young children, and (3) clinical and experimental studies.

Trance States. In many cultures trance states mark a rite de passage. As an illustration we cite one of Benedict's studies. She has described how, among the Plains Indians, an individual will experience many of the phenomena, including hallucinations, which are usually subsumed under the term hypnosis. The content of the hallucinations is relatively constant within groups but highly variable between groups. The role of the tranced subject is perceived from interaction with his own group. "The tranced individual may come back with communications from the dead describing the minutiae of life in the hereafter, or he may visit the world of the unborn . . . or get information about coming events. Even in trance the individual holds strictly to the rules and expectations of his culture, and his experience is as locally patterned as a marriage rite or an economic exchange" (Benedict, 1934, p. 77). In brief, the perception of the trance role is built up in social interaction.

Role - playing of young children. Space prevents the identification of the numerous studies which have been reported dealing with the fantasy-roles observed in young children. One can condense the findings for the purposes of this paper into this general statement: The roles which emerge in the fantasy and play activities of young children are dependent upon their being able to perceive other-roles (Axline, 1947; Bach, 1945; Cameron, 1947; Flugel, 1944). Some of the studies of imaginary companions are especially illuminating (Green, 1923).

Hartley et al. have recently reported a pioneering study in an attempt to understand how children perceive ethnic group roles and parental roles. As might be expected, children begin to have role-perceptions at an early age and there are levels of complexity in their formulations of role-perception (Hartley, Rosenbaum, and Schwartz, 1948).

Clinical and experimental studies. Dorcus, Bretnall, and Case (1941) have reported a study which shows clearly that college students--who make up most of the experimental population--are not naive subjects as far as hypnosis is concerned. For example, of 669 students questioned, 79 percent answered yes to the question: Is hypnosis possible? To the question, Could you be hypnotized?, 36 percent said yes, and 15 percent answered in the affirmative in regard to the possibility of hypnotic amnesia. These data may be interpreted to signify that most college students (the usual experimental population) have a perception of the role of the hypnotic subject. Not all who have such a role-perception, however, can enact the role. The proportion of college students who are successfully hypnotized is much less than would be expected from the Dorcus et al. data.

In a study by the author a sophomore class was asked to write descriptions of what takes place in hypnosis. This assignment was made a week before the lecture and demonstration of hypnosis. Volunteers from this class were subject to the induction procedures described by Friedlander and Sarbin (1938). The spontaneous acts, introduced by the subjects without instructions from the experimenter, were noted. Of the 12 subjects who volunteered, six subjects were classified as "good" subjects. The spontaneous actions of four of these subjects could have been predicted from their descriptions of the week before. For example, one subject spontaneously awakened from the trance each time she was given a task which called for opening her eyes. Upon a later perusal of her paper, we read "A person's eyes must be closed in order to be in a hypnotic trance." Another subject was non-hypnotizable on the first attempt. On the second trial he performed all the classical tests. His role-description contained the statement: "It takes time to learn to be hypnotized. Most people can't be hypnotized the first time." A third subject performed all the tests satisfactorily, except where she was asked to rise from her chair and write on the blackboard. She was resistant to all suggestions when on her feet. Her paper contained this statement: "The subject has to be reclining or sitting." The fourth subject was extremely stuporous, slow-moving, and unable to perform any of the tests. He required a vigorous shaking in order to wake him from the trance. His paper contained the sentence: "Hypnosis is like a deep sleep, the hypnotizer talks in a low voice and you go into a deep sleep." Of the remaining six subjects, all had a correct perception of the role. Their failure to enact it could be attributed either to unfavorable motivation or to a lack of role-taking aptitude (v. infra). These observations lend support to the notion that variations in role-perception influence role-enactment.

In a clinical study of 10 adult patients in a hospital ward, a standard hypnotic procedure was used except that the operator avoided any mention of the word hypnosis or trance. The words relaxation and restful state were substituted. By any of the usual criteria none of these patients was hypnotized. Five of them fell asleep, however. Later the same subjects were told that hypnosis was to be attempted. They were told about the phenomena of hypnosis, the manner in which it is induced, and the possible therapeutic outcomes. The same induction procedure was used as before but the words hypnosis and hypnotic trance were reinstated. Three of the ten subjects responded to the usual hypnotic tests. Thus, certain conditions leading to the perception of the role were prerequisite for enacting the role of the hypnotized subject.

Role-taking aptitude. Since motivational factors are necessary but not sufficient to account for the phenomena of hypnosis, and since role-perception does not automatically lead to role-enactment, a role-taking aptitude is postulated. However, since it is impossible to separate the motivational from the aptitudinal factors in studying hypnosis, White (1941) has suggested an experimental design. To a certain extent this design controls the factor of motivation and allows for an approximate isolation of the hypnotic aptitude. White recommends that all completely unhypnotizable subjects be eliminated for the reason that subjects with unfavorable motivations will thereby be discarded. The remaining subjects may be placed in two groups--somnambulists, showing marked amnesia, hallucinations and anesthesia, and light trance subjects who show eyelid and limb catalepsy. "It can be postulated that the first group possesses the hypnotic aptitude to a marked degree, the second to a moderate degree. There should accordingly be significant differences between their average scores on tests which measure the hypnotic aptitude." This design was adopted in a study conducted at the University of Chicago by the author on an original sample of 70 undergraduate volunteers. All were given the Minnesota Multiphasic Personality Inventory. All were subject to the same induction procedures. Of the 70, 36 were discarded as non-hypnotizable subjects. All verbalized role-perception (variations in role-perception were not

considered). Of the remainder, 16 fell into the category of
somnambulistic subjects, and 18 in the category of light trance
subjects. Of the various scales on the test, the Hy (hysteria)
scale differentiated the two groups. Using a T-score of 55 as a
cutting point, the following four-fold table depicts the
results.

	Somnambulists	Light trance
55 and above	12	4
Below 55	4	14

The chi-square value is significant to .01. (The mean T-score of
the somnambulists was 60, of the light trance subjects, 51.)
Thus a scale which differentiates hysterical patients also
differentiates hypnotic subjects. This finding recalls that part
of Charcot's theory which regards hypnosis as an artificially
induced hysteria. However, none of the subjects was known to be
a hysterical patient. We are led to the same conclusions made by
clinicians for many years--the good hypnotic subject and the
hysterical patient have something in common. We would suggest
the role-taking aptitude.

Auxiliary support is given to this conclusion in a study
reported by Lewis and Sarbin (1943). Here hypnotic subjects were
told to imagine eating a meal at a time when they were having
gastric hunger contractions. We found a high correlation between
the depth of hypnosis (Friedlander-Sarbin scale) and the ability
to inhibit hunger contractions. Those who could take the role of
the eater--to use an expression of Moreno's--who could imagine
themselves ingesting food, initiated a set of internal responses
which resulted in the cessation of the gastric contractions.
Subjects who could not be hypnotized, who could not take the
role either of the hypnotic subject, or of the eater in
imagination, showed no cessation of gastric contractions. That
role-taking is organismic is shown here.

When we say that the role-taking aptitude is organismic we
refer back to our "observations which must be accounted for." We
repeated the question raised by the laity and by other
theorists: How can such marked changes in behavior result from
such apparently innocuous stimuli? It is probably not far from
the truth to say with Goldstein (1939) that any act involves the
entire organism. When an individual places himself in the
hypnotic situation--when he takes the role of the hypnotic
subject--he does so organismically. When the subject acts as if
he is ingesting food, his actions are total. The variation in
his bodily responses, of course, will vary with the completeness
and intensity of the role-taking.

A further comment is required about the organismic basis of
the role-taking aptitude, especially as seen in acts which
transcend normal limits. In the case of actors taking a stage
role there are some who will enact the role without a
preliminary warming-up process, while others require
"preparation." In this warming-up or preparatory process the
director helps the actor perceive some of the necessary
attributes of the role. This might be considered a kind of
covert practice in role-taking. In hypnosis the frequent lengthy
induction may serve the same purpose, especially where the

subject requires time to shift to the type of attentional behavior which is a component of the hypnotic role. Relaxation, diffuseness, and uncritical passivity as components of the role may be perceived by the subject as a result of the experimenter's instructions. When the subject aptly takes the hypnotic role (whether immediately, or after warming up via the induction procedures) a shift occus from a sharp, alert, objective and critical attitude to a relatively relaxed, diffuse, and uncritical one. Because the alert orientation is highly valued and supported in our society some coaching or "preparation" is required for certain subjects. They must shift their focus to a relaxed, diffuse orientation which (as in the case of mystical states, for example) allows for more active motor-involvement and more intense affectivity. The variations in intensity or completeness with which one takes a role, and the concurrent motor and autonomic effects, are probably related to the subject's ability to utilize as-if formulations. It is to this notion that we now turn.

The As-If Formulation

Upon what does the role-taking aptitude depend? In a prior paragraph we noted the apparent relationship between the role-taking of the drama and role-taking in hypnosis. Mr. Arbuthnot, the actor, in taking the part of Hamlet, acts as if he is Hamlet and not Mr. Arbuthnot. The hypnotic subject acts as if he is an automaton (if automaticity is included in his role-perception). As a preliminary postulate we can say that the role-taking aptitude depends upon the subject's participation in as-if behavior. That this has a more general application is seen from a logical analysis of Rosenzweig's "triadic hypothesis" (Rosenzweig and Sarason, 1942). In this statement, hypnotizability as a personality trait, repression as an ego-defense, and impunitiveness as a response to frustration are shown to be related. These may be considered as-if structures. We have already noted the as-if character of hypnosis. In repression the subject acts as if an event threatening to the self had not occurred. In the impunitive response to frustration, similarly, the subject acts as if the frustrating event were no logner frustrating. The as-if formulation may be seen not only in the drama, in hypnosis, but in fantasy, play, and, in fact, all imaginative behavior. Imaginative behavior is as-if behavior (Vaihinger, 1924). Some data have been put forward by Jacobson (1938), Schultz (1932), Arnold (1946), and others which may be put to use in formulating our theory. From the proposition that all imaginative behavior is as-if behavior, we may state that role-taking aptitude depends upon imagination. The following statements give at least initial validity to this proposition.

In a series of carefully controlled studies Jacobson (1938) was able to demonstrate the influence of the subject's imagining certain events upon bodily functions. For example, in a condition of relaxation, a subject was told to imagine elevating his arm. The electrical recording showed activity in the muscles which were involved. Schultz (1932) reports many instances of the influence of imagination on various muscular and vascular characteristics. Varondenck (1921) tells how imaginary processes (implicit) can spill over into overt muscular movements during the act of imagining. Common experience verifies the same notion. In imagining a former embarrassing situation we can feel our ears reddening and our faces flushing; in imagining a former painful experience we may involuntarily withdraw from the direction of the imagined stimulus, or in imagining something extremely unpleasant or disgusting we may experience nausea.

Arnold has written the most complete analysis of the relationship between hypnosis and imagination (Arnold, 1946). According to her hypothesis,

> . . . in hypnosis the individual is actively striving to imagine what the hypnotist describes, and in so doing gradually narrows down his focus and relinquishes control of his imaginative processes . . . The individual focuses on a situation and actively selects the sensations which he will perceive; he actively focuses on possible situations in imagining, on symbols in logical thinking; and he refocuses on past experiences in remembering. Such focusing . . . is merely directed more efficiently, more intensely, during hypnosis than in waking life, and determined by the hypnotist instead of by the subject himself (Arnold, 1946, p. 127).

This writer would amend the last statement to read: The focusing is determined by the hypnotist only insofar as the subject's self-perceptions and role-perception permits such direction. This amendment would follow from a careful consideration of the data Arnold presents from her own experiment which reveals the individual character of the subject's own imagining over and above the directions of the experimenter.

Although Arnold's views are more sophisticated than most previous theories, we are left without any anchorage point for understanding differential responsiveness. The numerous experiments cited by Arnold show the influence of imagination on behavior and the kinds of exprimental and clinical situations appear to be of the same kind as the hypnotic situation. But what of the answer to the all important social-psychological question: What are the characteristics of those individuals who are not able to focus and thus cannot produce changes in overt or covert behavior?

In Arnold's data is concealed a partial answer to this question. She reports an experiment in which the postural sway technique is used. She tested the hypothesis that a suggestion is acted upon only if the subject actively imagines it. The subjects were told to imagine falling forward. The amount of postural sway was recorded. Comparisons were made between the amount of sway and the reported vividness of imagery. Her conclusion was: The more vivid the imaginative process, the more pronounced the overt movement. From this conclusion and from the long-accepted conclusion about the relationship between the postural sway test and hypnotizability a correlation between vividness of imagery and hypnotic depth could be posited. We could then deduce that hypnotic role-taking depended upon imaginative (as-if) processes. One might fit the previously mentioned findings of Eysenck and Furneaux into this formulation. Subjects who score high on postural sway tests and test of heat illusion are able to imagine vividly in these sense modalities. A fortiori, the experiment of Sarbin and Madow (1942) may be cited in which the depth of hypnosis and the Rorschach W/D ratio were shown to be correlated. The W or Whole response purportedly indicates a more active imagination.

How, then, does the role-taking theory apply to the four sets of observations previously identified as requiring explanation?

The apparent automaticity is apparent only. The subject varies his responses to the hypnotic situation in terms of his perception of the role of the hypnotized subject. If his perception includes automaticity, then he will act like an automaton.

The apparent discontinuity of behavior is also apparent but not real. The subject's behavior is continuous with his pre-experimental behavior--modified only by his enactment of the role of the hypnotic subject. Such "discontinuous" behavior as amnesia, post-hypnotic compulsions, etc., can be understood in terms of the subject's perception of the role, of his facility in as-if behavior and of the degree of participation of the self in the role.

The apparent disjunction between the magnitude of the response and the procedure for eliciting the response is a pseudo-problem. The magnitude of the response is not dependent upon the procedure except insofar as it coincides with the role-expectations of the subject. What appears to be disjunction is a vestigial remnant of an outmoded psychology which sought to find constancy between phenomenal experience and stimulus events. If the subject has an adequate perception of the role, if this perception is not incongruent with his self-perceptions, and if he has an appropriate amount of the role-taking aptitude, then he will produce all the dramatic phenomena of hypnosis merely because "the operator talks to him." If he does not or cannot perceive the role, if the role is not congruent with his self-perceptions, or he does not have a sufficient amount of the role-taking aptitude or skill, then he will not respond to the operator's commands. Thus differential responsiveness is declared to be a function of these three variables.

Summary

The known facts about hypnosis were grouped in four classes of observations: (1) apparent automaticity, (2) apparent discontinuity, (3) disjunction between the magnitude of the stimulus and the magnitude of the response, and (4) differential responsiveness. Because of the obvious dependence of the first three factors upon the fourth (differential responsiveness) this question was formulated: What are the characteristics of those individuals who, in response to hypnotic induction procedures, exhibit conduct which is apparently discontinuous and apparently automatic?

We sought to demonstrate that concurrent theories of hypnosis were tradition-bound: trying to explain hypnotic behavior in terms of conditioning, heredity, or vague neurological formulae. In order to establish a logical link between hypnosis and another form of social psychological conduct which is accepted without resorting to traditional formulations, we first indicated the similarity between role-taking in the drama and role-taking in hypnosis. We postulated that success in taking a dramatic role or hypnotic role depended upon favorable motivation, a perception of the role, and role-taking aptitude. The chief difference in the two forms of role-taking was the degree of participation of the self in the role (levels of consciousness).

The main portion of our presentation attempted to establish the validity of these conceptions. Favorable motivation was re-defined as congruence between the subject's self-concept and the role of the hypnotic subject. Role-perception is derived from the individual's interaction with various media of communication: the manner in which role-perception influences role-enactment is indicated. Finally, a role-taking aptitude is postulated. From our present state of knowledge this aptitude is probably dependent upon or continuous with the ability of the subject to use as-if formulations. Various research and clinical findings were introduced to supply a groundwork for the initial validity of the argument.

Footnote

1. Abridged from Psychological Review, 1950, 57, 255-270.

5

HYPNOSIS: THE DRAMATURGICAL PERSPECTIVE[1]

I

In this essay, my plan is to present a sketch of some world hypotheses that undergird the efforts of modern theorists of hypnosis. I shall show how most theorists of hypnotism have been guided by an implicit world view based on the root-metaphor of the machine. Fewer theorists have been guided by an alternate world view--contextualism--based on the root-metaphor of the historical event. It is this latter world view that provides the categories for the dramaturgical perspective. I shall assume that the reader is familiar with one form of dramaturgical analysis, the role-theoretical interpretation of hypnosis. For the present, when I employ the term hypnosis, I am referring to a social scene with at least two actors in which one actor enacts a role characterized by counter-expectational conduct.

I shall discuss in some detail an extension of the concept "skill in role-enactment" through the employment of the dramaturgical notion: credibility enhancement. I shall conclude with some suggestions for further theoretical development.

II

The first part of my analysis is guided by the work of the philosopher, Stephen Pepper. In his classic work, World Hypotheses (1942), he identified four useful world hypotheses, each flowing from a basic or root-metaphor. I shall mention three: formism, mechanism, and contextualism.

The formist metaphor--associated with Plato--depends on transcendental forms as the ultimate category. Events are described by classifying according to a priori forms. The root-metaphor is similarity. An event is identified according to its similarity with an a priori form. Causality is immanent, contained within the form. Psychological theories flowing from a formist metaphysic are those that depend on personality traits, neuropsychic dispositions, or dimensions of the mind. The futile search for correlates of the trait "hypnotizability" has been guided by an implicit formist metaphysic.

Mechanism is the dominant world view in modern western civilization. The root-metaphor is the machine. The kind of machine employed as the analogue may be a lever, a clock, a dynamo, or a computer. The mechanist world view provides categories for understanding events in terms of the transmittal of forces. Efficient causality--cause and effect--is the fundamental organizing principle of modern scientists, including scientists of hypnosis and other types of influence communication.

All of us are familiar with Mesmer's grandiose attempts to account for the counter-expectational conduct of his patients. His theorizing began from his noting a resemblance between the effects of a magnet when applied to iron filings and when applied to a human body. He coined the metaphor "animal magnetism." His use of the magnet as the vehicle to explain such happenings as crisis and cure was not random or casual. The Newtonian revolution had influenced all practitioners of physical science to build their models to conform to the root-metaphor of the machine. Animal magnetism was not such a wild idea when we consider one of the constructs of Newtonian science: the invisible ether. This concept was posited to help account for the pushes and pulls of natural forces.

Although many of Mesmer's propositions were self-contradictory, it appears incontestable that he believed the happenings that followed upon his gesticulations and manipulations could be accounted for by employing the same root-metaphor--the machine--that Newton had used so prodigiously. Of course, Mesmer's theories were overdrawn and extravagant, and authoritative commissions rejected his claims. Nevertheless, his theories were consonanat with the new world view that nature operated like a giant clockwork machine. In an influential work of the period, LaMettrie in 1747 espoused the belief that man, like an astronomical system or a clock, is a machine (Vartanian, 1960). This world view facilitated the acceptance of the belief that the conduct of Mesmer's patients could be accounted for in the language of the distribution of forces. The history of hypnosis records the appearance of other physicalistic metaphors to account for the communication of influence, for example, odylic force, electricity, ether.

The ultimate rejection of models of physical force had no effect on the popularity or utility of the root-metaphor of the machine. Physiological models replaced physicalistic models in efforts to discover the distribution of forces within the organism that was responsible for counter-expectational conduct. For example, the Abbe Faria made use of the Galenic theory of humours and posited the variable liquidity of the blood as the "cause" of hypnotic happenings. About the middle of the 19th Century, humoral models gave way to neurological models, models that continued to flow from the root-metaphor of the machine. Counter-expectational conduct was explained in terms of the distribution of forces in the nervous system. Except for refinement in language and the use of sophisticated technological aids, current neurological models follow the same lines as 19th Century models of hypnosis advanced by Braid, Charcot, and Heidenhain.

The root-metaphor of the machine continues as an implicit guide for most contemporary theorists. For some, the actions of hypnotized subjects and patients are regarded as happenings presumably caused by electrochemical forces in the nervous system. Only a few years ago, a prominent investigator, on the basis of some tenuous relationships between scores on hypnotic scales and pre-induction EEG profiles concluded that "hypnotic susceptibility is a function of brain physiology . . . ." (London, Hart and Leibovitz, 1968). As late as 1972--on the basis of a borderline significant correlation of .27 between fast EEG waves and the Barber Suggestibility Scale--a team of investigators stated that "hypnosis . . . exists in reality as a phenomenon demonstrable in the physiology . . . of the nervous system" (Ulett, Akpinar and Itil, 1972).

In addition to providing categories for physicalistic, physiological, and neurological models, the root-metaphor of the machine has guided the creation of psychological models of hypnosis. The vague concept of force was easily assimilated to the operations of the invisible, often ethereal mind, psychic apparatus, mental structures, and so on. With this assimilation, theorists of hypnotism could write accounts of the operation of psychic forces acting on mental faculties in the form of associations, stimulus response bonds, valences, and cathexes. Such psychic forces were not grounded in observation but were constructed to keep alive and intact the machine-like picture of the hypnotized subject.

The postulation of psychic forces weakened the structure of mechanistic psychological theories. The psychic forces doctrine led to an illicit eclecticism. Hypnotic conduct was described with categories drawn from two disparate world views: the metaphysic of transcendental platonic forms being employed when the metaphysic of mechanical forces failed to provide testable models. The trance concept illustrates the intrusion of a formist notion.

I have sketchily but critically reviewed the legitimate efforts of mechanistically guided scientists to make sense of counter-expectational conduct. It is no longer considered radical or impolite to declare that the causality category of the mechanistic world view has been singularly ineffective in understanding human social conduct. In the physical sciences, the machine metaphor has paid off handsomely. But in the psychological and social sciences, the pay-off has been scant. Psychologists, psychiatrists, and other scientists concerned with social conduct have not produced stable law-like statements such as are found in textbooks of physics and chemistry. Certainly, after 200 years of studying counter expectational conduct guided by the root-metaphor of the machine, it is frustrating that we have no formulae to help predict the outcome of a particular hypnotic interaction.

A different world hypothesis is available to guide our search: contextualism. Rather than the billiard ball universe with its implied linear causality, the salient imagery is the historic event. The contextualist is interested in an event in actuality, in all its complexity. He is interested in the dynamic, dramatic event. To illustrate the workings of models guided by the contextualist metaphysic, one would use present participles, e.g., persuading a crowd, solving a puzzle, performing a role, building a theory. The starting place for a contextualist analysis would be incidents or episodes in the study of a life in the plot of a novel or drama, or a social encounter.

To those who have been schooled in formist or mechanistic world views, contextualism at first appears chaotic. Events are in constant flux--the categorical statements assert change and novelty. The integration of the texture of an event alters the context of a future event. The contextualist recognizes the limits of mechanistic causality, and he seeks the strands that appear to influence the ongoing action.

To help convey my impression of the typical practitioner of each of the three world hypotheses, let me give my stereotypes: the formist is the medieval scholar describing the actions of the hypnotized subject as "in the nature of things"; the mechanist is the white-coated laboratory scientist describing the actions of the inert subject as happenings caused by antecedent stimuli; the contextualist is the playwright or novelist noticing the multiplicity of strands that influence the conduct of interbehaving actors: hypnotists as well as subjects.

III

The contextualist world view provides a set of categories that have evolved into the dramaturgical model. The metaphor of interest is: life is theater. Human actions are seen as episodes in a continuing drama. The metaphor calls up all the auxiliary concepts of the theater arts: roles, scripts, audiences, the stage, acting skill, scenes, rehearsal, preparation for role-enactment, props, and so on. The overarching concept is that the human being is an actor, a doer, a performer, and not an inert object that passively processes stimuli.

The dramaturgical perspective has been widely used by literary critics and by sociologists identified as symbolic interactionists. In the dramaturgical perspective, it is important to note that actors not only respond to situations, but also mold and create them. So-called mental processes and their sequelae have no place in the definition of the situation. The interactions of participants define the situation. The units of interest are not individuals, not organisms, not assemblages of traits, but interacting persons in identifiable contexts.

If there were more time, I would remind the audience of the observations made by myself and others that the conduct of the hypnotized subject can be most felicitously described as role-enactment. The subject or patient and the operator (experimenter or therapist or entertainer) come to the laboratory, the clinic, or the theater with certain beliefs, attitudes, skills, desires, expectations. The conduct of the subject and the operator are part of an episode, the meaning of the role-enactment of the subject depends in part on the meanings he assigns to the role enactments of the experimenter. As in any dramatic encounter, the actions of each actor may influence other actors as well as audiences.

Whether enacting a dramatic role, such as Hamlet, or a social role, such as presidential candidate, the person's actions must appear credible. That is to say, the actor has the job of demonstrating to his relevant audiences that he is legitimately ocupying his position, that he is entitled to enact the role. In order to enhance his credibility, then, the actor will make use of linguistic devices, motoric skills, gestures, costumes, badges of office, and any available props. The so-called bedside manner attributed to physicians is an example of actions to enhance credibility. The use of technical jargon is often designed to make one's adoption of a role believable. You will recall how Moliere, during the 17th Century when medicine was attempting to become scientific, made fun of a bogus physician's efforts to enhance his credibility through the use of Latin expressions and esoteric anatomical labels.

What does an actor do to enhance the credibility of his enactment of the role of hypnotic subject? Clearly, he must take into account what he believes to be the hypnotist's (and the audience's) criteria for a convincing performance. As discussed elsewhere (Sarbin and Coe, 1972), the subject who has agreed to perform the hypnotic role must exhibit conduct that will lead the hypnotist and audience to infer that the actor is performing appropriately and convincingly. The criteria of the role of the hypnotized person are widely shared in western society and are easily communicated: you must act in ways that are contrary to mundane expectations. If a person under ordinary conditions is told by a second person: "Your arm is stiff as a board, you cannot bend it," the first person might appear surprised and even question the sanity of the second person. But it is unlikely that his perception of his arm will be modified by the communication. If the communication is set in a scene identified as hypnosis, then the person, now assigned the role of subject or patient, will not be surprised nor will he question the sanity of the communicator, now assigned the reciprocal role of hypnotist. How does the "good" (i.e., skillful) subject perform convincingly? Not by passively complying with the communication. He will respond with vigor, enhancing his credibility by contracting antagonistic muscle groups, exhibiting great effort so that his audience will be convinced that in fact he cannot bend his arm, that he is legitimatly occupying the position of hypnotized subject. The role of the hypnotized subject calls for counter-expectational actions. The successful actor produces such actions with persuasive embellishments designed to add conviction to his enactment.

In our previous work Coe and I made use of the dramaturgical concept: skill in role enactment (Sarbin and Coe, 1972). To illustrate this concept, imagine the performance of a novice and a professional actor assigned the role of Hamlet. The novice might recite the appropriate lines on cue but his audience might declare the performance unconvincing. The professional actor's performance would be more convincing because he could activate certain skills, among them the subtle use of gesture, facial expression, posture, body language. Together with the recital of the "lines," these actions contribute to making the performance convincing.

A new metaphor is appropriate at this point: the rhetoric of role performance. The purpose of rhetoric is to convince, to persuade. Although rhetoric normally refers to the art of using spoken or written language to influence others, it is also employed to denote the expressive action of the body as an accompaniment of speech and also to refer to the persuasiveness of looks, glances, shrugs, and other bodily actions. (Parenthetically, the role of the hypnotist makes use of "passes"; the experimenter makes use of special vocal intonations.)

The current controversies in hypnosis center on phenomenal report as the sine qua non of hypnosis. Because motoric actions can be easily simulated, and because "the experience" has its own validity, we must pay special attention to the subject's self-report. Given that the subject tries to maintain his credibility, is the hypnotist prepared to separate dialectical from rhetorical expressions? This is an empirical question. It is my guess that most of us are attending to the content of the subject's self-report, and disattending to the rhetoric of performance; that is, the hypnotist may be insensitive to the components of the communication that make the content of the self-report convincing and credible. This is not to say that rhetorical cues are not available to analysis. Dimensions must first be identified. Birdwhistell (1970) and Spiegel and Machotka (1974) have already provided the impetus and some concrete proposals for the study of body language. Once the analyst of social communication has dimensions on which to sort non-verbal cues, then the rhetoric of performance can be separated from the verbal dialectic.

It is no great feat to acquire proficiency in analyzing spoken and written sentences for rhetorical elements, as in the study of propaganda. But body rhetoric, facial expressions, and gesture occur with such subtlety that the observer responds to the total communication without analyzing out the rhetoric of performance. A careful experimenter might write in his notebook "subject says 'I am three feet tall,' and the sentence is uttered with conviction. Therefore, I (the experimenter) am convinced that the subject believes the assertion, that to him the experience of being three feet tall is 'real'."

Let us return for a moment to our actors assigned the part of Hamlet. I point to the resemblance of the successful role rhetoric of the experienced actor to the convincing actions and report of the "good" hypnotic subject; also to the resemblance of the unsuccessful role rhetoric of the novice to the unconvincing report of the inept hypnotic subject. These conceptual resemblances lead me to mention three studies that provide some empirical support for the use of the concept: the rhetoric of performance. All three studies were guided by the dramaturgical model--that persons who are judged to be "good" hypnotic subjects engage in overt actions to enhance their credibility, and that such persons bring to the hypnosis context experiences and interests associated with the rhetoric of performance.

The first study (Sarbin and Lim, 1963) assessed the hypnotic responsiveness of a sample of college student volunteers. Later each student enacted five-minute improvisations in pantomine before a panel of judges who were experts in dramatic arts. Comparing the convincingness of the pantomime performances and the scores on hypnotizability showed a positive relationship. In this study, the concept skill in role enactment is nearly synonymous with the rhetoric of performance.

A second study (Coe and Sarbin, 1966) was directed to the question: what are the conditions that influence the accuracy of hypnotic role enactment? Again, taking our hypotheses from the dramaturgical perspective, we investigated the rhetoric of performance in an indirect way. We compared the hypnotic responsiveness scores of students majoring in dramatic arts with students majoring in the natural sciences. Choice of dramatic arts as a major is an indirect way of assessing the interest in, if not the aptitude for, role playing. Nearly all the dramatic arts students had participated in actual productions, and some had had leading roles. More important, they had practiced the same kinds of motoric behaviors and imaginings specifically required in the hypnotic role. Students in the natural sciences were considered to be low in role-taking skill because their present goals presumably required little practice in shifting from one type of role to another. The mean hypnotizability score for the dramatic arts students was much higher than the mean score for the science students. Since choice of major appears to be related to variations in socialization, it is likely that the drama students had acquired, along with the interest in the drama, skill in the rhetoric of performance, a skill that also influenced the subject's performance of the counter-expectational conduct called for in the hypnotic role.

A third study (Sarbin and Evanson, 1976) addressed directly the relationship between hypnotizability and the rhetoric of performance. In the vocabulary of the present analysis, interpretive dancers have the interest in and skill for performance rhetoric. We assessed the hypnotizability of students of interpretive dancing and compared their scores with unselected students. The interpretive dancers, as a group, had a significantly higher mean score on hypnotizability.

These studies, together with clinical material and reports of imaginative involvement, give support to the conclusion that persons who are skilled in the rhetoric of performance give convincing performances in the role of the hypnotic subject.

From the dramaturgical perspective, then, we have drawn a concept that stresses the theatrical qualities of the hypnotic performance. This is not to say that credibility enhancement is the central variable in hypnotic studies. However, given the arguments stated earlier--that the criteria for the hypnotic role include unspoken criteria of convincingness of counter-expectational performances--the concept of credibility enhancement cannot be ignored. Similarly, we cannot ignore the rhetoric of performance as a means of establishing and enhancing credibility.

IV

The foregoing remarks stress the action components of the hypnotic scene. The conduct of the hypnotist and the conduct of the subject are the topics of interest for us. The conduct of these actors make sense only if we try to locate the strands in the total context of action. It is instructive to point out that besides self-professed role-theorists, Barber (1969, 1974) and his associates have contributed to a contextualist understanding. Over the past twenty years, they have systematically uncovered the strands in the texture of the dramatic event labeled hypnosis. Among these strands are settings, instructions, motives, criteria held by observers, etc.

If we continue to regard the hypnotic scene as a dramatic episode, the dramaturgical model can illuminate some of the other dark corners of influence communication. Research for the past half-century has focused on individual differences in the quality of the hypnotic role-enactment. When we consider that the hypnotic scene is a multiply-elaborated event, it becomes futile to employ classical research designs. Rather, as I said before, we can reach an acceptable degree of understanding by approaching the hypnotic event from the posture of a playwright or novelist. I have already discussed how the judgment of the experimenter, "X is a 'good' subject," is influenced by (among other things) the skill in the subject's employment of performance rhetoric. But we cannot account for the complexity of the dramatic episode if we entertain only one hypothesis about the origin of individual differences in responsiveness. The dramaturgical perspective directs us to another feature of the hypnosis setting: the dramatistic possibilities of a particular role assignment as imagined by the hypnotic subject.

I should like to suggest as a strand in the texture of the hypnotic scene the degree to which the actor can imagine theatrical possibilities, given his role assignment. We may posit a dimension: at one pole is the actor who is unwilling or unable to imagine himself as a player of roles, as part of a drama. He rigidly performs his one role, neglecting other enactment possibilities. In the middle of the dimension is the actor who is sometimes willing and able to view his performances as dramatic role playing. It is as if the actor momentarily stands aside and views his actions from the vantage point of the audience. Imaginatively standing aside, the actor can entertain the possibility of molding the actions of others, thereby altering the developing script. At the other pole is the actor who deliberately stands apart from the action. To him the action is a dramatic performance; he can perform with apparent engrossment. An exemplar from dramatic literature is Cyrano. He is a role player who is excited by the theatrical possibilities of his own role. He is a part of the action, at the same time, he stands apart from the action. In the theater, the audience shares the same perspective as Cyrano.

This dimension makes use of imagining, a concept employed in connection with explaining counter expectational conduct at least since the French Academy investigated Mesmer's claims. The imagining is directed by the actor's assumption that his actions and the actions of co-actors are constrained--but not fully determined--by the structural properties of roles; that social conduct need not be ritualized; that the content of any role may be altered by the actions of the reciprocal role player.

Let us apply this conception to the person who agrees to enact the role of the hypnotized subject. For most candidates for this role, the introduction of the concept "hypnosis" frames the scene. The model for the frame may be derived from observing others in the same scene, from reading novels, seeing movies, etc. If the subject's style of action is literal, if he does not recognize the role-playing possibilities for himself in the hypnosis scene, if he avoids the use of "as if" (hypothetical) formulations of social encounters, then he is not likely to depart from his everyday mundane roles and imaginatively prepare himself for the dramatic role of the hypnotic subject. The actor located at the non-theatrical pole of the posited dimension would be the typical non-responsive subject. Most of our subjects are drawn from the middle of the dimension--they are able to recognize some theatrical possibilities in the hypnotic scene and shift from mundane to dramatic roles and vice versa. Our unusually responsive subjects are located at the dramatistic pole. They can imaginatively place themselves in the hypnotic scene and they can silently entertain the effects of performing counter-expectational acts. The clinical studies of Josephine Hilgard (1970) are instructive in this connection. This dimension--the ability to recognize the dramatic possibilities of a scene--may be regarded as a cognitive skill, parallel to the motoric skills involved in the rhetoric of performance.

The implication of these remarks for research and theory is clear. We must give up our reliance on the machine metaphor, constructing hypotheses and testing them as if the subject is an object involved in the transfer of energy. If we conduct our post-experimental inquiries as if our subjects (and operators) were engaged in a dramatic adventure, we would acquire more useful information about the complexities of the hypnotic scene.

V

My current efforts to extend the utility of role theory make use of the actions of participants as the text of a drama and the silent constructions of each actor before, during, and after a performance as the pre-text. These conceptions, together with those already discussed, provide a framework for explaining some of the complexities involved in the act of believing one's imaginings.

Text and pre-text are conceptions that flow from employing the metaphysic of context . They can be employed to answer questions arising from looking at hypnosis, not as a form, not as the distribution of forces, but as a historical event. The recent development of the "hidden observer" concept by Hilgard lends itself to dramaturgical analysis. The questions could be framed: How do experimenters, clinicians, subjects and clients create and employ such dramatistic characters as "hidden observers" to account for counter-expectational conduct?

Footnote

1.   Prepared for the 1976 meetings of The Society for Clinical and Experimental Hypnosis. I am indebted to Professor William C. Coe for help of many kinds. This essay has not been previously published.

PART IV
Transformations of Social Identity

The basic theoretical work for the material that appears in this section was begun in the summer of 1965, when Sarbin, together with Karl Scheibe and Rolf Kroger, prepared a series of working papers on the topic of social identity. The impelling problem for this work was that of formulating a conception of identity that would lend itself well to interpreting the process of social degradation as exemplified in typical careers of the prisoner, the mental patient, the poor, and the stigmatized. Such a conception of social identity must also apply to the process of social upgrading--the making of heroes, champions, and social leaders. The general question was, "How is it that human beings come to have such enormously different evaluative significance?" The formulation that emerged in response to this question is clearly based on role-theoretical conceptions, in particular on the elaboration of the simple distinction between achieved and ascribed roles. The theory is not about individuals enacting particular roles, but about the individual as a composite of social roles--as a social identity.

The first paper in this section is essentially a refinement and synthesis of original working papers. It sets forth a three-dimensional model of social identity and with it an explication of how the model might be applied generally to "transvaluations" of social identity.

From this model, dozens of applications have been made, of which the next two papers in the section are examples. In the first paper, application is made to "the dangerous individual" and, more generally, to the concept of danger. Sarbin argues that to be endangered by another person is to be in a condition of real or potential domination by that person. Danger in this sense is shown to derive from a differential social evaluation of persons and is manifest as the threat or possibility of dramatically revising the existing ordering of social evaluation.

The final paper in this section extends the model of social identity to accommodate the radical "self reconstitution" processes that are illustrated by thought reform, religious conversions, political radicalization, or cult indoctrination. This is an attempt to make intelligible the kinds of dramatic personality changes described in James' Varieties Of Religious Experience. Sarbin examines a wide range of literature on radical personality changes and suggests a series of five themes that are common to all of them. He also identifies three major processes of transformation that are common to all such cases.

One consequence of this examination of the ways in which social identities are transformed is that the form of change seen in psychotherapy becomes a special case. Also, the process of becoming a mental patient is now clearly something that happens in the context of a society that holds to certain metaphors about how deviant or unusual conduct is to be explained. Part V will explore the applications of the contextualist position to the concept of mental illness in more detail.

6

THE TRANSVALUATION
OF SOCIAL IDENTITY[1]

Our purpose in this chapter is to present a model of social identity that will facilitate an understanding of the processes of social degradation and the processes of social upgrading. Relevant to theories of individual and societal change, degradation and upgrading are forms of transvaluations--a reorganizing of the valuations declared on a person.

Reference observations for the process of social transvaluation are many. Degradation is illustrated in the treatment meted out to convicts, mental hospital patients, prisoners of war, political rivals, members of minority groups, traitors, and the disreputable poor. Advancement is illustrated in the ceremonies of job and school promotion, elections to office, wedding celebrations, prison pardons, and the honoring of heroes.

By the application of these social procedures of degradation and promotion, human beings acquire differential valuation. This differential grading, we shall demonstrate, has powerful implications for the conduct of individuals and groups. The consequences of degradation are the loss of freedom, loss of respect, loss of esteem, and the limitations of power and privilege. The consequences of promotion are increased esteem, increased freedom of movement, and an expanded set of powers and perquisites.

I

The theoretical idiom of choice for these issues can be provided by modern social role theory (Sarbin and Allen, 1968). In the arguments to be set forth, the underlying premise is that a person's social identity at any point in time is a function of his validated social positions; validated through appropriate, proper, and convincing role-enactments. The model provides a means for the comparison of different patterns of roles specific to individuals or for the same individual at different times.

We begin from the postulate that the survival of human beings is dependent on their ability to locate themselves accurately in their various ecologies. Efficient behavioral choices are dependent upon the correct placements of self in the world of occurrences. Among the various ecologies into which the world may be differentiated is the social ecology or role-system. A person is constantly faced with the necessity of locating himself in relation to others. Misplacement of self in the role system may have embarrassing, perilous, or even fatal consequences.

The self is located in the role-system through an inferential process. On the basis of available clues and of knowledge of the role-system, an individual infers the role of others and concurrently of himself. One's social identity is defined as the multiple product of attempts to locate oneself in the role-system--symbolically represented by asking and answering the question, Who Am I?

It follows that planned or unplanned changes in role-relationships will modify inferences about social identity because different information is available to the person concerning who he is. That is, one's location in social space is different when interacting with an adult or with a child, with a policeman or with a physician, with a friend or with a stranger, with a victim or a victimizer. Such induced transitory modifications in social identity should not be confused with the substitution of one identity for another. The question of the limits of the modifiability of social identity as a function of changes in social reference individuals and groups should properly remain open.

The necessary features of the proposed model may be expressed in terms of three dimensions which jointly describe a solid of roughly specifiable shape. (Various perspectives are presented in Figures 1, 2, and 3.) Again, the reader should be reminded that the shaped model is presented as a device for illustrating the relationships we are positing among variables. While the metric significance of the dimensions is weak, the generally important relationshhips can be clearly represented in this manner. The three dimensions are: (a) the status dimension; (b) the involvement dimension; and (c) the value dimension. First, we show how the value of a person's social identity is related to characteristics of his component roles, and then we take up the problem of transvaluations of social identity.

II

Status

The present usage of the term status is synonymous with "position in a social structure." The relationship between role and status is conventionally described as follows: A status or position is an abstraction defined by the expectations held by members of the relevant society. Role is a set of behaviors enacted by an individual in his efforts to make good his occupancy of a particular status or position.

Linton (1936) first made the conventional distinction between ascribed and achieved statuses. That is, some statuses are given: they are ascribed to a person in virtue of sex, age, race and kinship. Other statuses are achieved by a person following decisions and choices made by and about the person during the course of life. This distinction, which has been found convenient and acceptable by a number of authors, is not sufficiently clear since the differentiating criteria for achieved and ascribed statuses have never been explicitly specified. However, even using the major implied criterion in Linton's distinction--the presence of choice prior to adopting a role--it would seem that the classification of statuses should be more than two-valued.

Contained within the meaning of "ascribed" is the notion of "granted" or "givenness." In the discussion that follows, the term "granted" will frequently be used as a synonym for the more opaque term "ascribed." The term "achievement" has a surplus meaning in current usage that does not always contribute to the sense of this discussion. The terms "attained," or "selected" will generally be used in its place.

The difficulties with Linton's dichotomous conception are: (1) that clear criteria are unspecified for deciding whether a given status falls into the granted or the attained category; and (2) that many instances show the contribution of both kinds of factors. Is the sex role of the successful transvestite granted or attained? Does the father who deserts his family and establishes himself as a bachelor fit the granted or attained category? Does the natural successor to a king win his position by ascription or by achievement? These and other difficult cases may be dealt with consistently if social statuses are regarded as falling along a continuum based upon the degree of choice prior to a person's entering a given social position. Thus, occupying a given status may under some circumstances be a great attainment and under other circumstances be almost completely "taken for granted."

The degree of choice for any status may be determined by considering the number of alternatives for action available to the actor and the degree of optionality of these alternatives. More choice is exercised prior to a person's entering the position of lawyer than for the position of factory worker. The potential lawyer may choose, in principle, many occupations below that of lawyer in the occupational status hierachy while the potential factory worker has fewer occupations below him from which to choose. Similarly, less choice is involved in becoming a parent than in becoming a godparent. The social forces toward parenthood are more compelling than those producing godparenthood.

It should be clear that choice is being used here in a sense that is consistent with selectivity and not in the sense of freedom or lack of determining constraints. Decisions may be made for or about the person who is placed on the path to great attainments--one may have little sense of choosing one's own destiny. Nonetheless, it is meaningful to consider choice to have operated to a very high degree in the development of virtuoso attainment, for during the course of life many selective decisions must have been made that were instrumental in the attaining of high status.

Social statuses and their corresponding roles, then, may be ordered with respect to optionality. For any society, the position of cultural participant, or person, is placed at the granted end of the status continuum. Sex roles, age roles, and kinship roles are in the same region. Occupational and recreational roles, such as member of the Book-of-the-Month Club, member of a political party, and physician are relatively more attained positions.

Roles in the granted region may be further characterized as less differentiated and as applying to a large proportion of society's membership. Thus, every person may be initially granted the role of cultural participant. As such he is expected to act according to certain basic propriety rules that preempt the requirements of any particular attained position. This grant carries with it the legitimacy of claims for certain "inalienable" rights.

The concept of fundamental human equality, the origin of which has been attributed by Cassirer (1946) to the Stoics of ancient Greece, is a prescriptive injunction against the witholding of a human birthright from any person on a priori grounds. The kind of social progress represented or instigated by the Magna Carta, the Declaration of Independence, the 19th Amendment of the constitution, and the Civil Rights Act of 1964 is an approach to this ideal.

Skipping now to the other extreme of the status dimension, highly attained roles are highly differentiated and apply to relatively few members of society. Examples are Supreme Court Justice, violin virtuoso, or Secretary-General of the United Nations. Legitimate power and social esteem accrue to occupants of attained positions.

Social roles can be ordered along the status dimension by another operation. A certain probability of attainment exists for every distinct social position. Probability, in this context, has the conventional relative frequency interpretation; the probability associated with a position is determined by the proportion of individuals who opt for a position successfully attaining it.

Choice is exercised prior to occupancy of an achieved position through several means. A person attains a position by election, nomination, special training, responding to a revelation or "calling," volunteering, or by demonstrating some special skill. In each of these cases the process of promotion to an achieved position is reciprocal--the person must choose (or at least accede) and at the same time the relevant social reference groups must recognize and certify the promotion. The initial choosing is done either by the person or by the social reference groups, or by both. Characteristically, then, achievements are a joint product of choosing and of being chosen. The selectivity involved in both of these choosing processes compounds to form the degree of choice prior to achievement, which in turn is the means of indexing the location of a given position on the status dimension.

III

Involvement

The second major dimension to be considered is opportunity for variation in involvement, to which we shall simply refer as involvement. Role enactments vary in the degree to which the actor is involved in the role. But statuses also vary in the extent to which they allow variations in role-involvement. Before discussing this point systematically it is necessary to define the present usage of the term Involvement.

Involvement may be considered a dimension of the intensity of enactment of a role (Sarbin and Allen, 1968). With low involvement, role and self are clearly differentiated, few organismic systems are activated, and little effort is expended by the actor in enacting the role. At the other end of the continuum, self and role are undifferentiated, the entire organism is activated, and much effort is expended.

Other than degree of organismic involvement (and concurrently, degree of self-role differentiation), time is an index of role-involvement. A role is defined as highly self-involving if the person is "in the role" a large proportion of the time. Being "in the role" means engaging in activities (performances) that are role-specific. To be cast in the role of adult female, for example, means being "on" almost continuously.

Given great situation and temporal variability in role involvement for some positions and little for others, the problem is to account systematically for these differences. Our observations suggest that the potential for variability in role-involvement is a function of placement on the status dimension. The closer a status is to the granted end of the continuum, the less the potential for differential involvement. Conversedly, the closer a status is to the attainment end of the dimension, the greater will be the observed variations in role involvement.

For the ultimate ascribed role, that of "person" or "human being," it is difficult to think of a case of less than continuous high involvement. In singular cases, individuals succeed by meditation, disease, or drugs, to lose involvement in the role of "person" or its negative counterparts, but our language is impoverished in descriptive terms for this state of affairs.

By contrast, attained roles may be put on and off like cloaks. Most attained roles are cyclical, and while intense organismic involvement may be demanded for certain periods, temporal involvement is rarely continuous over long periods of a person's life. A professional baseball player may be highly involved in his role when on the diamond, when in spring training, when reviewing batting averages. He may be relatively uninvolved in the baseball player role when attending a funeral, when writing letters, or when visiting friends.

Involvement at the attained end of the status continuum can be as high as at the granted end. While a man is President of the United States, he is just as involved in that role as in the more granted roles of human being, man, and citizen. But for any attained role, there is the opportunity for complete disinvolvement--for escape. The resignation of Richard Nixon from the presidency is a case in point. Opportunities for disinvolvement are fewer for positions in the granted region.

This posited relationship between potential for variability in involvement and the status dimension is roughly represented by a triangle, coming to a point at the granted end of the dimension. (See Figure 1.) In the relatively totalistic setting of prisons, mental hospitals, and forced labor camps, opportunities for variation in involvement are restricted. In these settings the statuses are heavily weighted with ascriptive features and involvement is typically high--not by choice, but by the demands of the total situation. The social identity of a member of these classes does not include attained roles, the enactment of which may be cyclical. Legitimate opportunities for obtaining role-distance (Goffman, 1959) are absent when one's identity is composed exclusively of granted roles. That is to say, when an individual is enacting a granted role he is "on" all the time and has little or no opportunity for gaining "distance," for taking a view of his conduct from the perspectives of another role.

IV

Valuation

Positive and negative valuations bear an orderly relation to the two dimensions of status and involvement. The valuation continuum is constructed at right angles to the status and involvement dimensions and is marked with a neutral point and positive and negative limiting extremes. The question may be phrased: What is the potential gain and loss in the value of a social identity associated with various statuses and various levels of involvement?

Consider first the range of potential valuation applicable to the occupancy of statuses in the attainment region of the model. (See Figure 2.) Valuations declared on nonperformance or poor performance are near the neutral point. That is, strongly negative valuations are not applied for failures to validate highly attained statuses. Being fired from a glee club, dropped from a team, or dismissed from college does not enrage or perturb a community. Such failures are considered to be due to lack of practice, underachievement, poor judgment, limited talent, or misfortune, and are met with verbal expressions of sadness, disappointment, sympathy, regret and so on. On the other hand, the proper performances of attained roles earn tokens of high positive value, such as prizes, public recognition, monetary rewards and other indicators of public esteem. For attained statuses, then, values range from neutral to positive--there is much to gain and little to lose.

By contrast, the potential for gaining positive value from granted statuses is diminished. (See Figure 2.) An individual is not praised for participation in a culture as a male, an adult, a father, a person. One is expected to enact such roles without positive public valuations. The nonperformance of such roles, however, calls out strong negative valuations. Consider the valuations declared on a male who fails to perform according to the expectations for masculine sexuality and the subsequent labeling: sissy, fairy, homosexual. Consider the sanctions imposed when a mother fails to be interested in the care and welfare of her children and is labeled an "unfit mother." Consider the value-judgments rendered upon people who fail to act according to age standards and are called immature, childish, or regressive. Consider the negative valuations applied to individuals who are considered to act in opposition to fundamental principles of law: criminal, felon, or outlaw.

It follows that the most universal common expectations for behavior are associated with the extreme granted status of person. While there are cultural variations in conceptions of the nature of man, all persons within a given culture are expected to conform to a basic definition. Especially strong negative sanctions are reserved for acts that are held to be non-human or "unnatural." Commonly, expectations associated with the basic grant of personhood are concerned with reciprocal social interaction (communication) modesty, property, and ingroup aggression. When these norms are violated the person is marked more or less permanently with a strongly perjorative label. While many forms of the label are used, they have the common function of denoting the social identity of a nonperson. Once the pejorative label is applied, the society begins to treat the individual as something less than a person.

The concept most widely used to represent non-person status is that of "brute," sometimes rendered as beast, animal or low-grade human being (Platt and Diamond, 1965; Sarbin, 1967a). In the vernacular, these valuations emerge in such epithets as pig, dog, worm, jackass, and son-of-a-bitch. For example, Dostoevsky said, "In the eyes of this shining world, I was no more than an unclean and useless fly."

A further qualification must be added to the valuation dimension. Although represented by a single line, the quality of the valuation below the neutral point differs from the quality of valuation above the neutral point. Positive valuations appear to coincide with the meanings usually held for the conventional expression "esteem." The public performances of attained roles is the basis for the according of esteem. By contrast, the quality of valuation associated with the granted extreme of the status dimension is denoted by the term "respect." When an individual fails to perform an ascribed role, the respect that inheres to the associated status is withdrawn. Motherhood is respected until a mother publicly fails to meet minimal expectations of the group concerning child care. The performance of granted roles, however, earns no special tokens of esteem. One is expected to perform granted roles without special incentives; disrespect and associated negative sanctions follow non-performance.

V

Transformation Of Social Identity

At any given point in time a person's social identity is composed of a set of validated statuses, which might be indexed in terms of the extent to which they are granted or attained and in terms of degree of involvement. In this fashion are determined the social valuations that are applied to a person. The major purpose of this conception is to provide a heuristic guide for understanding the dependency of significant psychological change upon changing social interactions. For convenience we consider separately the process of degradation and the process of enhancement or upgrading.

Degradation. It is an implication of the model that there are two ways by which the value of a person's social identity may be lowered: derogation and demotion.

The root meaning of derogation (to rescind, annul, or reverse a previous privilege) and the present sense of the term make it appropriate for the process of transformation from a role with potential for esteem to its negative counterpart. To derogate is to identify a person as a "bad" actor, an ineffective incumbent of a status. Further, the model accommodates the differential significance of derogation for roles at different points along the status dimension. A person's identity is damaged greatly by allegations that he is a "bad person," a "bad son" or an "impotent male" (loss of respect).

The alternative means of degradation is demotion--the stripping away from a person of certain attained statuses. For this process, it is also appropriate to use the term "disparagement" with its root sense of suggesting a comparison between inferior and superior elements. To treat an adult as if he were a child is degrading in this sense, as are actual demotions such as an officer being removed from his rank, or varsity player assigned to the second team. Demotions (or disparagements) from achieved positions deprive the person of opportunities for enjoying esteem.

It follows that the most degrading processes are those which combine derogation and demotion. If a person is relieved of all achieved statuses--professional and avocational--and is derogated with respect to all ascribed roles, including sex, age, kinship, and citizenship roles, then he would be reduced to the lowest possible value. It is an extreme degradation to treat a person as "nothing but a beast," ("nothing but" implies demotion, and "beast" implies derogation).

Upgrading. The model applies equally well to the enhancement of social identity. The development of heroes, champions, successful persons, and "self-fulfilled" individuals is typified by the logical opposites to the processes of derogation and demotion. These processes might be called, respectively, commendation and promotion.

The occupant of a status may receive special commendation for proper performances. Not all members of the same social position are given equal esteem for their performances. Medals, grades in school, merit citations, and ordinary forms of praise and positive regard are some of the mechanisms by which this form of upgrading is carried out. It should be noted that commendation is provided in the form of verbal and symbolic acts that serve as social reinforcers. The varieties of commendation are many: the roar of the crowd in athletic contests, curtain calls in the theater, prizes and awards for scientific achievement, honorific titles, and so on. It is frequently the case when a speaker is introduced that the audience is informed of the validated statuses of the speaker, "a father, a citizen of the commonwealth, a senator" and also the commendations he has received, "oak leaf clusters, man-of-the-year award, Guest prize for poetry."

A newly attained status or promotion opens up fresh possibilities for the gaining of esteem. In general, the greater the jump in rank, the greater the gain in esteem.

The most highly valued human beings, then, are individuals of great achievement who: (1) have achieved rare social positions and have been commended highly for their performances in them, and (2) at the same time have maintained their respectability. These, then, are the basic mechanisms of social transvaluation. To explore the implications of the model for various configurations of roles, we begin by discussing the statuses illustrated by the vertices of the status-involvement triangle (see Figure l).

Extreme Granted Roles (Vertex a)

We have previously argued that involvement for the most granted role is consistently high. The social category employed at this point is that of human being, member of a society, participant in a culture, or person. It remains to consider the values that might be attached to effective validation of the most granted status, human being, as well as the valuation for insufficient or improper performance in this position.

The negative consequences of being classified as "inhuman" or a "beast" are very great indeed. Platt and Diamond (1965), in tracing the history of the "wild beast" theory of criminal insanity, support the view that no other categorical appellation has had such consistent negative potency. Partridge (1950) provides evidence that derogatory slang is often a literal allegation that a person is not human. Nineteenth century California ranchers disported themselves by exterminating "varmints," the remnants of a tribe of Digger Indians. Until the modern era, death by being drawn and quartered was reserved for those judged to be no better than animals. Hitler decreed that those responsible for the 1944 assassination plot be slaughtered like pigs and their carcasses hung on meat hooks, and so they were. While Mussolini was given an animal execution, the world was cheated of revenge on Hitler by his peremptory, and very human, suicide.

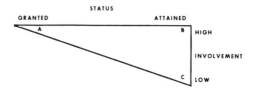

Fig.1. Opportunity for variation in involvement related to status.

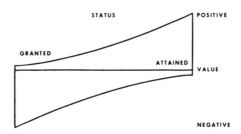

Fig.2. Positive and negative valuation in relation to status.

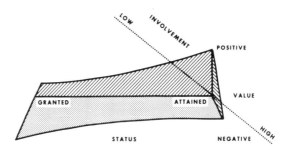

Fig.3. The three dimensional model of social identity:
status, value, and involvement.

Relative to the great negative value of being declared an object of disrespect by the classification "non-human" or "non-person," positive validation of human status carries a weak payoff. In absolute terms the difference in value for social identity between person status and non-person status is enormous. However, mere status as a person carries no positive value for social identity. Validation of this status is universally expected, and is a minimum necessary condition for any form of promotion.

Highly Involving Achieved Roles (Vertex b)

The position of President of the United States is one of maximum achievement and involvement. In the same region are virtuoso musicians, Nobel prize winners, athletic champions, eminences of the Church. Clearly, the positive value for social identity associated with proper performance in these positions is maximal. These positions provide access to power, prestige and wealth.

What of the negative counterparts of these achieved roles? As examples we might cite an ineffective President, a losing coach and an incomprehensible philosopher. If it is agreed that the failure in each of these cases is only with respect to the demands and requirements of the attained roles of President, coach, and philosopher, respectively, then the value declared on the occupants of these positions would not be negative, i.e., would not be noted by terms of disrespect. The inability of a President to halt inflation, for example, could result in declarations of disesteem, but no disrespect. The President may still be regarded as a kindly and basically honest man, good to his family, and a great servant to his country. The coach may still be regarded as an accomplished raconteur and teacher, and the philosopher may still be regarded as an inspiration to students and ardent civil libertarian.

With respect to value, extremely achieved roles which are highly involving present just the opposite case from that of granted roles. (See Figure 3.) The absolute difference between maximal success and maximal failure for achieved roles is again enormous. But most of the potential is for positive value rather than for negative value. There is much to gain and little to lose in trying for attained positions. One does not invoke sanctions against a virtuoso for missing a note or playing badly: but sanctions are invoked for a temporary lapse from the requirements of being human.

Examples could be cited of the profoundly degrading consequences for the person of loss of attainments--as in the case of the French pastry chef who committed suicide upon learning that his restaurant had lost its four star rating. Such cases are newsworthy because of their infrequency, and more complete account of the antecedents of such profound negative consequences of demotions would also demonstrate the existence of actual or imagined defects of some of the granted components of social identity.

Minimally Involving Attained Roles

When a person ceases to be involved with attained roles, the status is latent. Examples would be retired generals and executives, members of honorary societies, and professors emeriti. Zero involvement in a role implies no value for social identity. Zero involvement in attained roles indicates that a person is not active in that role, though involvement could recur. Obviously, degree of involvement depends upon social context. The Grand Plenipotentiary of the Secret Dragons might enjoy great esteem at his meetings and conventions, but derive little social recognition for this position at his place of work. Ph.D.'s, scholastic honors, and publication records are without value when one is trying to board a subway. In such cases, the individual can derive satisfaction from implicit role-involvement by thinking about his achievements. However, it seems patent that self-esteem as well as public prestige is dependent upon valuations assigned by reference groups and individuals. Reference groups and individuals make their evaluations on the basis of convincingness of the actor's performances which in turn is a function of involvement.

Linked Roles

While it has been only implied in the foregoing discussion, it is appropriate to make explicit the importance of role linkages in the degrading and upgrading processes. For upgrading to occur, the person must have satisfied the codified and informal regulations of society regarding prerequisite validated positions. Once upgrading has occurred, the actor must not violate norms pertaining to prerequisite statuses. If a medical superintendent were to admit that he has forgotten his medical knowledge, then he would probably be demoted. Such a demotion would occur not because the forgotten knowledge has any direct function in the discharge of his daily duties but because powerful medical societies have created and supported the linkage between qualified "physician" and "medical superintendent." Similarly, the White House official in the Johnson administration who was revealed as a homosexual was no longer allowed to function in his attained position because of the linkage involved; he was demoted from his job and derogated as a man.

Many positions that are highly achieved are not closely linked with a number of more ascribed statuses. Thus, a man can attain esteem as a great actor without having graduated from college, without working his way up through the corporation, without being a respectable family man, and without adhering to conventional religious beliefs. However, if he wants to be a politician, he must take care to touch the requisite bases, i.e., he must not violate granted role prescriptions, before he attempts to gain promotion. Similarly, pecadillos are tolerated with amusement in movie stars that would outrage the public were they exhibited by a magistrate. A well-known musical conductor and a Hollywood actress lived together and had a child without benefit of clergy. There was no public outcry. However, resignation from office was the only option for a high government official who maintained an intimate relation with a "secretary."

The Faust legend provides an excellent example of transvaluation in which the long term effects of degradation differ markedly from short-term effects. When Faust bargains his soul away to the Devil in return for earthly favors, he effectively degrades himself with respect to the most ascribed component of his identity--his claim to conventional humanity, to being a normal person. In return he receives a set of "achievements," conquests in love and other affairs. In the terms employed here, he has traded respect for esteem. In the modern idiom, he has "sold out"--he has accepted promotion without legitimizing his claims to the most ascribed component of his identity--his humanity.

VI

To summarize: We begin with an acknowledgement that neither behavioristic nor phenomenological models can convincingly account for personal transvaluations. Current psychological theories--useful as they are for certain purposes--fail to employ as a central construct that form of the self variously rendered as the socius, the social self, or social identity. Our preference is for the label "social identity." Without such a construct, the problem of understanding the transparent fact that people assign valuations to others and to self remains bound to post hoc stimulus-response propositions or to idiosyncratic phenomenalism.

The valuation of persons--whether in the form of degradation or upgrading--is a social process. That is to say, its form and direction depend upon the nature of the social organization in which the valuing behavior occurs. The model of social identity presented in this essay provides a social psychological language for the analysis of social valuation. The model itself is a heuristic device: its utility is to be measured by its success in establishing the processes of degradation and upgrading as knowable events to be illuminated by social psychological research and analysis.

Beginning from the standpoint of role theory, we have proposed that a person's social identity may be regarded as a composite of social positions or statuses--the occupancy of which he has made good through performing appropriate acts.

The extent to which each of the components of social identity contributes value to the composite depends upon the extent to which the position was granted (ascribed) as opposed to attained (achieved), and the degree of involvement of the person in his role-enactment. A person's social identity is not an absolute, for obviously differently composed reference groups will not assign the same valuations to any particular presentation of self. Valuation is a reciprocal social process--values inhering neither in the subject nor object of valuation but emerging from their interaction.

From this perspective, respect is seen as a maintenance of status grants--birthrights, political and religious orthodoxies, and other minimal expectations for personal conduct. This provides a person with a grant of social credit, which if taken from him amounts to a loss of respect (or respectability). Esteem, on the other hand, is earned. It is acquired as the socially proffered wages for attainments--the more selective the attainment, the higher the wages, i.e., the greater the esteem.

The social identity of the individual concerned is considered to be composed of a complex of references at various points along the status dimension. In contrast to the religious conception of man, which emphasizes ascribed or granted features, and to the economic conception, which places high value only on man's attainments, we argue that the nature of social organization demands of the effectively functioning person that he have grants of respect as well as (but not to the exclusion of) opportunities to gain esteem. Observations of alienation, anomie, depersonalization, and so on, can be conceptualized according to this model, particularly in terms of the improper validation of granted statuses.

Footnote

1. Reprinted in abridged form from the chapter by T. R. Sarbin and K. E. Scheibe in C. Bellone (ed.), Organization Theory And The New Public Administration. Boston: Allyn and Bacon, 1980.

7

THE DANGEROUS INDIVIDUAL:
AN OUTCOME OF SOCIAL
IDENTITY TRANSFORMATIONS[1]

The goal of this paper is to achieve an understanding of the concept of danger, particularly as it is applied to felons and other persons who are negatively valued. Through a more penetrating analysis of the concept of danger, we might reach a set of conclusions that informs us how a man becomes dangerous. Such conclusions may point the way to practices designed to reduce the probability of offenders (or others) becoming dangerous.

Any exposition of the concept of danger requires a concrete reference as a point of departure. Since our focus is on the employment of the concept in connection with law-breakers, I shall use as a reference case the inmate of a total institution, namely, a maximum security prison. The arguments to be presented in this paper are applicable to inmates of other institutions than those that are obviously total. Modern urban ghettos, to a large degree, may be defined by the same variables as are used to define such total institutions as prisons, concentration camps and mental hospitals. When the necessary changes are made, the arguments may be applied with equal validity to "inmates of such non-obvious total institutions.

The present exposition does not lay claim to analyzing the equally important concept of violence. The concept of danger and the concept of violence are not coterminous. Violence denotes actions; danger denotes a relationship. I shall only assert that the antecedents to violence are not necessarily the same as the antecedents to danger. The unfolding of my argument will give support to this assertion.

The analysis of danger, like the analysis of any complex phenomenon, is helped along by a semantic study. This is especially true if we take a backward glance at its metaphorical beginnings. Words, as we know, do not arise without motivation. They are molded and they survive to fill the needs of human beings to make known to others their intentions, plans, and wants. We might expect the origins of the word "danger" to be related to physicalistic conceptions because of its widespread use for denoting physical objects and events that may damage property or maim and kill people. Surprisingly, this is not the case. The term seems to have been shaped out of linguistic roots that signified relative position in a social structure, a relationship between roles on a power dimension. The root is found in Latin in a derivative of "dominium," meaning lordship or sovereignty. According to the Oxford English Dictionary, the word came into Middle English through Old French and carried the meaning of "power of a Lord or master, jurisdiction; power to dispose of, or to hurt or harm; especially in phrases such as "in a person's danger," within his power or at his mercy; sometimes meaning specifically in his debt or under obligation." If we follow the implication of this brief etymological analysis, it will lead us away from a purely descriptive denotation, such as in the phrases "danger--falling rocks" or "dangerous curves ahead" to the conception of danger as a symbol denoting relative power in a social organization. A possible consequence of this implication is that persons concerned with dangerous offenders might direct their curiosity to the social psychological antecedents and concomitants of such labeling, instead of, or in addition to, the hypothesized internal character traits that supposedly render a man dangerous to his fellows.

If we revive the older meaning of danger as dominium, as a relationship between positions in a social structure based on relative power and esteem, an interesting network of conceptions emerges. This network includes the notion of role-system, the reciprocity of rights and obligations, the complementarity of power and responsiblity, the shaping of social identity through placement in the role system, and the transformation of social identity through police, legal and penal practices. In the present paper I can only sketch some of the main conceptions of this network. The thesis that I shall try to advance is that the assaultive or violent behavior that leads us to attach the label "dangerous" to an offender can be understood as the predictable outcome of certain antecedent and concurrent conditions. Among these conditions are degradation procedures which transform a man's social identity. At a certain point this identity transformation places the man in a condition of strain where he is faced with the choice of accepting the identity of a non-person, a brute, or engaging in instrumental behavior that radically alters the social system, and reverses the "dominium," the power relationship, thus affording him a more acceptable social identity. Such a solution, of course, is perceived as danger by those whose grant of power is thus repudiated.

II

In order to develop this thesis, it will be necessary for me temporarily to lay aside the concept of danger and present some conceptions drawn from modern social psychological theory. An explicit assumption in most psychological theories is that effective functioning is facilitated through accurate placement or location of self and others in the role system. In the

simplest terms, such locating of self is achieved through overt
or covert answers to the question: Who am I? The answers to such
a question are usually constructed in role terms--I am a doctor,
I am a husband, I am a citizen, I am a prisoner, etc. It must be
emphasized that such answers are empty if they are not validated
through actual   or symbolic interaction with   occupants of
complementary positions. For a man convincingly to declare I am
a doctor   requires   that he engage in healing behavior with
reference to patients; validly to say I am a father requires
that he perform certain conduct with reference to sons or
daughters. Thus, the complex of answers to the question who am I
defines one's social identity.

Since role-relationships are the definers of one's social
identity, planned or unplanned changes in role-relationships
will produce changes in the answers to the "Who am I" question
and in the beliefs about one's social identity. A moment's
reflection will inform us that changes in social identity occur
all the time, such as when one interacts in turn with a
colleague, a devoted friend, a stranger, a child, etc. It is
clear that the changes that occur in one's social identity as a
result of shifting from one such role to another are not of the
magnitude that would set the stage for the extreme behaviors
that are considered dangerous. It is necessary to construct a
set of dimensions that make it possible to determine the
relative contribution of particular roles to one's social
identity and to show the effects of shifting one's placement in
the role-system. For this purpose, a three-dimensional model
gives us the means for assessing the total value of a person's
social identity at any point in time. The three dimensions, for
convenience, may be identified as (1) the ascription-achievement
dimension; (2) the ' value dimension; and (3) the involvement
dimension (see the previous selection in this volume).

Every role may be placed in a three-dimensional space that
allows grading according to degree of choice and legitimate
power and esteem prior to entering the role, grading according
to valuational standards, and grading according to degree of
self-involvement. The invalid enactment of roles at the granted
end of the first dimension, roles that are at the same time
highly involving, invokes negative valuations from others and
leads to pejorative labeling. The extreme of this labeling
process is represented by the term non-person or brute. I have
already argued that the social identity of an individual is
formed out of his role relationships. When he is cast in the
role of a non-person he is denied a social identity. Another way
of phrasing this state of affairs is that the ultimate
derogation, to be labeled and treated as a non-person, arises
out of the valuational practices of significant persons in one's
society who have the legitimate power to declare such
valuations.

III

This audience requires no reminders that the attitudes,
customs and conventions of police officers, jailers, court

employees and prison personnel contribute to the shaping of the social identity of those we typically call offenders and inmates. Goffman (1961a) and Sykes (1958) as well as others have carefully documented the depersonalizing or brutalizing effects of being caught up in the web of total institutions. In our model, an individual enacting roles at several levels of the model, if apprehended and sentenced, is unceremoniously stripped of nearly all his roles; at first, a process is employed of breaking relationships with persons and events that support roles of choice; then, through enforced dependency, constant surveillance, and demeaning activities, he is deprived of support for most of his granted roles. It is axiomatic that all men on the way to becoming participants in a culture acquire a social self--and with it the need to be regarded as a person with some potential for positive social reinforcements. The desocializing process of apprehension, detention, sentencing and imprisonment sets up a high degree of cognitive strain. Stated as a syllogism, the typical offender holds the major premise that all persons are entitled to certain minimal rights, such as reciprocal communications. He also holds a minor premise, acquired through early socializing influences, that he is a person. His experiences with police and prison personnel lead to the contradictory premise that he is a non-person. Such a state of affairs is the epitome of cognitive strain. What adaptive techniques are available to the typical offender whose history, no matter how inimical, led to the belief that he was guaranteed some minima of choice and reciprocal conduct and who now finds the vehicle for realizing his expectations degraded?

In the case of the incarcerated offender, only three classes of adaptive techniques are possible. The first is to reject the life-long belief that he has a right to minimal choice and other social prerogatives; such a rejection and the concurrent perception of self as a degraded thing produces no strain. Belief and perception are congruent. The passive acceptance of the identity of a non-person or brute leads to psychological deterioration and psychosis. The second class of adaptive techniques begins from the point of departure that the major premise is valid; that all men may lay claim to identity as a person. To upgrade one's social identity in a total institution requires the development of what Goffman calls an underlife: an artificial and often illicit social system that makes possible the validation of the offenders' minimal social identity through interaction and communication with other offenders. Such artificial social systems are brittle, however. When they are disrupted by prison officers or by the patent difficulties inherent in maintaining an artificial society, the offender is again in a state of strain. To keep alive the belief that he is a person rather than a brute, in the condition where he perceives the prison world as incapable of validating his identity, only the third alternative is available: forcibly to change the role-system, to change "dominium" so that he may occupy an upgraded status in the system. To change the system, of course, requires instrumental behavior of a violent sort. Even though the offender may calculate the risk and the almost certain failure of his rebellion, he is left with no alternative. We have no hesitation in calling such offenders dangerous. Their efforts to re-locate themselves in the social system demand direct instrumental behavior of a violent sort. For a prisoner to be dangerous, then, is to try to rebuild the social system so that the perceived brutish identity can be altered. We have come full circle now and can see how the modern word danger still carries much of its old sense.

A word needs to be said about individual differences in the readiness to take action to change the dominium. I think research now in progress will show that some offenders have a low tolerance for the frustrations coincident with degraded statuses. These may be individuals who cannot make their way into the artificial role-structure of the inmate population. They are left with only two of the three choices we mentioned before: (a) changing their beliefs so they can accept the brutalized status, or (b) upsetting the role structure. It is my belief, however, that individual differences in frustration tolerance do not account for the major variance in the creation of danger. Rather, I think we shall find, if we are creative and thorough, that instances of dangerous conduct follow from practices that transform a man's social identity downward and leave no room for substitute identities. The inmate uses violence to change the system when no other alternatives are available for maintaining an acceptable social identity.

IV

The individual in the chosen role of guard (keeper, policeman) must be on-the-ready to classify the conduct of an inmate as potentially dangerous. Thus, the guard's role is one with high involvement; he is motorically prepared to engage in instrumental activity immediately upon noticing any sign that the "dominium" is threatened. Thus, he may further contribute to the degrading and brutalizing of his charges and unwittingly provoke danger.

Experiments by Langer, Werner, and Wapner (1965) at Clark University, have demonstrated that the experience of time and the experience of space are markedly altered under conditions of physical peril. Time is over-estimated and the space between the dangerous object and the self is interpreted as diminished. If we extend these conclusions to danger as the reversal of the power relationship, then we can more easily understand how a guard might perceive the potentially dangerous individual as being closer than he really is (by objective measurement). Such a misperception could lead to his taking instrumental action to suppress the potentially dangerous inmate. Similarly, the inaccurate perception of time could lead to fast action without taking time to check the validity of his perceptions. The often premature power display may serve as an additional cue to the perception of self as an untrusted non-person; somewhat in the same category as a "wild beast" that must be continually controlled.

V

To summarize: First, danger is not to be construed as the expression of a personality trait, but rather as a relationship of relative power in a role-system. In all societies, roles are ordered on the basis of choice prior to entry and may be placed on a dimension with granted roles at one end and chosen roles at the other. The ultimate granted role is that of the person with the expectation that he who adopts this role is guaranteed certain minimal rights.

Second, an individual's social identity is the complex of validated roles enacted. Changes in social identity are coterminous with changes in role-relationships. When any validated role is stripped away, the individual may form his identity out of his remaining roles. The ultimate degradation is to eliminate an individual's claims to identity as a person.

Third, the management practices of personnel in total institutions tend to degrade and disparage inmates. To deal with the strain created by the incongruity between (a) the beliefs about the inviolacy of the granted role of person and (b) the perception of self as a non-person, three solutions are theoretically available: the autistic solution--to repudiate one's beliefs about the inviolacy of the person role and accept the status of non-person; the social solution--to form and maintain an artifical society which validates at least the granted role of person; and the danger solution--through violence to attempt to reverse the power relationship.

Fourth, the experience of potential danger alters the perceptual accuracy of guards, policemen and others in reciprocal positions to non-persons. Misperceptions may lead to premature power displays which in turn exacerbate the degradation process.

The implications of this analysis are transparent. The dangerous offender is a product in large measure of the institutions we have created to manage and mold him. The enlightenment that is gaining ground in criminology is bringing this implication under scientific scrutiny. As a result, we may expect that the form and function of such institutions will change to accommodate the stubborn fact that human beings cannot survive without acceptable social identities.

Footnote

1. Abridged from British Journal of Criminology, 1967, 7, 285-295.

8

SELF-RECONSTITUTION PROCESSES[1]

At least since the middle of the nineteenth century, psychologists interested in changing the conduct of individuals have leaned heavily on rationalistic models and have consistently avoided, neglected or rejected models that included nonrationalistic components. The theories of Freud, Rogers, and Sullivan, for example, are suffused with rationalism and focused upon an almost exclusive concern with verbal transactions, i.e., talk, as the mediator of rationality.

This emphasis on rationality in the transactions that are directed toward altering behavior has been in the nature of an ideological commitment to science. Nineteenth- and twentieth-century psychological theorists, hoping to emulate the progress of their contemporaries in the natural sciences, organized their efforts toward discovering "scientific" methods that would be congruent with contemporary science and its rationalistic imperatives. A by-product of the limits thus imposed was the rejection of any model of behavior change, no matter how effective, whose basic metaphors were inconsistent with the vocabulary preferred by contemporary scientists. Thus, any method of behavior change that employed theological metaphors, or exploited such procedures as ritual, dancing, isolation, fasting, prayer, and other means that departed from apparent rationality (polite talk) was declared unscientific and unworthy of serious study. Parenthetically, misled by surface appearances, we have failed to recognize or to make explicit that often our standard, official models of change masked rituals where the "irrational" quality was attenuated or disguised.

Because of this rationalistic emphasis, most systematic writers have failed to take advantage of the world literature on conduct and personality alteration, such as the writings of William James, McNeill, Loyola, Kierkegaard, and others. For

example, William James' observations in his Varieties of
Religious Experience, in spite of his own rationalism, makes use
of metaphors that have not been assimilated into contemporary
rationalistic models. In one essay, he posits two kinds of
persons. The first are the healthy-minded who need to be born
only once, and others are "sick souls" who must be twice-born in
order to make some tolerable adjustment to an imperfect world.
James employed a number of metaphors that were congruent with a
humanistic ethos but which were ignored by most rationalistic
theory-builders.

> Such unification or rebirth may come gradually or it
> may occur abruptly; it may come through altered powers
> of action: or it may come through new intellectual
> insights, or through experiences which we shall later
> have to designate as "mystical."
> In all these instances we have precisely the same
> psychological form of event--a firmness, stability,
> and equilibrium succeeding a period of storm and
> stress and inconsistency. (James, 1902)

Similarly, McNeill's History of the Cure of Souls makes use
of another metaphorical system. That he is interested in conduct
reorganization through reconstitution of the self can be readily
inferred from the following excerpt:

> The cure of souls, then, is the sustaining and
> curative treatment of persons in those matters that
> reach beyond the requirements of the animal life. Man
> is a seeker after health, but not health of the body
> alone. Health of body may be contributory to, but it
> does not guarantee, health of personality. It may be
> possessed by man who suffers painful disorders of mind
> and spirit. On the other hand, it may be destroyed by
> mental or emotional disease. The health that is
> ultimately sought is not something to be secured by
> material means alone: it is the well-being of the
> soul. (McNeill, 1951)

McNeill traces the history of cures from the rationalistic
approach of Cicero and Seneca, through the "rebirth" of
Nicodemus by his faith in Jesus, to the concepts of confession
and reawakening of Luther and Calvin.

The Spiritual Exercises of Saint Ignatius of Loyola, a
system of reconstitution of the self employing the death and
rebirth theme, offer a simplicity unmatched by any system of
contemporary behavioral science. One must be prepared to find in
the theological vocabularies and metaphors the same underlying
behavioral operations and processes. The exercises of St.
Ignatius are carried out during a "retreat," in which four
phases are identified as "weeks" of irregular intervals. During
these four "weeks" the aspirant passes through stages of
reconstitution of the self (soul) reminiscent of exercises in
other Eastern and Western religions, and involving processes of
"Purgation" or catharsis, "Illumination" or insight, and
sanctification or reorientation. Metaphors of Death, Transition
and Rebirth order events familiar to us in secular programs.

The exercises in the first week require the subject to
meditate on sin and its consequences, to contemplate hell and to

meditate upon his own death, picturing in detail his last moments and their agony. Is this dissimilar from the "anxiety" that brings the patient to therapy from the compulsive repetition and circularity of failures and injured self-esteem of the initial anamnesis? Meditations for the second week involve the Saviour as a means of salvation. The aspirant contemplates the humility, agony, poverty and love of Him. In theological metaphor is this not the externalization of the ego-ideal, the aspiration level for the individual's self? The third "week" is a phase in which the exercises seek to confirm the election to Christ; i.e., working through to confirm the way of holiness. The fourth week is characterized by the setting aside of dreadful thoughts and sadness, meditating instead on the life eternal. It is not necessary to match absolutely identical events and processes to suggest that similar generic elements are involved.

When, at the turn of the century, psychology was breaking away from philosophy and attempting to affirm itself as a natural science, the human organism was construed as a passive entity inactive unless prodded by instincts or pushed by external stimuli. To reconstruct the forces in the "mind," or to change personal habits, rationalistic psychologists and psychiatrists turned to manipulating verbal stimuli as levers. The study of myths and their effect on conduct, let alone such literary works as those of James Joyce or Dylan Thomas, makes compelling the conclusion that verbal transactions provide no automatic warrant for "rationality." An additional difficulty of this conceptual model was that it encouraged the partition of the subject who is isolated from his social milieu and regarded as a kind of solitary specimen in the laboratory, where verbal utterances could be analyzed through the use of rationalistic schemata.

Recent developments in general psychological theory make apparent the gross limitations of earlier association models and call for the construct of an active self. Psychological theory no longer finds plausible or useful the image of a passive, stimulus-bound organism; instead, contemporary theory is moving toward a conception of an intrinsically active organism whose ongoing knowledge seeking activity leads to broader and more structured resolutions of the distal field. The passive organism, waiting for the stirrings of tissue needs or the promptings of "anxiety" signals and only then looking for an external tranquilizer, is an obsolescent construct. The newer view of man as an active creature requires a metaphor that embraces the fact that he is an inveterate, ongoing decision maker, rehearsing possibilities on the basis of expectancies garnered from the environment. And such rehearsal involves not only organized beliefs about the ecology ("Moving heavy objects requires strength"), but also beliefs about the self ("I am weak"). Like all abstractions, the active self is not an ideal metaphor, but it does reflect the changing view of the human organism. For the present we restrict ourselves to the statement that to be an effective decision maker a person must locate (assign meanings to) self as object as well as other persons and things. To do this, he must be able to construct abstractions about himself as well as the behavioral environment.

A set of concepts has proved useful in our attempts to account for the kinds of changes referred to variously as the process of conversion, reconstitution of the self, transvaluation of social identity, and profound conduct reorganization. This set of concepts deals with the source of information from which persons make decisions regarding action. Two categories are posited: (1) the proximal ecology (or the proprium) which provides sensory input from posture, movement, proprioception, imaginings; (2) the distal ecologies. It has been useful to differentiate five distal ecologies: the self-maintenance ecology, the spatial-temporal ecology, the normative ecology, the social ecology, and the transcendental ecology. The human organism defines a smooth course of action for himself by making sense of the data gleaned from these input sources; in other words he is able to answer ecologically relevant questions, What am I in relation to the self-maintenance ecology?, Where am I?, Who am I?, and so on, in terms of existing cognitive organization. Although the construct of the self involves placement in all ecologies, in this paper we single out the social (or role) ecology, the source of inputs for constructing a social identity, and the transcendental ecology, the source of inputs for constructing the self as abstraction in relation to other abstractions such as God, the universe, humanity, and justice.

In this prolegomenon we can only sketch our conceptualization of the self. The self is regarded as a set of knowings or beliefs that accumulate as the result of efforts actively to locate oneself with reference to differentitated habitats or ecologies. Such efforts are facilitated by searching behaviors, by the person asking questions of the form Who am I? (the self in relation to others) and What am I? (the self in relation to the cosmos), as well as other questions. Both the everyday object world and the transcendental world of meaning and value are included in the latter. Answers to the Who am I? question represents the socius, the subjective aspect of social identity. Answers to the What am I? questions, drawn from inputs generated both proximally and distally, represent the self as cosmological object--the subjective aspect of "thingness."

Inasmuch as the answers to these questions are directly relevant to the person's choice of actions, usually with social reference, we posit that social roles are perceived and enacted against a background of self. Self and role may be viewed as coordinates. The construct, self, refers to the inferences the person makes about the predicates for "I"; the "I" in turn is the subjective aspect of identity.

Our point of departure is this: significant conduct reorganization can be understood as the sequelae of a reconstitution of the self. Such reconstitution comes about as the result of efforts to change the conditions for locating of self in the cosmological and the social ecologies. Such efforts are not recondite nor mysterious. For example, they may include such knowable antecedent operations as altering body-image boundaries through motoric activity, fasting, or hyperventilation, and altering identity supports through degradation rituals, isolation, ostracism, or aversive social reinforcements.

II

Our model is derived from a review of the literature that has been virtually ignored and rejected by behavioral scientists. Among the sources consulted are works on spiritual exercises, conversion, enthusiasm, shamanism, ecstasy and other processes of conduct change operating in a religious setting. We have examined the procedures of Thought Reform, military indoctrination in boot camp and officer candidate schools, and other processes in the political arena; we have looked into socially oriented change conditions such as Synanon, Alcoholics Anonymous, rites de passage, as well as hypnosis and sensory deprivation. Examining the behavioral operations involved in profound and critical conduct reorganization, we have been able to identify a number of variables that have been ignored or neglected by theorists and expositors of one or another traditional psychotherapeutic system.

Common Themes

Our initial excursion into the literature suggests that there are communalities that can be abstracted from the multiplicity of systems developed over the centuries. We have isolated a number of themes and the steps or operations that lead to the reconstruction of the self as preliminary to, or concurrent with, profound changes in conduct.

Theme I. Symbolic Death and Rebirth. One theme is recurrent in these diverse systems--the theme of symbolic death and rebirth or the annihilation and reconstruction of the self. How this is conceptualized depends upon the metaphors employed in the thought models carried by the persons involved. The theme characterizes a central feature of a number of currently voguish therapies--the encounter, confrontations, action, and Gestalt therapies. Our concepts are intended to provide a means for establishing the validity of these "therapeutic systems." We have kept an eye open to the possibility that the recurrent and reemergent theme of symbolic death and rebirth may be more useful in establishing a generic model of conduct reorganization than the older themes of insight, shift in dynamic equilibrium, or deconditioning.

Our analysis of the literature leads to the proposition that, at first, certain personal behaviors diminish or cease altogether, at the same time being replaced by a new set of overt behaviors and corresponding self-definitions. The metaphoric use of the words dying, being reborn and saved, is well known in Catholic and Fundamentalist literature. These metaphors are used frequently in autobiographical and literary descriptions of conversions. The dual process is noted in such metaphors as "death and rebirth," "death and transfiguration," "the spiritual awakening," "degradation and renewal." In all the

systems we have reviewed we have found the recurrent theme of
death and rebirth, whether it takes the form of a ritualized
dying ceremony, "surrendering" before one begins a new life,
"hitting rock bottom," "renunciation" of worldly and bodily
pleasures, penance, humiliation, or being forcibly degraded to
justify a spiritual death. The specific operations by which this
"death" is brought about, the point at which the "death" is
reached, the "rebirth" phenomenon and the group acceptance which
follow are keys to understanding the coversion process in all
its forms.

C. Eric Lincoln, in his analysis of the Black Muslim
religion in America, discusses the initiation of an individual
into the Muslim sect--a process which exemplifies the
death-rebirth theme:

> To clinch the conversion of those true believers who
> approach the Movement in simple curiosity, Muhammad
> offers the lure of personal rebirth. The true believer
> who becomes a Muslim casts off at last his old self
> and takes on a new identity. He changes his name, his
> religion, his homeland, his "natural" language, his
> moral and natural values, his very purpose in living.
> He is no longer a Negro, so long despised by the white
> man that he has come almost to despise himself. Now he
> is a Black Man--divine, ruler of the universe,
> different only in degree from Allah Himself. He is no
> longer discontent and baffled, harried by social
> obloquy and a gnawing sense of personal inadequacy.
> Now he is a Muslim, bearing in himself the power of
> the Black Nation and its glorious destiny. His new
> life is not an easy one: it demands unquestioning
> faith, unrelenting self-mastery, unremitting hatred.
> He may have to sacrifice his family and friends, his
> trade or profession, if they do not serve his
> new-found cause. But he is not alone, and he now knows
> why his life matters. He has seen the truth, and the
> truth has set him free . . . This change of name is,
> of course, only the most outward token of rebirth.
> Perhaps the deepest change promised--and
> delivered--is the release of energies
> that had been dammed or buried in the old personality.
> This release may account in part for the regeneration
> of criminals, alcoholics and narcotic addicts which is
> a hallmark of the Movement. (Lincoln, 1961)

The death-rebirth theme in this context may be viewed,
then, as the death or loss or relinquishment of one social
identity and the rebirth of formation of another. The point of
death, to use a metaphor of the social sciences, is when the
individual becomes a "nonperson." The individual is treated by
relevant others as not being able to meet minimal cultural
expectations; he is perceived as not being able to perform
actions to make good the occupancy of the most undifferentiated,
granted social roles. Being a nonperson, with reference to his
social ecology, it is as if he were dead. This symbolic death
process is characterized by a mounting of high arousal and
cognitive strain. Restrictions are placed on the employment of

adaptive techniques for reducing cognitive strain so that the nonperson, to make sense of the confusion of inputs, must change the structure of his belief system. The process may be viewed as an "assault" upon the individual's conception of self as a cosmological object and as a social identity. The modification, reevaluation, and transformation of these "knowings" is brought about by planned events so that alternative, more congruent, and more easily instantiated views of self are available. The new self (after the rebirth) is tagged with labels carrying connotations of wholeness (healed, holy) rather than fractionated (cracked, crazed, split, schizoid).

Postures and artifacts required in diverse systems of conduct change, all support the ceremonies of symbolic death and rebirth, and are instruments of change. Examples of such symbolic support are the couch, the horizontal position, the hypnotic "trance," the waiting period, the ritual fractionation of time into weeks of spiritual exercises or hours of therapy, the ritual separation of spiritual and therapeutic exercises from the routines of the customary world.

Models that emphasize warmth, support, "tender-loving care," and that focus solely on the nurturant role of the therapist, fail to recognize that a therapy that aims at reorganization of the personality has other functions too. Failure to appreciate the wide range of therapeutic roles, and the extremely different phases in the ongoing process, and insisting on the passive receptive role alone may be responsible for the frequently observed stalemate in therapy. The need for the active induction of stress, of directed organismic involvement, is a central factor in all the systems we have reviewed. This is perhaps more easily recognized in radical techniques developed outside the mental health profession but as readily recognized in the classic forms of psychoanalysis. The assault on the self is brought about in numerous ways: the "meat-axe" and "hot seat" therapy of some group procedures, the synanon "haircut," the exhaustion, toxicity, and the sensory deprivation of "marathon" therapy.

Similarities among diverse systems of change are noted in recognizing that converts or patients may avoid or delay the "death" or degradation process. Thought reform techniques in China differentiate the earlier false confession from the ultimate true confession. The addict initially comes to Synanon for reasons other than "the cure." He begins with a false confession which must be exposed as a maneuver. A central myth of Synanon is the "Night of the Big Cop-out." The junkie is compelled to break the code of his group and "squeal" as a repudiation of his old self and the beginnings of a commitment to a new self. In the psychoanalytic idiom, Kris has referred to the initial anamnesis as the "myth of the hero" that serves defensive functions and stands in the way of degradation of self. Such defensive maneuvers must be overcome before change can occur. It is often the case that patients come to psychoanalytic treatment to try by new means to achieve their goals and to avert their suffering rather than to demean the self through repudiating such goals as a step toward reorganization.

The application of the death-rebirth theme to modern psychotherapy depends upon the readiness of the mental health profession to shift metaphors, to overcome current nonutilitarian myths and to displace them with new or revived metaphors that are more continuous with observations. Angyal (1965) talked about psychotherapy in an idiom more in keeping with the death-rebirth theme. He wrote about the patient being faced with the futility of his customary ways, hopeless and degraded, who had to acknowledge his bankruptcy and confront his damaged self esteem. "The neurotic structure melts in the fire of an intensive and persuasive emotional experience . . . There is profound despair." Such a situation may not have to occur in the minor first aid type of therapy that is essentially "mask repair." But where fundamental unmasking and recasting of the self is the goal, this step is of central importance. "There is no other way," Angyal maintains, "than the way that leads through despair . . . a sweeping experience of bankruptcy must come if the person is to break out and take a chance on a different mode of existence."

Crucial to the process of behavior change is the involvement of self in role. It may vary from precipitously waking one morning to assume a new life to persisting experiences of terror and ecstacy. The greater the involvement, the greater the probability of the shift in self-conception, and the more probable the renunciation of the former self. The beliefs and values held antecedent to immersing oneself in actions characterized by high involvement becomes the "before," not completely forgotten or denied, but reorganized and reconstructed to justify and maintain the newly adopted self. The degree of conduct change necessary to meet the demands of the converted covers a wide range. At one end of the distribution we could place the ex-alcoholic in Alcoholics Anonymous who now drinks coffee with his companions; at the other end, the Yogi Guru, once a successful businessman who now literally contemplates his navel for days. In this conversion process what is converted is the self as social identity and the self as a cosmological abstraction, i.e., the complex of answers to the Who am I? and What am I? questions.

Theme II. The Group and Other. The relationship between the convert (or patient, novice, plebe, etc.) and the group varies according to the degree of involvement and specificity of role perception. At one pole this relationship may take the form of an individual who comes into contact with a particular group, such as a religious or millenial culture. The group, then, provides the setting for change. Not only does the group provide role models which specifically furnish the objects of emulation, imitation and identification, but also the conditions that demand certain performances from the initiate.

The individual (self) is further located in abstract ephemeral reference groups: the generalized other in a theological or transcendental reference. Locating oneself, then, with reference to God, One, Unity, Nature helps to provide answers to the individual struggling with the "What am I?" question. The demands imposed on the individual not only dictate which social roles he is permitted to enact but also influence self-assessment. The individual not only changes overt behavior to meet role expectations and demands, but in the process his conception of self becomes modified.

In the reconstitution of the self, the role of an Other as a role model and source of information is required. This mandatory role, whether occupied by a group or an individual, or a symbolic surrogate (oracle, Book, icon) has been found in each of the systems we have studied. This role might best be designated as "teacher," although different systems adopt other names: sponsor, priest, therapist, shaman, doctor, guard, guru, or captor. This Other or teacher is an esteemed member of the group in which the actor desires membership, such membership being a prerequisite for the invalidation of the old self and the confirmation of the new identity. What appears to be most relevant is that the role of the teacher serves to socialize the activity; that is, it serves the purpose of an evaluative audience for the adaptive measures the actor takes in handling the strains involved in the change process. What the actor does is under observation and scrutiny by the teacher who has the power (legitimate or coercive) to apply reinforcements for approved behavior, and also the power (expert) to guide the actor into appropriate role behavior. The presence of the therapist, even in silence, makes the activity public and shifts from exclusive concern with existential questions to concern with identity questions--a shift from the proprium to the socius dimension.

As we have mentioned with Alcoholics Anonymous, public testimony is a widely used method of assault that takes into account the importance of group coercion. The Salvation Army, Alcoholics Anonymous, and revivalist conversions are well known exemplars of the public testimonial. It is usual for several converts to give their testimony. More than affirmation of faith, they tell the audience their experiences, their joys and their sorrows; they speak of sins, failures and weaknesses, and of their temptations, once irresistible but now overcome through the intervention of a transcendental force, e.g., Grace of Christ. The reported experiences of members of the audience give validation to the new converts' testimony. The words of the speakers and the preachers are reaffirmed in chants and songs, recited or sung in unison. Symbolic reinforcement comes not only from the leader but from peers.

The use of drugs to facilitate conduct reorganization tends to operate at cross-purposes to the social facilitation provided by the Other group. Drugs tend to turn the actor to his "private" experiences rather than to events with a group reference. Drugs confirm private time and idiosyncratic conceptual forms. This is not to say that under some conditions drugs may not have value. They may disrupt the relations of self to surroundings, breaking through habitual and perhaps rigid conceptualizations of self. Under such conditions, given the group control of distal inputs, the actor may become more manipulable.

The group and its representative, the Other, hold a key position as primary component in this model of conduct reorganization. It is, of course, the group or Other that manipulates sensory input from the distal ecologies, that creates situations that activate inputs from the proximal ecology (e.g., proprioceptive inputs), and holds the key to reinforcement.

Theme III. Ritual Behavior. Overlapping the death-rebirth theme and the group theme is the theme of ritual behavior. We can further divide this theme into two components: the varieties of ritualized activity per se, and its relationship with the changing concept of self; and the use of such activities to manipulate time into concentrated or limited spans of individual attention, i.e., time binding.

The isolation of time increases concentration and limits the span of attention. The waiting period, the postponement of the initial appointment, the setting aside of the therapeutic hour, and the use of the retreat, can be understood as the ritual manipulation of time. Such manipulation of time may be independent of the content of the time. The bracketing or isolation of time prepares the actor for the nonconfirmation of earlier specific roles and, given the absence of customary audience feedback, initiates the stripping of achieved statuses, a prerequisite for "dying." Time can be ritually manipulated so that it appears to contract to a pinpoint or to expand otiosely. The ritual manipulation of time can shift the perspectives of the ongoing present and of past and future. In such a shifting of time, attention moves from socius to proprium and back again, depending on the form of conversion. Depersonalization and fugue, as drug "trips" suggest, can be induced. Such acts as staring, closing the eyes, praying, speaking in tongues, repeating sentences monotonously, singing, chanting, dancing, jumping, regulating the breath, and other methods are used in the various systems to limit the convert's span of attention and enhance his concentration on the objects, goals, and means of conversion.

The learning and perfection of ritual acts may also serve to neutralize arousal and reduce strain during the process of conversion. Ritual activity may be required in the performance of new roles. Incorporating various aspects of ritual into one's repertoire of instrumental acts provides for a shift from viewing oneself as agency to that of agent, from a possessed victim to one who (again) may actively cope with the distal ecologies. Prayer, for example, may be viewed as an active involvement of oneself in manipulating one's own destiny. In most of the systems of conduct reorganization we have encountered, the use of ritual has been to allow for the smooth transition from "old" to "new" lives. The repetition of sacred sentences or prayers, the strict regulation of physical habits, all are important in the reestablishing of the boundaries of the self. The performance of such tasks may serve as means of mastering basic definitions of new roles and, particularly, may initiate social ecological responses of a positive nature, i.e., reinforcement from the distal ecology. The convert, like the infant, learns to master his own behavior through elementary ritualistic and imitative activity. It is a mastery of a new and alien world, the world of the "new life."

Theme IV. Proprioceptive Stimuli. Sensory inputs from the proximal ecology play a crucial role in all systems of conduct reorganization. When the somatic components of the proximal ecology are not readily instantiated, when they"make no sense" the person actively seeks constructs or premises to help make sense out of a baffling situation. The locating and manipulating of core anchorages of the self can be managed by variations in proprioceptive stimuli. Emphasized in all of the systems we have investigated are those positions and states of the body which allow the subject or convert to shift his perception of the world, for example, kneeling, standing, lying and prostrating. Fatigue states, cramps, hunger and sleeplessness are induced and the subject's sensory dependence on external stimuli is challenged. Ritualized activity plays a role in disrupting the boundaries of the self by reorganizing stimulus inputs in the proximal ecology. Psychoanalytic procedures can be understood in this light. They establish a stimulus restructuring and withdraw attention from the location of self in social dimensions and, instead, guide the patient to inputs that provide answers to the What am I? questions.

Excitement and relaxation to induce quietude and calm are specific procedures used by many systems of behavior change that intend to achieve relaxation after periods of high involvement. In this activity the self-other relations are modified. Field dependence or independence as a perceptual function is modified, and, therefore, such modifications and manipulations of field dependency shift one's subjective view of "thingness." Thus, the shifts brought about by variations of stimuli within the proximal ecology provide a somatic basis for the process of symbolic death and rebirth.

The components of ritualistic time-binding and proprioceptive inputs are not mutually exclusive categories. Both components are used in the various systems of conduct reorganization to shift attention from external to internal events, to increase involvement, to emphasize the convert's passivity, and to arouse and heighten cognitive strain and physiological arousal. Also, as we have seen, the components may be used to provide sources of gratification and reinforcement, calm and serenity, support and nurturance.

Theme V. Triggers. The final theme is used to denote an event of unusual texture or quality that is likely to produce or enhance the process of conversion. The exact function of the trigger is uncertain and possibly idiosyncratic to the subject, but the presence of a trigger or "high value stimulus" is undeniable. A dramatic occurrence becomes the critical incident in the transition from old to new selves. John Dewey (1910), using a different metaphor, noted the importance of a sudden intense stimulus in the reorganization of thought. The trigger is most effective if it occurs at the moment of transition in the death-rebirth process.

Summary

These themes on the self-reconstitution process are not

mutually exclusive, nor do they necessarily exhaust the number of elements involved in the process. It is our concern, as we continue our study, to isolate and specify their limits. The operations necessary for the reconstitution of the self, whether found in thought reform and brainwashing, in religious conversion or in orthodox therapy, in shamanistic rites or in psychedelic cults, differ from each other, we believe with Lifton, only in degree. To the prisoner of war the reform camp has a different meaning than Loyola's exercises have for the volunteer at a retreat, or than 12 Steps have for a member of Alcoholics Anonymous. However, in terms of organismic involvement, the resolution of cognitive tension in the modes of challenging central beliefs and values, the procedures used by the various systems, are functionally equivalent. In all these procedures three central processes appear to be at work: (1) a physical or psychological assault (symbolic death); a developing confusion about self and other beliefs (the bridge between death-rebirth); (2) surrender and despair (becoming a nonperson), and (3) a working through, active mastery, reeducation of adaptation process (the rebirth experience). We have found the forms of the process to be constant, though the metaphors vary to meet the needs and values of groups or individuals. In the West the convert seeks to uplift and raise himself, while in the East the experience may be formulated as a sinking, or deepening or descent to the material depths of nature. The West may focus on the salvation of social identity, the East on cosmological properties.

In the Annual Review of Psychology, the persistent criticism of the literature on psychotherapeutic processes notes the lack of useful units of measurement, confusion and variability in identifying the relevant interactional factors, and difficulty in establishing significant intervening variables. The paucity of meaningful parameters and of criteria for change is perennially deplored. Many take refuge in this situation in the argument that therapy is essentially a matter of art and style. This only retreats from the question.

Our formulation, we believe, offers a rationale for studying the occurrences when conduct changes. It suggests a systematic formulation of the role and operations of both the subject and of the change agent. Further, it orders the kinds of interventions and their appropriate timing and position. Our continuing investigations will, we trust, establish a theoretical framework that can account for the multifarious techniques of conduct reorganization and the various modes of psychotherapy as instances of an underlying, structured generic process.

Footnote

1. This chapter is a combination and abridgement of two published articles: "Self-reconstitution processes: A preliminary report", The Psychoanalytic Review, 1971, 57, 599-616, written jointly with Nathan Adler, and "Self-reconstitution processes: A proposal for reorganizing

the conduct of confirmed smokers, " Journal of Abnormal Psychology, 1973, 81, 182-195, written jointly with Larry P. Nucci.

PART V
Critique of Concepts
of Deviant Conduct

This section consists of two chapters that present a critical analysis of the prevailing way of conceptualizing deviant conduct, with special attention devoted to the category of deviant conduct that is labelled as "mental illness."

The salient feature of deviant conduct--that is, behavior that violates social norms--is that it is puzzling to observers, and therefore evokes a need for causal explanation. Readily available for use in labeling or categorizing deviant behavior is the well-entrenched model or paradigm of "mental illness." Sarbin provides a trenchant critical analysis of the concept of mental illness in these two chapters; furthermore, he goes beyond criticism by offering viable alternative models that can be used to conceptualize deviant behavior.

In the first chapter in this section the origin of the concept of mental illness is discussed, its implications are specified, and a new conceptual model is proposed. In a stimulating and scholarly analysis of the linguistic and historical roots of the concept of "mental illness", Sarbin shows that it was employed initially as a metaphorical device in the 16th century. But with the passage of time, the metaphor was transformed into a reified entity. The choice of a metaphor for discussing behavior is not without significant implications. In the case of the mental illness concept, perhaps the most important consequences are the stigmatization and the degrading of persons categorized as "mentally ill." As an alternative to this metaphor, it is proposed that deviant conduct can be conceptualized in terms of the transformation of social identity.

In the second chapter in this section a spirited challenge to the "mental illness" or disease paradigm of human conduct is continued by focussing on the problem of involuntary hospitalization. The utility of the disease paradigm is questioned by critically examining its conceptual foundations. Among the ideological premises that seem to support current practices in dealing with deviant conduct are the apparent legitimacy of civil proceedings, the perception of the mental hospital as a legitimate institution, the belief that certain types of persons are dangerous, and the attribution of special authority to the physician. It is this ideology or system of beliefs that leads to the labeling and the involuntary hospitalization of persons who exhibit deviant conduct.

The basic thrust of both chapters in this section is that a new paradigm is needed for interpreting unconventional or norm-violating behavior--a paradigm that does not possess pernicious consequences for the individual. Sarbin points out that one important consequence for the present system of viewing deviant conduct is the denying of liberty to certain persons on the basis of "unreliable and invalid psychiatric diagnosis." In Sarbin's words, such practices "cannot be tolerated"--and it is likely that we all will agree with this sentiment.

9

THE SCIENTIFIC STATUS OF
THE MENTAL ILLNESS METAPHOR[1]

One of the most perplexing problems in contemporary behavior science is that of defining instances of conduct that are not easily assimilated to concurrent norms. The persons who exhibit such misconduct are frequently labeled disordered, insane, psychotic, mentally ill, crazy, lunatic, aberrant, deranged, and so on. The problem may be stated simply: Under what conditions should certain acts be defined as a basis for applying a label to a person, the result of which may have far-reaching consequences?

Our problem is not unique. In every age and in every culture, acts that violate certain (but not all) normative prescriptions pose a problem to the immediate or remote observers of such acts. The need to locate such misconduct on meaningful dimensions is as urgent for the illiterate Chukchee as it is for the modern behavior scientist. Perplexing conduct that cannot readily be accounted for by rule-following models--based on the concept that man's conduct is rational, purposive, and intelligible--invokes a causal explanation. When the observed conduct is an exception to a rule, and when the conduct under consideration is not inconsequential, a causal explanation must be invoked, and the posture of the observer reflects a why? or what for? question. Entrenched cultural thought models provide the starting point for such causal explanations.

We have fallen heir to a deeply entrenched thought model that is symbolized by the term "mental illness." Although the model is part of everyman's stock of conceptual equipment, certain specialized agencies and professionals employ it to form and to justify decisions about persons who fail to enact certain expected and required roles. More specifically, the person whose conduct is designated, through a series of inferential steps, as "symptoms" of "mental illness" is then subject to isolation, segregation, degradation, incarceration, surgery, chemical or psychological treatment, and so on. The assignment of a person to the class "mentally ill" is its own warrant for decisions related to management and treatment. Historians of science have concluded that entrenched thought models of the type that includes "mental illness" are particularly resistant to change or abandonment. They become convenient myths that are unbending against the flow of rational argument or empirical nonconfirmation. It is not until a new metaphor is introduced and accepted because of its kinship to other tolerated or acceptable thought models that the old myth is exposed and exploded.

The mental illness model has been attacked from a number of quarters. Szasz (1961), Goffman (1961a), Scheff (1966), and Sarbin (1964, 1967, 1968), among others have argued that mental illness is best regarded as a myth; a myth that, among other things, supports these status quo in the medical profession, giving to physicians the power (and obligation) to pass judgment on the acts of others.

This chapter is intended:
1. to uncover the metaphoric roots of the concept "mental illness" and to show, from our present perspective, how the metaphors were illictly transformed and combined into a myth;
2. to review the social implications of maintaining the mental illness concept;
3. to propose a new metaphor for labeling persons whose actions embarrass, annoy, perturb, or endanger others; and
4. to sketch some of the heuristic and pragmatic implictions of the new metaphor.

History of the Mental Illness Concept

The answer to our first question requires a brief excursion into historical linguistics. Where and when did the expression "mental illness" arise? We may stipulate at the outset that from the dawn of civilization individuals have performed acts that were judged by their contemporaries to be extra-ordinary, bizarre, inexplicable, and perturbing. Our concern is not with the truth of the statement that an individual's performances may set the stage for his being declared possessed, psychotic, or mentally ill. Our concern is with the cultural conditions that led our predecessors to regard the inexplicable event (1) as an illness or sickness and (2) as being located "in the mind."

Lest the impatient reader offer the criticism that semantic analyses fail to illuminate problems, let me declare that the choice of metaphor to denote a set of observations is not merely a rhetorical exercise. Every metaphor is potentially rich in connotations; each connotation is potentially rich in implications; each implication is a directive to action. Appropriate here is Szasz's (1961) argument that we regard deviant conduct as "problems in living." The connotations (and concurrent implications for action) of the predicate in the statement "He is mentally ill" are dramatically different from the connotations of the predicate in "He has problems in living."

It is important to note that the label "mental illness" represents a combining of two unrelated concepts, the mind and illness. Our first focus is on the illness concept; the mind will be discussed later. The basic referents for illness, and for synonyms such as sickness and disease, have not changed in any substantial way over the centuries. To medieval man, no less than to contemporary man, the referent for the symbol "illness" or for its cognate "disease" was discomfort of some kind, such as fevers, chills, aches, pain, cramps, shaking, and so on. Parenthetically, the word disease was originally equivalent to discomfort, or "not at ease" (dis + ease). Some of the meaning has been retained in "malaise" (aise = ease). In both cases, the referent is a self-assessment through attention to compelling stimuli located "inside" the organism. These internal (proximal) stimuli, when they occur simultaneously with dysfunction or incapacity of bodily organs, are the so-called symptoms or signs of illness. A diagnosis of illness or disease meant not only that a person complained of discomfort but that the associated somatic dysfunction rendered him incapable of performing some of his customary and expected roles. This general paradigm of sickness, illness, and disease is widespread and may be noted in ancient writings as well as in the observations by anthropologists of esoteric societies.

How did the class name "illness" come to include misconduct, a term relating to behavior, rather than somatic symptoms and complaints, the defining criteria of pre-Renaissance medicine? What other criteria were employed to increase the breadth of the concept "illness" in the absence of self observations described as aches, pains, chills, fevers, or other discomforts?

A search into historical sources suggests that the inclusion of conduct disorders in the concept "illness" did not come about suddenly or accidentally. Rather, the label illness was at first used as a metaphor. As is the case with metaphors, they are frequently transformed into reified entities, thus setting the stage for myth-making. The history of the employment of the concept "illness" seems to fit this sequence.

The beginning of this metaphor-to-myth transformation appears to have been an achievement of the sixteenth century. The demonical model of conduct disorders, so thoroughly exploited in the fifteenth-century "Malleus Mallificarum," had embraced all deviant or perplexing conduct. The most significant outgrowth of the model was the Inquisition, a social movement that reached into every nook and corner of Western civilization, including the diagnosis and treatment of perplexing behavior, unusual imaginings, esoteric beliefs, and so on. Such diagnosis (nearly always witchcraft) and treatment (invariably burning) was the special province of the priestly hierarchy.

The sixteenth century witnessed a number of reactions against the excesses of the Inquisition. The discovery and serious study of Galen and other classical writers, the beginnings of humanistic philosophy, in fact, the whole thrust of the Renaissance was opposite to that of the Inquisition.

One of the outstanding figures of this period was Teresa of Avila. Her efforts to save a group of nuns from the Inquisition contributed to the shift from demons to "illness" as the cause of conduct disturbances. The nuns exhibited conduct that at a later date would have been called mass hysteria, a condition arising from cloister life. By declaring these women to be infirm or ill, Teresa could fend off the impending Inquisition. That illness is something that happens to a person, rather than something over which one has control, was (and is) the traditional and thoroughly accepted viewpoint. However, the appeal that a diagnosis should be changed from witchcraft to illness did not result from a direct straight-foward fiat. Rather, Teresa asked whether the observed behavior could be explained by natural causes. Among the natural causes that she suggested were (1) melancholy (Galenic humoral pathology) (2) weak imagination, or (3) drowsiness. Persons whose conduct could be accounted for by such natural causes were to be regarded not as evil, but comas enfermas--"as if sick." By employing the metaphor "as if sick," she implied that physicians rather than priests should be the social specialists responsible for dealing with the problem (Sarbin and Juhasz, 1967).

When employing metaphorical expressions, there is a common human tendency to drop the qualifying "as if." That is to say, the metaphor is used without the label that designates it as figurative rather than literal. In the case of illness as a metaphor for conditions not meeting the usual criteria of illness, the dropping of the "as if" was facilitated by the practitioners of "physik" (predecessors to medical practitioners). It was awkward for them to talk about two kinds of illnesses, "real" illness and "as if" illness. The "as if" was dropped, especially when Galenic classifications were reintroduced. Thus, Renaissance and post-Renaissance practitioners could concern themselves with illness as traditionally understood and also with misconduct as illness. A review of the sixteenth- and seventeenth-century treatises on "physik" reveals clearly that Galen's humoral theory was widely accepted. In many cases, writers copied verbatim the declarations of Galen and of others of the Greco-Roman period. Hunter and McAlpine (1963), historians of psychiatry, in reproducing some excerpts from Barrough (1583), explain that the treatise

> shows the main divisions of mental and neurological disease based on Galen's classification which remained in use into the nineteenth century. Equipped with only the crudest notions of pathology, the presence or absence of fever measured by the pulse was the main diagnostic guide. In consequence there was much confusion between organic and nonorganic conditions; that is, between neurological and psychological disorders (p. 24).

That Barrough (and nearly every other writer on "physik") was influenced by Galen's humoral theory is readily documented. The point is clearly illustrated in the following description of "madness," one of a dozen disorders differentiated according to the then-current beliefs about the conditions, amount, and even location of actual or imaginary humors within the body.

Mania in Greeke is a disease which the Latines do call Insania and furor. That is madnes and furiousnes. They that have this disease be wood and unruly like wild beastes. It differeth from the frenesie, because in that there is a fever. But Mania commeth without a feaver. It is caused of much bloud, flowing up to the braine, sometime the bloud is temperate, and sometime only the aboundance of it doth hurt, sometimes of sharpe and hote cholericke humours, or of a hote distempure of the braine. There goeth before madnes debility of the head, tinckling of the eares, and shinings come before there eies, great watchings, thoughtes, and straunge things approach his mind, and heavines with trembling of the head. If time proceed, ther is raised in them a ravenous appetite, and a readines to bodily lust, the eyes waxe hollow, and he do nether wincke nor becken. But madness caused of bloud only, there followeth continuall laughing, there commeth before the sight (as the sicke thinketh) things to laugh at. But when choler is mixed with bloud, then the pricking and fervent moving in the braine maketh them irefull, moving, angry and bold. But if the choler do wax grosse and doth pricke and pull the brain and his other members, it make them wood, wild, and furious, and therefore they are worst to cure.

Greco-Roman medicine provided Renaissance scholars with the basic model of illness, a model that continues into the present. The patient's complaints of pains, aches, fevers, and so on, are integrated with observations of skin color, pulse, respiration, and so on, and an inference is constructed as to the probable humoral imbalance. Similarities among persons in complaints and observed signs were taken to indicate similarities or identities in the underlying etiological agent--the presence or absence of humors in certain parts of the body.

The decline of the importance of the Church in matters of unusual imaginings and conduct was parallel to the rise of science. The prestige of the scientist and his utility in filling the gap left by the withdrawal of the temporal priesthood helped in establishing the model of Galen for all kinds of illnesses--those with somatic complaints and observable somatic symptoms and those without somatic complaints but with conduct disorders substituted for somatic symptoms.

Whereas the concept of illness had been satisfied by the exclusive use of conjunctive criteria (complaints and observable somatic symptoms), now it was satisfied by the use of disjunctive criteria (complaints and somatic symptoms or complaints by others of perplexing, embarrassing, or mystifying conduct). As a result of the uncritical acceptance of the humoral pathology of Galen as the overriding explanation for both somatic and conduct disorders, the latter became assimilated to the former. That is to say, to meet the requirements of the basic Galenic model, symptoms of disease had to be observed. So the form of the conduct disorder was regarded as if it were the observable symptom. Thus, the verbal report of strange imaginings, on the one hand, and fever on the other, were both treated as equivalents. As a result of shifting from a metaphorical to a literal interpretation of conduct as symptom, Galenic medicine embraced not only everything somatic but also all conduct. Now, any bit of behavior--laughing, crying, spitting, silence, imagining, lying, and believing--could be called a symptom of underlying, internal pathology.

Such a state of affairs held until the nineteenth century, when neurology, influenced by the development of the telephone, precipitated the distinction of organic and functional disorders. The former, of course, had demonstrable pathology, but the latter had no demonstrable organic signs. Organic medicine continued to use the conjunctive criteria of Galen: self-report of discomfort and observed symptoms leading to a search for neoplasms, germs, toxins, and so on. Probably because of the intrinsic dissimilarity of the "functional" disorders, psychiatry arose as a medical specialty that concerned itself exclusively with conduct perturbations as symptoms of underlying disorders. However, nineteenth-century replacements for humors, specific microbes, localizable neoplasms and specific toxins, were inadequate to account for the behavioral symptoms of misconduct, particularly those bits of misconduct called hallucinations, delusions, phobias, and compulsions. In this connection, it is important to note that patients with somatic complaints in general seek out physicians for help. Patients whose conduct is not assimilable into current norms are usually referred to psychiatrists by relatives or law-enforcement agencies.

The basic Galenic model was not rejected by psychiatry and its immediate antecedents. Microbes, toxins, and growths, which were material and operated according to mechanical principles, were appropriate "causes" of diseases of the body. They were inside the body. The appropriate causes for abnormal behavior had to be sought along different lines. Since the dualistic mind-body concept was everyone's heritage, the hypothesis could be entertained that the causes of abnormal conduct, conduct already considered as nonsomatic disease, were in the mind. If this were so, then the most appropriate label for such nonsomatic diseases would be mental illness.

Before considering the meaning of "mental" in the phrase "mental illness," let me recapitulate. I have tried to show that "illness," as in "mental illness," was an illicit transformation of a metaphorical to a literal concept. To save unfortunate people from being labeled witches, it was useful to regard persons who exhibited misconduct of certain kinds as if they were ill. The Galenic model facilitated the eliding of the hypothetical phrase, the "as if," and the concept of illness was thus stretched to include events that did not meet the original conjunctive criteria for illness. A second transformation assured the validity of the Galenic model. The disturbing modes of behavior could be treated as if they were symptoms equivalent to somatic symptoms. By dropping the "as if" modifier, observed behavior was taken to be symptomatic of underlying internal pathology.

Our question has now become this: How did the notion of illnesses "of the mind" become so widely accepted that it served as the groundwork for a medical specialty? A searching analysis of the history of the concept makes clear that "mind" was originally employed as a metaphor to denote such events as remembering and thinking. (Colloquial English still uses mind as equivalent to remember, as in "mind your manners.") The shift of meaning to that of a substantive and an agency can best be understood as still another instance of the metaphor-to-myth transformation (Ryle, 1949).

The modern practitioner of Galenic psychiatry operates from the principle that the illness about which he is concerned is in the mind (or psyche, or psychic apparatus). Further, just as special techniques may be employed to examine the body, so are there special techniques for examining the mind. But the mind, even for Galenic practioners, was too abstract and undifferentiated a concept. It had to have certain properties, just as the body had specific properties.

Since visual, palpable organs were obviously assigned to the material body, the differentiating characteristics of the invisible, impalpable mental entity were expressed as states. States of love, fear, anxiety, apathy, and so on were invented to account for differences in observed conduct. Since the mind was invisible and immaterial, it could not have the same properties as the body--properties that could be denoted by physicalistic terms. A new metaphor was required--the metaphor of states of mind. The practitioner now had the job of discovering through chains of inferences which mental states were responsible for normal and abnormal conduct.

For our purposes we can begin our linguistic analysis of mental states with the language of the Middle Ages. The natural history of word formation seems to be, first, the forming of words to denote objects and events in the distal environment, such as sun, fire, water, people, clouds, and so on. These distal objects are primarily mediated by the receptors of vision and audition. Later, terms are invented for denoting proximal events, such as pains, itches, pressures, soreness, and so on. Words already in existence to denote distal objects are borrowed through metaphor to denote proximal events. Just as distal events are mediated by visual and auditory receptors, proximal occurrences (and not mental states) are mediated by somasthetic receptors. The construction of a language to denote distal and proximal events was no mean achievement. Such a language served the purposes of men who had to communicate about things of importance to their survival.

The achievement of language to denote mental states--the purported object of study by mentalistic specialists--required a tour de force, a special set of circumstances. What were these special circumstances? In short, how did the concept of mental states, whose relation to empirical events was unknown or presumed to be inconsequential, derive from the distal-proximal language?

Before the great religious and scientific transformations of the Renaissance, the language of conduct was essentially a distal-proximal language. The available stock of words denoted objects and events in the distal and proximal ecologies that had concrete reference. This is not to say that terms were not at hand for denoting imaginary things such as angels, leprechauns, and demons. However, these imaginary objects were regarded as if they belonged to the distal world, not to a shadowy inner world. A review of early writers, such as Chaucer, reveals almost no reference to internal mental states. The motivation to go on pilgrimages, for example, is in the world of nature and in the changing of seasons--it is not a result of the activation of a special mental state.

Three developments contributed to the postulation of a mind as the repository of mental states--a postulation that made possible the further invention of illnesses of the mind: (1) a linguistic factor--the availability of dispositional terms, (2) the introduction of new terms of faith and religion that located religious experience "inside" the person, and (3) the development of scientific lexicon that tried to break away from theology.

(1) Dispositional terms are shorthand expressions for combinations or orderings of distal or proximal events--in principle a dispositional term may be reduced to a series of observable occurrences. For example, "courage" implies a set of concrete behaviors under certain conditions. There is no necessary implication that the referent is an internal mental state. The development of dispositional terms, however, appears to be a necessary (although insufficient) prerequisite for the postulation of mental states. In time, the detailed, concrete occurrences (for which the dispositional term is a sort of shorthand) became elided and remote from the original metaphoric beginnings. It is as if some dispositional terms were free-floating and distant from their empirical moorings.

(2) Terms of our second class were conveniently borrowed when religious conceptions shifted from emphasis on ritual and ceremony to "inward," personal aspects of faith. Theologians and preachers gave a new set of referents to these dispositional terms, referents that changed dispositional terms from shorthand descriptions of conduct to descriptions of states of mind.

The context in which mental states are employed is best expressed by the polarity inside-outside. The problem for the medieval thinker was to find a model for locating events on the inside. Such a model could have been constructed from the following observations and inferences: Two classes of proximal inputs may be identified. The first occurs in a context of external events. For example, pain in the ankle occurs in a context of tripping over a curb; discomfort in the head occurs in the context of a blow from a baseball bat; a burning irritation in the fingers occurs in the context of accidentally leaning on a hot stove. The second class of proximal inputs occurs in the absence of recognizable distal events, such as toothache, headache, gastritis, neuritis, and so on. Since the antecedents of the latter inputs could not be located in the outside world by medieval man, the locus of the somatic perception was taken as the causal locus--inside the body. Medieval man had little reliable knowledge of anatomy save that there were bones, sinews, tubes, and fluids, and there were also empty spaces. Under the authority of the priests, he acquired the belief that an immaterial and invisible soul resided in these otherwise empty spaces. Within this system of beliefs, events for which there were no observed distal contexts could be attributed to the workings of this inner entity or soul. Proximal events that could not be related to occurrences in the distal environment were related to the spiritual happenings inside the person.

Such an analysis probably prepared the way for locating dispositions inside the person and calling them states of mind. If the cause of an event had no obvious external locus, then it must have had an internal locus. Dispositions, when they are codified as substantives, tend to be treated in the same way as other nouns, as possessing "thingness." Thus, courage, lust, conscience, purity, devotion, all dispositional terms originally tied to orderings of behavior were framed as nouns. If some nouns are names of things--and things are frequently located on spatial dimensions--then dispositional terms may refer to things that have location. But how to locate the disposition? In the same manner as locating the cause of pain in the absence of external occurrences--inside the person. Thus, anger, joy, courage, happiness, and so on came to be located in the soul.

(3) The displacement of theologians by scientists in the sixteenth and seventeenth centuries in matters pertaining to strange and mysterious conduct made necessary a shift from theological to scientific metaphors. The soul had too much surplus meaning to be useful to materialistic scientists. However, they could not break completely with the entrenched dualistic philosophy so well enunciated by Descartes. Renaissance scientists took as their point of departure the facts of thinking and knowing, and, as a substitute for the soul, employed mind as the organ for such activities. With the development of classical scholarship, Greek terms were substituted for the vernacular, the most popular being "psyche" (Boring, 1966). The efforts of the post-Renaissance Galenic practitioners, then, were directed toward analyzing states of mind and psychic processes. Those sequences of perplexing conduct that could not be related to external occurrences were declared to be outcomes of internal mental or psychic processes.

In the preceding paragraphs I have tried to show that mental states--the objects of interest and study for the diagnostician of "mental illness"--were postulated to fill gaps in early knowledge. Through historical and linguistic processes, the postulation was reified. Contemporary users of the mental illness concept are guilty of illicitly shifting from metaphor to myth. Instead of maintaining the metaphorical rhetoric "it is as if there were states of mind" and "it is as if some states of mind could be characterized as sickness," the contemporary mentalist conducts much of this work as if he believes that minds are "real" entities and that, like bodies, they can be sick or healthy.

Implications of "Mental Illness" Conception

Having sketched the metaphoric history of the phrase "mental illness," we now address ourselves to its implications. As we suggested earlier, the choice of metaphors is not inconsequential. The concepts embraced by a particular term contain their own implications; and implications are directives to action.

The most potent implication of the metaphor is that persons labeled mentally ill are categorized as significantly discontinuous from persons labeled with the unmodified term "ill." Of course, referring to persons as simply ill or sick suggests that they belong to a class different from the mutually exclusive class "not ill" or "healthy." Assigning persons to the class "ill" carries the meaning of objective signs and symptoms of a recognized or named disease in addition to subjectively experienced discomfort. In most societies, persons so classified are temporarily excused from the performance of selected role obligations. The label carries no hint of negative valuation. Sickness, in general, is something for which one is not responsible.

However, when the modifier "mental" is prefixed, a whole new set of implications follows. Contrary to the humane intent of those who resisted the diagnosis of witchcraft by employing the nonprejorative diagnostic label of illness, present usage is transparently pejorative.

In adding the word "mental" to "illness," the whole meaning changes. In the first place, the necessity for adding a modifier to "illness" imposes a special constraint on the interpreter--he asks, "What is it about this person or his behavior that calls for a special designation?" Since it is a special kind of illness, does the same expectation hold that he is to be temporarily excused from the enactment of his roles?

The answer to these questions may be found in a number of studies (J. Cummings and E. Cummings, 1962; Goffman, 1961a; Nunnally, 1961; Phillips, 1963). Persons who are labeled mentally ill are not regarded as merely sick, but are regarded as a special class of beings, to be feared or scorned, sometimes to be pitied, but nearly always to be degraded. Coincident with such negative valuations are the beliefs that such "mentally ill" persons discharge obligations of only the most simple kinds. Elsewhere I have argued that the process whereby a person is converted into a mental patient carries with it the potential for self-devaluation. The stigmatization, then, may work in the nature of a self-fulfilling prophecy (Sarbin, 1968c).

Further, because of the inherent vagueness in the concept of mind, its purported independence from the body, and its permanence (derived from the immortal soul), there is a readiness to regard this special kind of sickness as permanent. Thus, a person who has a broken leg or suffers from barber's itch, that is, a sick person, may take up his customary roles upon being restored to health. A person diagnosed as mentally ill, however, is stigmatized. Although "cured" of the behavior that initiated the sequence of social and political acts that resulted in his being classified as mentally ill, his public will not usually accept such "cures" as permanent. It is as if the mental states were capable of disguising the person as healthy, although the underlying mental illness remained in a dormant or latent state.

Another implication of the mental illness concept, stemming from the demonstrated utility of germ theory for nonmental illness, is the internal causal locus of mental illness. The interior of the mind, rather than the interior of the body, is the object of study and inference. But that shadowy interior is not easily entered. The experts must depend on chains of inference forged out of the patient's verbal and nonverbal communications. From such communications the experts draw conclusions about the mental structures, their dynamic properties, and their relation to observed behavior. One outcome of the exclusive verbal preoccupation with the interior of the mind is the neglect and avoidance of events in the exterior world that might be antecedent to instances of misconduct arbitrarily called symptoms.

The heuristic implications of the mental illness metaphor are no less important than the practical implications. Scientists of many kinds have discovered the causes for many (nonmental) illnesses by looking inside the body. By adding a postulate that all mental states are caused by organic conditions (the somatopsychic hypothesis) and also accepting disordered conduct as symptomatic of underlying disease entities, one is then forced to consider the corollary that the ultimate causal agents will be discovered through biochemical, toxicological, and bacteriological investigations. Again, such search methods deploy attention and effort away from the distal ecology as the source of possible antecedent conditions of misconduct.

A further implication of the illness metaphor is that physicians should be assigned the task of diagnosing and treating mental (along with non-mental) illness. But those persons assigned the mental patient role, characteristically allowed to meet only minimal social demands, required special kinds of medical treatment. Since the middle of the nineteenth century in the United States, such treatment has been carried on in asylums and hospitals where policies and practices were within the province of physicians. Szasz (1961) has convincingly discussed the biases introduced into legal procedures as a result of labeling a person "mentally ill."

It is interesting to note that a euphemism is only effective for a short time. "Asylums," at first a term used to suggest a haven of safety and security, deteriorated in meaning along with the degrading practices of the keepers and inmates. Its pejorative character made it inappropriate for the new humanism of such forceful figures as Dorothea Lynde Dix. "Hospitals" became the new euphemism. However, when "hospital" is now employed as in State Hospital or Mental Hospital, the image of bedlam is reconstructed, including locked wards, barred windows, keepers and wardens, and so on. The degraded status of the inmates has generalized to their institutional residences.

In the interest of brevity, we must eschew further discussion of the implications of the mental illness myth. To recapitulate, the choice of "mental illness" to denote conduct that violates certain cultural norms carries with it some definite implications for practice and theory. Among these implications are the following:

1. The diagnosis "mentally ill" is a pejorative; its use has the effect of publicly degrading a person and also of providing the basis for self-devaluation.

2. The belief in the "reality" of mind and mental states has directed the attention of scientists to the interior shadowy mind. The effect of this concern for the "inner life" has been a systematic rejection of possible causal factors in the exterior world.

3. The force of the illness metaphor is that physicians should be the specialists of choice. Along with this implication is the continued search for internal mental state causalty on the model of germ theory.

4. Special kinds of illness require special treatment centers. Euphemistically called mental hospitals, such centers are managed by physicians and in the main serve merely to segregate the diagnosed mentally ill from the community.

A New Model: The Transformation of Social Identity

In the natural history of science, a myth is exploded when evidence of its inutility accumulates concurrently with the exposition of a new metaphor that better captures the essence of the events under examination. The remarks in the preceding pages were aimed at "undressing" the metaphor (Turbayne, 1962) of mental illness. The purpose of this undressing was to show that "mental illness," originally a pair of metaphors introduced to facilitate communication about certain kinds of conduct, has been transformed to the status of a myth.

Metaphors have great utility in opening new frontiers of exploration and in suggesting new directions for research and practice, as well as in modifying the connotations of a concept. The time has come for replacing the old myth with a new metaphor. The assertion can be readily supported that the mental illness model of dysfunctional conduct is no longer helping us to understand, predict, or control disordered behavior. The current trend for dealing with deviant and disordered persons is away from the tradition of the physician's being sought out by the patient or by his relatives. The efforts of professionals are no longer exclusively directed toward the more dramatic instances of disordered conduct for which our predecessors coined sesquipedalian Greco-Latin terms such as agoraphobia, pyromania, catatonic schizophrenia, and psychasthenia. Modern efforts are directed toward controlling the mystifying conduct denoted by such opaque metaphors, as well as the garden varieties of disordered behavior. The grand strategy is to reach out into the community and help those people who lead lives of quiet desperation, some of whom occasionally break out of their social entrapment with bizarre conduct or violence. To be effective, this new strategy must take into account two postulates: (1) that man as a social creature must confront and solve certain ongoing problems, and (2) that man as a social creature acquires modes of solving problems that may be successful under some conditions and not successful under others. These postulates are irrelevant to practitioners and theorists of Galenic medicine, whether ancient or contemporary.

As a replacement for the older concept, I propose that disordered conduct follows from, or is concurrent with, attempts to solve certain problems generated in social systems. The metaphor of choice is "the transformation of social identity." The conception flows from a dramaturgical stream of ideas. The establishment of a social identity occurs in a context of enacting roles in such a manner as to make good one's granted and attained roles. The dimensions of social identity are formed out of the components of the role system in which the person operates. (2)

People with degraded social identites are the potential, if not the actual, candidates for the diagnosing, judging, helping, and treatment facilities usually called "mental health services." To degrade an individual's social identity, one need only remove from him the opportunity to enact roles that have elements of choice. The more one's identity is made up of granted roles, the fewer opportunities he has of engaging in role behavior that may be positively valued. The best he can hope for is to be neutrally valued through the proper, appropriate, and convincing enactment of his granted roles, all of which are highly involving. Such a state of affairs is achieved, if at all, only at the cost of high degrees of strain, a neutrally valued social identity being the maximum possible reward. At what point does the individual raise the question of whether the payoff is commensurate with the high degree of strain? Indexes of social pathology are highest among populations that exhibit these characteristics. If a man's job and other vehicles of his achieved identity are removed, he has few chances of displaying conduct that may be positively valued by self or relevant others. The difference is only one of degree between the unemployed urban ghetto dweller and the more commonly used examples of degraded identities, inmates in a maximum security prison, patients in back wards of mental institutions, and prisoners of war in thought-control camps. Totalistic social organization and control of achieved statuses leads to extreme degradation, to the identity of a nonperson.

The implications of this model--designed to displace the entrenched mental illness model--are transparent. In the first place, our technique for case-finding is to be guided by a theory of social identity and the socially dysfunctional outcomes of degradation. That is to say, we would try to locate those individuals and groups whose efforts to establish acceptable social identities have been unsuccessful. These persons would show the characteristics of degraded identities, as indicated before. In the second place, the theory makes possible the construction of a set of propositions to be tested empirically. These propositions include hypotheses about the behavioral effects of prolonged degradation, the outcomes of upgrading social identities through commendation, promotion, and so on. Further, the heuristic implications are not to be minimized. The search for "causes" will be in social systems, not in mythic internal entities.

The process of reorganizing conduct takes on a new set of characteristics. In the place of "psychotherapy"--a derivative of Galenic medicine--opportunities arise for the use of a social systems approach. Rather than direct the efforts of the helping professions to the "insides" of the individual, the focus is the role-set, the constellation of persons in complementary and reciprocal relations one to the other (Kahn, Wolfe, Quinn, Snoek and Rosenthal, 1964). Further, the degradation and upgrading metaphors suggest an entirely new approach to behavior change or conduct reorganization. From an analysis of systems of behavior change that have been successfully employed in religious, military, and other non-medical settings, we have been able to isolate components that bear a striking resemblance to the components of the model presented here under the heading: the transformation of social identity (Sarbin and Adler, 1971).

Traditional metaphors for conceptualizing socially dysfunctional conduct are unsatisfactory. The illness and mind metaphors have led us astray. We suggest a fresh perspective--that we follow the implications of social role theory and concern ourselves with the shaping and transforming of social identities. To approach the etiology of dysfunctional conduct, we must take into account the effects of the degradation of social identities. The new metaphors must flow from a comprehensive social theory; they must replace "mental illness"--the older metaphor-turned myth, the heritage of Galenic medicine.

Footnotes

1. Reprinted, in abridged form, from S.C. Plog and R.B. Edgerton (Eds.), Changing perspectives in mental illness. New York: Holt, 1969. pp. 9-31.
2. This model is presented in detail in Chapter 6 (The Transvaluation of Social Identity), and therefore is omitted from this chapter.

10

IDEOLOGICAL CONSTRAINTS ON THE SCIENCE OF DEVIANT CONDUCT[1]

We have anguished and complained and protested about involuntary hospitalization and its degrading consequences. Protestations without a conceptual foundation are, however, futile--they can lead nowhere unless we can illuminate the ideological underpinnings, expose the prevailing myths, and dissolve the metaphors that give rhetorical sustenance to judicial, psychiatric, and bureaucratic practices that deal with persons who exhibit unwanted conduct. This paper is intended to make our protestations more potent by analyzing the conceptual foundations of involuntary hospitalization.

Two major elements in my title need to be elaborated. For ideological constraints, I could have substituted other words, such as hidden assumptions, paradigms, tacit models, myths, or guiding postulates: I chose the phrase "ideological constraints" because it has certain connotations not carried by the other terms. The term ideology is more often employed in the analysis of political beliefs, i.e., beliefs about the appropriate distribution of legitimate power, but it also carries the notion of being highly valued. The second term in the title, "deviant conduct," is intended to convey something other than individual differences in behavior, and something other than mere departure from so-called normality. "Deviant conduct" connotes departures from an assumed norm that make contact with the moral standards of persons who are empowered to apply such standards. I prefer the word "conduct" rather then "behavior" because of its placement in a family of terms that have to do with special interactions and transactions. Unlike the more antiseptic word "behavior," the word "conduct" denotes the involvement of other people--other people who make value judgments.

The contemporary study of deviance is moving away from exclusive concentration on the identified norm-violator as an abstract individual. Instead the accent is on the social system: the identified norm-violator is but one actor in an ongoing drama, and those who pass judgment on him are other actors. If we extend this kind of analysis to its logical limits, we find ourselves not only undertaking a simultaneous study of the target person and the other persons who make the value judgments, but also the codified and uncodified rules that the valuing person employs to construct his judgments about the target person (Mancuso and Sarbin, 1977).

This introduction reveals my bias: I regard as an exercise in futility the search for disturbance within the individual, originating within an abstraction called mind or psyche or personality; my emphasis is on the social system that supports beliefs about unwanted conduct. Involuntary hospitalization, I shall submit, can best be understood if examined in the context of historical and political events. Whether one deplores or accepts current practices, the social, legal, and political problems raised by involuntary hospitalization force us to re-consider freedom as one value in the context of competing values. In this country, involuntary hospitalization is carried out under the apparent protection of court procedures. Either as the result of statutes or of custom, such proceedings make use of the expert testimony of physicians, where possible, physicians who profess competence as psychiatrists. It is not my intention to discredit psychiatry--some criticism of certain aspects of the profession may occur as fallout. My intention rather is to understand why the paradigm that has prevailed in psychiatry (and, I might add, in clinical and abnormal psychology for over 100 years) does not assimilate the increasing fund of knowledge that would change that paradigm.

My use of the word paradigm takes us into the helpful analysis that Professor Thomas Kuhn presented about fifteen years ago on the structure of scientific revolution--an analysis that has been widely accepted and used in a number of settings. He made the point that every scientific enterprise constructs a paradigm, i.e., a patterned way of looking at the world of occurrences, together with a set of experimental and conceptual procedures that are regarded as the givens for performing the everyday tasks of that science (Kuhn, 1962). General psychology is still pre-paradigmatic, still searching for a single paradigm. But abnormal psychology and psychiatry function according to a vigorous and well articulated paradigm--the diagnosis and treatment of disease. It has respectable antecedents in somatic medicine, and a review of its contemporary literature would lead to the conviction that, in spite of efforts to challenge it, the paradigm remains intact.

Without the disease paradigm modern medicine could not have made its great advances in understanding the cause and cure of many somatic illnesses. The same paradigm is used by the practitioners of psychiatry who, as physicians, acquire skills to diagnose and to treat patients suffering from disease. The general disease paradigm has given rise to the medical model as the basis for the everyday science of abnormal psychology and psychiatry (Sarbin, 1967a; Scheff, 1966; Szasz, 1961, 1970).

For various reasons, a sufferer may voluntarily consult a practitioner of psychiatry or clinical psychology and establish a doctor-patient relationship. Such an application of the medical model is not my concern. The patient is free to seek help from a broad spectrum of helpers, professional or other wise. Whether mental health professionals are more effective than other kinds of helpers is an empirical matter. I am concerned, rather, with persons whose conduct is the object of complaint by others, and who do not complain of pains, aches, bleeding, discharges, engorgements, tickles, pressures, itches or any of the other discomforts or suffering that bring people to physicians.

II

As a result of historical events (described in Chapter 9), the entire vocabulary of medicine could be applied to unwanted conduct re-named "mental illness": diagnosis, treatment, prognosis, etiology, etc. As a consequence of shifting from a metaphoric to a literal interpretation of gross behavior as symptom, the practice of medicine could embrace not only every physiological and anatomical condition, but also all conduct. As a result, any item of conduct--laughing, crying, threatening, spitting, the reporting of imaginings, writings on yellow paper, the expression of unpopular beliefs, wearing unconventional clothing, resisting authority and denouncing myths--could be called symptoms of underlying internal pathology.

I have so far addressed myself to a brief statement of the paradigm that guides modern psychiatry and the related mental health professions. My next task is to present evidence that contradicts the basis for contemporary practice, that challenges the utility of the disease paradigm. If contradictions of such magnitude were introduced into most other disciplines, the resulting condition would be identified as a paradigm-in-crisis, a stage in the development of a science preliminary to scientific revolution.

From a large array of facts and arguments that challenge the continued use of the mental illness model, I have selected four: (1) the lack of reliability of psychiatric diagnosis, (2) the lack of validity of psychiatric diagnosis as demonstrated in the Rosenhan (1973) study, (3) the effect of extraneous factors such as political attitudes on psychiatric diagnosis, and (4) the mythic quality of mental illness.

My first set of observations has to do with unreliability of psychiatric diagnosis. Numerous studies and reviews of studies have appeared and all of them converge on one conclusion--that psychiatric diagnosis is unreliable (Spitzer and Wilson, 1975). The highest degree of consistency reported is represented by an error rate of about 20%, which occurs under conditions where two diagnosticians work closely together and agree that certain signs and symptoms will be used as criteria for employing certain diagnostic labels. If we assume that the first diagnostician is correct in 100% of the cases, under the most ideal circumstances, the second diagnostician would disagree in 20% of the cases. In some studies the error rate between diagnosticians is as great as 75%.

Mental health professionals in private practice and even in hospital work are aware of the futility of psychiatric diagnosis. However, entrenched bureaucracy in government agencies and in insurance companies--wedded to the medical model--insist on the use of these diagnostic categories. The Diagnostic and Statistical Manual of the American Psychiatric Association provides the categories, complete with descriptions, and even with code numbers.

For example, to know "what schizophrenia is" one could refer to the Diagnostic and Statistical Manual. This widely used Manual has provided psychiatric practitioners with definitions that in principle would enable them to recognize schizoprenia or any other mental disease when they saw it. I quote the definition taken from the 1958 edition :

...It represents a group of psychotic reactions characterized by fundamental disturbances in reality relationships and concept functions, with affective, behavioral and intellectual disturbances in varying degrees and mixtures. The disorders are marked by a strong tendency to retreat from reality, by emotional disharmony, unpredictable disturbances in stream of thought, regressive behavior, and in some, a tendency to "deterioration."

Over half the words in this definition allows for almost unlimited interpretation. It is no wonder that psychiatrists, when making their judgments in clinical or in court settings, have such high rates of disagreement (Ward, Beck, Mendelson, Mock and Erbaugh, 1962).

In 1968, a second edition of the Manual appeared. Presumably the language was made more precise so that diagnosis would be more reliable. The description of schizophrenia appeared as follows:

This large category includes a group of disorders manifested by characteristic disturbances of thinking, mood, and behavior. Disturbances in thinking are marked by alterations of concept formation which may lead to misinterpretation of reality and sometimes to delusions and hallucinations, which frequently appear psychologically self-protective. Corollary mood changes include ambivalence, constricted and inappropriate emotional responsiveness and loss of empathy with others. Behavior may be withdrawn, regressive and bizarre. . .

Recent studies indicate no increase in agreement as the result of the newer language. Again more than half the words are abstract, ambiguous and opaque.

As I said before, many professionals avoid the language of diagnosis. The court appointed physician, however, does not have the luxury of choice. Even though diagnosis is characterized by a lack of reliability, the deprivation of liberty cannot be suitably carrried out unless the "quasi-defendent" is first assigned to a psychiatric category.

My second set of observations has to do with lack of validity of psychiatric diagnosis. The proposition that a diagnostician can regard any bit of conduct as a symptom of underlying psychiatric diseases has been elaborated by Goffman (1961a), Sarbin (1967a), Szasz (1961), and others. That psychiatrists and other mental health professionals are biased toward psychopathology is a well-established fact. David Rosenhan's (1973) study nicely illustrates the invalidity of psychiatric diagnosis. In brief, eight of his associates volunteered to enter mental hospitals as pseudo-patients. We can speak of 12 pseudopatients inasmuch as some of the volunteers participated more than once. The presenting symptom was an "auditory hallucination" that said "empty," "thud" or "dull." This symptom was selected because such an atypical form of conduct does not ordinarily come to the attention of diagnosticians. The pseudopatients were instructed to be 100% truthful about everything except this one symptom. In every case, the person was admitted to the hospital; 11 cases were diagnosed as paranoid schizophrenia, and one case was diagnosed as manic depressive. On discharge from the hospital, the pseudopatients, it is important to note, were diagnosed as "schizophrenia: improved," or "schizophrenia: in remission" or "manic depressive in remission."

The second part of the study, which is equally important, was Rosenhan's response to a challenge made by the staff of another hospital. Rosenhan agreed to send one of his pseudopatients into this hospital, but did not identify the date. During the period of the study there were 193 admissions. Twenty one percent of these were diagnosed by at least one staff member as pseudopatients, 12% by at least one psychiatrist, 10% by one psychiatrist and one other staff member. Because of illness, the assigned pseudopatient never appeared during the interval of the study. Rosenhan's conclusion is worth repeating: ". . . we have known for a long time that diagnoses are often not useful or reliable, but we have nevertheless continued to use them. We now know that we cannot distinguish insanity from sanity." Not only are psychiatric diagnoses unreliable, like those funny elastic rulers sold in sport shops for measuring the length of fish, but this study demonstrates that diagnoses are not credible. This labelling of the pseudopatients on discharge as paranoid schizophrenia, in remission, in the absence of any reliable or valid diagnostic signs, raises the most important point of all: the mythic nature of mental illness.

The study has been criticized by supporters of the medical model. Professor Seymour Kety (1974), for example, offered a criticism in the context of deception. He said "if I were to drink a quart of blood and, concealing what I had done, had come to the emergency room of any hospital vomiting blood, the behavior of the staff would be quite predictable. If they labelled and treated me as having a bleeding peptic ulcer, I doubt that I could argue convincingly that medical science does not know how to diagnose that condition." Professor Kety does not go on to say that when no bleeding was observed the next day, and when all diagnostic tests had proven negative, the patient would be discharged as "bleeding peptic ulcer: improved, or in remission," a label that he might carry around with him for the rest of his life. More probably, the final diagnosis would be listed as "unknown." But Professor Kety leads his readers to believe that the deception of a medical or psychiatric staff is easy because the medical staff is obligated to diagnose and treat people in distress. He overlooked entirely the fact that when a person is diagnosed or misdiagnosed as paranoid schizophrenic in the absence of criterial conduct, the diagnostician is illigitimately applying a stigmatizing label that may stick permanently.

The third set of observations has to do with the influence of extraneous factors on diagnosis. That psychiatric diagnosis, the basis of expert testimony in civil hearings, is influenced by extraneous factors is a fact now well-documented. If, for example, a "suspected patient" or "quasi-patient" appears to be of lower class origins, he is more likely to be declared psychotic then if he appears to be of middle class background (Hollingshead and Redlich, 1958). Another extraneous factor that influences psychiatric diagnosis is political attitudes. The doctors Braginsky and their co-workers have illuminated this rather murky area (Braginsky and Braginsky, 1974).

In the first of two studies, they assessed certain political attitudes of hospitalized mental patients and mental health professionals in the same institution. They were particularly interested in attitude toward new left philosophy and attitude toward the use of radical tactics. The new left attitude scale assessed a philosophy of support for social change, the "Radical Left" attitude scale assessed a philosophy of support for social change, the "Radical Tactics" scale assessed attitudes toward various strategies to achieve social change. On both these scales, patients scored significantly higher than mental health professionals and, incidentally, higher than a reference group of high scoring university students. Among the mental health professionals, psychologists and psychiatrists were the most politically conservative.

Having established that mental hospital patients, as a group, are politically different from mental health professionals the doctors Braginsky and their colleagues undertook a second study to determine whether such an extraneous variable as political attitudes could influence psychiatric diagnosis. Two videotaped interviews between a doctor and a pseudopatient (enacted by a college senior) were put together. Each interview was composed of four distinct segments: Segment 1, presenting complaints; Segment 2, expression of political philosophy; Segment 3, expression of political strategy; Segment 4, evaluative comments about mental health professions. For both interviews the first segment consisted of complaints made by the patient in response to the doctor's question, "How are you feeling?" The complaints were listlessness and fatigue, poor appetite, restless sleep patterns, irritability with friends, and so on.

In the second segment of the tape, the patient expressed either a new left political philosophy or a middle of the road

political philosophy. In the third segment, the patient who
expressed the new left attitudes endorsed the use of radical
tactics to bring about social change, while the moderate patient
decried the use of radical tactics. Both patients in the fourth,
and final, segment criticized mental health professionals, but
did so from different perspectives. The new left radical accused
mental health workers of being the handmaidens of a repressive
society, labelling, drugging, and incarcerating anyone who
disagreed with conventional values. The middle of the road
patient asserted that mental health professionals have done more
harm than good by destroying traditional values, by encouraging
permissiveness, and by being, in general, too radical.

Each videotaped interview was shown (on separate occasions,
of course) to audiences of mental health professionals who were
asked to diagnose the patient and to describe the severity of
his illness after each of the four segments. Thus, after Segment
1 was shown, the video recorder was stopped, the observers
completed their rating, turned the page of their test booklet,
Segment 2 was shown, and so on through Segment 4.

The results of this study clearly indicate the significant
effect political attitudes have on psychiatric diagnosis. As the
new left radical patient's complaints shift from his own person
to society, he is seen as increasingly psychologically
disturbed. When he suggests action to be taken to correct what
is wrong with society, he is perceived as still more
pathological. The moderate counterpart's psychopathology remains
stable as he vocalizes anti-new left sentiments, and somewhat
decreases when he criticizes those who would radically change
our social institutions. The judgment of severity of pathology
of both the new left and the middle of the road patients
dramatically increase when they criticise mental health
professionals. Even the politically "rational" young man seen as
moderately disturbed (despite being presented as a hospitalized
mental patient) is then diagnosed as being quite psychotic
following his attack on the mental health profession. (In this
connection, I wonder what diagnostic label will be used by
psychiatric diagnosticians who read this paper?)

The most spectacular change in the perception of the
patient occurs in the sequence when he directs his derogatory
remarks to mental health personnel. The question that
immediately comes to mind is: What would happen if the patient
uttered flattering comments? That is, if his insults to
psychiatry are seen as a function of a "paranoid" disturbance,
would complimentary remarks be perceived as the functioning of a
non-psycho-pathological person? Returning to the video recorder,
the experimenters constructed a new fourth segment where the
patient accentuated the positive aspects of mental health
professions. This new Segment 4 replaced Segment 4 of the new
left radical interview. Another group of hospital staff was
convened and the same procedure followed.

The results for the first three segments were similar to
those obtained before. On Segment 4, however, the very disturbed
mental patient was suddenly "cured" of his mental illness--he
was perceived as having given up his symptoms, of being
"normal." The "cure" consisted of communicating to mental health

personnel that they were helpful, kind, competent, and, in general, very special people.

These studies would appear to support the assertion that diagnosis is a moral rather than a scientific enterprise, that psychiatric diagnosis is not like the diagnosis of pneumonia or fractured pelvis.

The fourth set of observations considers "mental illness" as a scientifically empty term. In a paper published earlier (Sarbin, 1972b), I presented a preliminary report to show that schizophrenia (a subcategory of mental illness) could best be conceptualized as a myth. The main features of my argument centered on illicit transformation of a metaphor (first employed to describe unwanted but puzzling conduct) to a reified or mythic status. Although myths, like fairy tales and legends, are useful for some purposes, they provide no basis for empirical science. Professor Mancuso and I set out to discover if the massive research programs of the past 15 years have identified any stable correlates of schizophrenia. If we could identify no stable, objective defining criterion, then our declaration would be supported that schizophrenia (and mental illness) be considered as mythic (Sarbin and Mancuso, 1970).

The raw data for this analysis are taken from 300 articles on schizophrenia published between 1959 and 1973 in the Journal of Abnormal and Social Psychology. This Journal was selected because it enjoys the reputation of enforcing the most rigorous standards for research in the field of abnormal psychology.

There is an almost universal prototype in studies of schizophrenia. The basic design is as follows: The experimenter advances a hypothesis. It is usually of the form "compared to normals, schizophrenia patients will perform poorly on such-and-such an experimental procedure." The investigator then selects, say, 30 to 50 hospitalized patients each of which serves as an experimental subject. It is important to note that the experimenter (a) employs only cooperative patients and (b) accepts the psychiatric diagnosis as the basis for his independent variable. He compares the average score of his schizophrenic sample with the average score of a non-schizophrenic sample, often called "normals." The experimental task might be the solving of logical problems, the completion of incomplete sentences or drawings, the interpretation of proverbs, manipulating a dial, the recognition of partially concealed pictures of nude figures, etc. In principle, the experimental task is designed to test a hypothesis about schizophrenia that derives from a particular model of schizophrenia. For example, a model that regards loosening of associations as a criterial attribute of schizophrenia will suggest a hypothesis to be tested by a word association test, by interpretation of proverbs, or by a concept formation task. A model that places disturbances in feelings in a central position will suggest a hypothesis to be tested by the quality of the subject's response to stressful stimuli of varous kinds, and so on.

The experimental variable is intended to provide a way of defining the schizophrenia-non-schizophrenia dichotomy. Not content with the subjective impression of psychiatrists, experimenters look for objective, verifiable signs. There is hardly a laboratory or clinical exercise that has not been employed in the effort objectively to identify schizophrenia. Here is a partial list: size estimation tasks, resistence to cognitive interference, performance on the prisoner's dilemma game, performance on tests of short term memory, performance on tests of long term memory, accuracy of report of felt discomfort, span of apprehension, scores on tests of field dependence and independence, conditioning, accuracy of object sorting, blood chemistry, urinalysis, E.E.G., etc., etc.

If I had to make a general statement about the results of the 300 studies, I would say that most of the investigations show small differences that favor the normal sample. That is, normals on the average get "better" scores. A few studies report no differences, and at least one reports a difference where the normals do worse. The statistical operations are designed only to show that the small differences between averages of the samples are probably not related to chance factors. The statistical tests are not designed to locate the subjects precisely as belonging to the class "schizophrenia" or to the class "normal." With this standard procedure, the distributions of the scores on the experimental tasks can be nearly identical.

In nearly every study, so long as there is a statistically reliable difference between the means of the two samples (no matter how small), the investigator implies or asserts a claim for the validity of his model and then makes the logically inappropriate inference that schizophrenics function differently from normals. From inspection of the data, it is clear that most schizophrenics function no differently on these experimental tests from most normals. It would be the height of folly to try to identify a person as schizophrenic or normal by his score on any known experimental variable. This is an alternate way of saying that every study contains a high proportion of cases that are counter instances to the predictions of the particular hypothesis.

The fact that no objective procedure can reliably differentiate schizophrenics from nonschizophrenics leads to the bold conclusion: schizophrenia, like Santa Claus, is a myth. (2)

Of course, a tenacious (and patient) supporter of the disease paradigm might reject the conclusion with the statement that 80 years of experimental science has not yet produced the appropriate dependent variable.

I have just presented examples of the evidence that the models arising from the disease paradigm have been particularly unfit as guides for explaining norm-violating conduct. The evidence notwithstanding, polemical efforts, sometimes tortuous, to vindicate the mental illness model appear with predictable regularity. What accounts for this tenacity?

To be sure, all paradigms, ideologies, and myths tend to be conservative. Changes are more likely to occur as the result of a "death-rebirth" experience than from the gradual accrual of facts that question the utility or truth of the belief system.

The history of science is a record of observation and experiment that supports the displacement of one paradigm by a concurrently more useful one. A paradigm remains useful, after all, when it presents its users with puzzles to solve as well as presenting the categories within which such puzzles may be solved. Even when an attempted solution is unsuccessful, a scientist is inclined to retain the paradigm, with the hope that future investigations will yield the reluctant solution.

At least for the last century the disease paradigm has not been fruitful as a generator of categories to illuminate the conditions of unwanted acts. No convincing causality statements have been developed. In the biological sciences, where the **disease** model has certainly been eminently successful, investigators have demonstrated their success through specifying antecedent events as independent variables which as it were "cause" the resulting symptoms--the dependent variables in causal statements. Clearly, from the brief sampling of studies already reported, causal statements cannot be made for mental illness. In reviewing the course of the scientific enterprise devoted to understanding unwanted conduct, it becomes clear that the proponents of the disease model are aware of its failure, but they continue to hold to the paradigm on the belief that the appropriate causal variable is yet to be discovered and defined. Such proponents hold the belief that the cause of mental illness will ultimately be discovered as the result of continuing efforts of puzzle-solvers who stay within the circumscribed limits of the traditional paradigm.

III

I have tried to show that the science of deviant conduct may be characterized as a paradigm in crisis. The paradigm borrowed from traditional medicine is unworkable. I have only to remind you of the unreliability or inconstancy of diagnosis; in addition, I remind you of the failure to deal with the empirical research and penetrating criticisms of many scholars.

My task now is to identify some of the ideological premises that support--often unwittingly--the practitioners of the normal science of deviance. I accent again my caution that unwanted, unacceptable conduct is not to be construed as equivalent to psychopathology--the latter term focuses on the abstract individual as the object of scientific study. Unwanted conduct refers simultaneously to the actions of at least two interacting participants: the target person (the identified patient or defendant) and a second person who has declared a negative valuation on the actions or on the reported imaginings of the target person. I say at least two participants. In actual practice, where the second person, most often a relative, has an interest in the target person and--more important--has legitimate or coercive power to bring the latter to the attention of the local or state mental health establishment, the number of persons involved is much larger than two. For example, a county prosecutor may receive the petition from the interested relative or from a police officer. A probate or superior court judge participates in a civil hearing preliminary to the decision to commit or not to commit to a state hospital. One or more physicians may be called upon to examine the patient and to provide expert testimony. In addition, the personnel of a hospital or of a county or city jail where the target person is temporarily detained become part of the social system of interest to the behavior scientist.

In examining the social system that I have just identified, two positions are of special interest: the judge and the physician (usually a psychiatrist) who is called upon to advise the judge. The remarks that follow are pertinent to the beliefs held by the occupants of these positions. Such beliefs help to legitimize the enactment of their roles within the civil proceedings for involuntary hospitalization.

In order to focus my arguments, I shall ask you to imagine a courtroom drama with but three roles: the judge, the psychiatrist, and the target person. This drama is perforce fictional--the actual situation may include relatives, bailiffs, hospital attendants, hangers-on, and occasionally a lawyer representing the target person. But the central roles are the three that I have already identified: the person whose liberty is at risk (whom I shall call the "quasi-defendant"), the judge who has the legitimate power to deprive him of his liberty, and the physician whose expert knowledge or advice may be employed by the judge in arriving at a decision. In the presentation to follow, the actor taking the part of the "quasi-defendant" becomes a shadowy figure and the spotlight is beamed at the other two actors. As we proceed, the spotlight will narrow on the physician, the judge joining the "quasi-defendant" in the shadows. Parenthetically, the metaphor of "shadowy figure" is an apt one. Unlike criminal proceedings, where the person whose liberty is at risk is identified with a label "the defendant" or "the accused," the object of judgment in the civil proceedings has no status, at least no status that can be dignified with a standard label. No better example of the nonperson status of the "quasi-defendant" and its implications for prejudgment could be cited.

As I said in my introductory remarks, an ideology is a set of beliefs organized around a small number of values and are accompanied by strong feelings. I have identified a number of these ideological premises. I shall have time to discuss only four. These conjoined premises provide a mute context for the role enactments of judges and medical doctors in assigning the status "mentally ill" to the person whose conduct comes under their evaluative scrutiny.

The apparent legitimacy of civil proceedings. The judicial procedures for denying liberty are of two kinds. Professor Dershowitz (1970, 1973) has made the case most convincingly. Two strategies may be entertained for denying a person his liberty: performance-punishment and prediction-prevention. The first is predicated on the premise that an alleged offender has performed certain acts in violation of the law and should be deterred from further violations through punishment or other sanctions; the second is predicated on the premise that an individual is alleged to belong to a certain class of objects. The class possesses the attribute potentially violent or disorderly. Merely being a member of the class rather than performance of an unlawful act, then, becomes the defining criterion for the denial of liberty. It is the responsibility of the court to prevent the potential offender from engaging in unlawful conduct; therefore, he is prevented from harm-doing on the basis of his status: membership in a class with certain attributes.

It should be evident that the concept of involuntary hospitalization is similar to, if not identical with, the concept of preventive detention. Professor Dershowitz pointedly asks whether the United States Constitution permits detention of a person on the ground of a probabilistic prediction that at some time in the future he may engage in harm-doing. His answers to the constitutional question in part hinge on the arbitrary decision by prosecutors to label a proceeding as criminal or civil. If the proceeding is "criminal," then certain constitutional safeguards must be observed. If the "civil" label is invoked, the court is not constrained by due process and equal protection safeguards.

The arbitrary labelling of a proceeding as "criminal" or "civil" has the effect of an accusatory proceeding similar to continental justice systems. The "alleged offender" is treated as "guilty until proven innocent." The quasi-defendant must in effect establish his innocence of crimes not yet committed. Complaints about the arbitrariness of courts in labelling a hearing as "criminal" or "civil" is parallel to the frequently heard complaints about police officers arbitrarily dispensing "curbside justice" (Skolnick, 1966).

Given the ambiguous status of civil proceedings in a democracy that guarantees due process, it is no wonder that jurists seek the help of expert witnesses, namely, physicians. The presence of the expert lends an atmosphere of credibility to the court proceedings. After all, the arbitrary decision to label the proceeding "civil" follows from the premise that the defendant has not overtly violated the criminal code. Rather, he may in the future violate the criminal code. The court looks to possible actions in the future. Since prediction of behavior is a subtle art, especially if the behavior is mediated by mysterious mental processess, the quasi-defendant is presumably protected from arbitrary decisions based on ignorance when a physician provides expert testimony. The physician's diagnosis gives the appearance of scientific legitimacy to the "civil" proceedings.

The mental hospital as a legitimate institution. The second item in the ideological background of the psychiatrist is the knowledge of the availability of the mental hospital. I might add that the imagery of "mental hospital" is markedly different from the imagery of "hospital." It is important to note that the decision made by the judge, which generally follows upon the expert testimony of the psychiatrist, is implemented by the fact that there is a place to send the "mentally ill" person. Diagnosis, then, it not idle. To justify the denial of liberty, the claim is often made that involuntary hospitalization is for the patient's own good. Here is where the court invokes the "parens patriae" tradition. Parens patriae (originally meaning the king as father) has come to mean that the interests of both the person and the state are served by the denial of liberty, especially in the belief that help and rehabilitation will be forthcoming and will improve the conduct of the person. Even though the psychiatrist may have available pessimistic statistics on rate of improvement, the knowledge of the stigmatizing and degrading effects of hospitalization, and the knowledge that labelling is pernicious, he conducts his diagnostic work on the premise that a place exists for "mentally ill" patients to be segregated from the rest of society.

It is instructive to remind ourselves that the state hospital, a standard feature of the contemporary landscape, is the outgrowth of a noble experiment. Its predecessor, the asylum, was regarded by many observers as a reform. On the surface, "it was an obvious improvement not only over existing conditions, but over other possible alternatives ..." the historian, David J. Rothman (1971), writes. "But such a perspective," he goes on to say, "is bad logic and bad history. There was nothing inevitable about the asylum form, no self-evident reason why philantropists should have chosen it. Indeed, the subsequent history...should make historians somewhat suspicious of any simple link between progress and the asylum. Was an organization that would eventually turn into a snake pit a necesary step forward for mankind ?" Rothman's question is worth pondering in the light of recent and much belated judicial opinions on the patient's right to treatment when incarcerated. (The prior constitutional problem is the right to non-interference.)

The promise of the early asylum humanely to regulate the conduct of its inmates came to an end. In the middle of the 19th century, numerous waves of immigrants entered the U.S., industrial and commercial developments changed the nature of the economy, and cities and slums grew at a rate without precedent. These developments contributed to the increase in the distinctions between social classes. The time-honored mechanisms for maintaining order became unworkable. The concept of "dangerous classes" became a slogan for pamphleteers and led to repressive legislation. Under these conditions, segregation and imprisonment became the method of choice for controlling those subsets of the population that violated concurrent propriety norms. The reform movement of the Jacksonian era had created the asylums, but their utility as centers for custody made them indispensible. When, through accidents of history, medical superintendents were appointed to administer these custodial centers, "asylums" became "hospitals," but their basic function remained the same: the maintenance of public order through the incarceration of actual and potential norm-violators.

Certain types of people are more dangerous than other types of people. In 1958, Hollingshead and Redlich published their monumental study of social class and mental illness. Among other things, they demonstrated the docility of psychiatric diagnosis to indicators of social-class membership. Persons identified as lower-class were over-represented in the diagnostic class "schizophrenia;" those identified as middle-class were more often diagnosed as "neurotic." Recent reports give experimental support to the conclusion that a silent assumption about social class membership guides the practitioner in his use of diagnostic labels (Lee, 1968).

What is the ideological source of this bias? The readiness to attribute mental illness to lower class people (with its attendant high risk of being deprived of freedom) may be interpreted within the context of the Protestant Ethic (Rotenberg 1975). Concern with success and failure in meeting life goals, especially economic goals, had its origins in the writings of the influential 16th century theologian, John Calvin. The essence of his teachings is contained in a sentence that declares favorable destinies for some people and not for others" . . .eternal life," he wrote, "is foreordained for some, and eternal damnation for others." The doctrine of predestination was widely circulated in Protestant countries.

In the context of diagnosis leading to involuntary hospitalization, the identification of a person as one of the damned carries with it the belief that that person may be dangerous. We have not outgrown the beliefs of the 19th and 20th centuries, that poor people--especially recent immigrants and blacks--besides being "damned," were to be regarded as members of "dangerous classes" and in need of control (Sarbin, 1967b).

In order for a psychiatrist or other professional to declare a person dangerous in the absence of clearcut violent behavior, he must first construct an inference of dangerousness. This is accomplished through cognitively equating 16th century Calvinistic damnation with 20th century mental illness. Being mentally ill or psychotic, then, is a variant of being forever damned. And the mentally ill could be "dangerous" to the elect and to their social institutions.

Professor Hayden White (1973) has written a fascinating account of the origin of the myth of the "wild man within." The lingering myth is supported in part by the Wild Beast theory of insanity drawn from early English law (Platt and Diamond, 1966), and in part by the entrenched position of Freudian doctrine in psychiatry. To the diagnosticians it provides a silent ideological premise to support his beliefs that the "mentally ill" person has failed to become fully socialized or civilized, and may not be able to contain the "wild man within" and is, therefore, potentially dangerous. A further conclusion follows: dangerous persons should be removed from society.

Authority of the physician. In the light of contemporary knowledge about the difficulty of predicting conduct, a reasonable question may be asked: why are physicians (rather than other professionals) identified by statute or by custom as having the appropriate expertise to participate in the judicial proceedings? To be sure, the assimilation of so-called mental illness to somatic illness, discussed earlier, would be a partial answer to the question. However, the repeatedly demonstrated fact that psychiatric diagnoses lack reliability and credibility ought to have influenced the courts and legislatures that psychiatric testimony should be replaced by other procedures.

The physician, unlike other professionals, possesses a unique kind of authority, a combination of expert, moral, and charismatic authority which Paterson (1966) labeled "Aesculapian" (after the Greek god of healing). Siegler and Osmund (1973) elaborated this conception. The medical doctor's unique authority resides first in his claim to being taken seriously in virtue of his knowledge or expertise. The physician possesses expert power because he is assumed to have knowledge of the field of medicine. The second aspect of Aesculapian authority is moral authority. It is based on the belief shared by both doctor and patient that the doctor intends to do good, to alleviate pain, to prolong life, to defeat death. The third element is charismatic authority: possessing this kind of authority entitles the doctor to order and control others in virtue of a remnant of the priestly role; he is perceived to have a god-given grace. Charisma is a certain quality of an individual that sets him apart from others. He is treated as if endowed with exceptional powers. The quality is lost if the individual is recognized as not having special features or powers. Charismatic authority depends upon the doctor conducting himself in ways that are consistent with the attributions that others assign to him. He makes use of his Greco-latin vocabulary, his technical skills and his rituals, to confirm his charisma. Siegler and Osmund (1973) regard the Aesculapian authority as necessary in order to confer the sick role. They go on to say that without Aesculapian authority, "one cannot function as a doctor, and indeed cannot even be a successful medical imposter." The similarity of this description to that of shamans is striking (Levi-Strauss, 1963).

While Aesculapian authority may have utility in the doctor-patient relationship, the use of such authority in quasi-judicial proceedings is to be deplored. The decision to deprive a quasi-defendant of his liberty requires attention to cold, hard facts, not to the effects of magico-religious features of the healer.

To expose some of the ideological underpinnings of the practice of involuntary hospitalization is one thing. It is another thing to recognize that some people conduct their lives in ways that may be judged by other people as silly, shameless, unconventional, eccentric, irrational, perplexing, mystifying, and sometimes even dangerous. When other people become the intentional targets or innocent bystanders of such conduct, they may perceive themselves or their valued institutions as threatened. Under such conditions, the threatening person is given a moral label, "bad." The implication of such moral labelling is that the "bad" person be reformed or removed. It is clear that the identification and labelling of deviant conduct is a moral, not a scientific enterprise.

IV

We may have to reform our thought models. We may have to begin from a different paradigmatic base. For example, behavior that would mystify us and lead to psychiatric diagnosing can be seen from another perspective as unconventional, nonconforming, or even creative efforts of a person to make sense out of a complex, probablistic and changing world. It is not that such a paradigm has been absent from the premises of ordinary men and women. Else how can one account for the fact that many norm-violators are spared from being labelled mentally ill and from being subsequently launched on a career of stigmatized patienthood? The contingencies of the moment make the difference, among them the beliefs and values of relevant others, and the readiness to accept the proposition that more than one metaphysical perspective is credible (Sarbin and Juhasz, 1975). The readiness to withhold moral judgment of persons operating from other perspectives is an important contingency, especially during those periods of social and personal upheaval when individuals are struggling to find solutions to fundamental problems of existence.

Throughout this presentation, I have implied that individual liberty is a sacred value. At the same time, I want to declare that other values are also sacred, such as equality and security. The optimum balancing of these values cannot be achieved by laws that are forever valid. The problem of balancing values must be faced anew by every generation. But wherever one places individual liberty in his hierarchy of values, the present system of denying liberty to certain persons on the basis of unreliable and invalid psychiatric diagnosis cannot be tolerated. Liberty is too precious to be cavalierly manipulated by the silent workings of unrecognized ideological premises, especially the ceremonials of civil commitment, and the ritual behavior of doctors performing within their Aesculapian authority.

Footnote

1. Keynote address, fifth annual meeting of the American Association for the Abolition of Involuntary Hospitalization, April 19, 1975, New York, N.Y.
   The problem of defining madness has a venerable history. The relativity of the diagnosis of madness to situations has been a fertile topic for satirists. DePorte (1974) in an analysis of the work of 18th century writers shows how Jonathan Swift handled the relativity:

   > It is a concern sometimes expressed as a fear that madness will escape detection if it is common. In Prior's dialogue between Cromwell and the mad porter, for example, the porter insists that the difference between Bedlamites and "Public madmen" like Cromwell is only that the later have been lucky enough to gather others around them who share their dementia: "You all Herd together and it is a very hard thing to catch one of You but we are fewer in number, divided, unarmed, and different in our principles. If the least disturbance happens from any impetuosity of our Temper the Neighborhood has an Eye upon us, and away we are hurried the next dark Night to Morefields or Hodgdon . . . but you have commonly the majority on your Side, which as your Excellency very well knows, is no small advantage in England."

The whole question of judging sanity is raised with particular acuteness in Spectator No. 576, August 4, 1714, where Addison reports a curious anecdote about an inexorably rational country gentleman: "he would not make use of a Phrase that was not strictly true: He never told any of them (his friends) That he was his humble Servant, but that he was his Well-wisher: and would rather be thought a malcontent than drink the king's health when he was not a-dry." In short he was so rational his friends thought him mad. Addison comments by way of a quotation from Fontenelle: "The Ambitious and Covetous are Madmen to all Intents and Purposes, as much as those who are shut up in dark Rooms; but they have the good luck to have Numbers on their Side; whereas the Frenzy of one who is given up for a Lunatick, is a Frenzy hor d'oeuvre, that is . . . something which is singular in its Kind, and does not fall in with the Madness of a Multitude."

The problem thus set forth is a perplexing one, and one which since the Nuremberg trials has become especially painful in our own time. What if the norms of society upon which a man models his behavior are unworthy? What if they are base and ignoble? What, in other words, if the common forms sanction a kind of madness? A true skeptic would have to reply that it is not meaningful to speak of madness in any absolute sense since we can have no absolute knowledge of anything, that it is defined by a particular community or group.

PART VI
Belletristic
Psychology

The title of this section, "belletristic psychology," refers to that portion of Sarbin's research in which linguistic or historical analysis and conceptions taken from literature have been used effectively to illuminate problems in psychology. In several papers, he has creatively applied the technique of etymological analysis to the dissection of current psychological concepts.

The first chapter in this section, published here for the first time, uses a concept taken from a literary work to help explain "believed-in imaginings," which includes phenomena such as hypnosis and hallucinations. Derived from Cervantes' novel, the "Quixotic Principle" is a concept that refers to an individual's adopting an identity from the fictive world of literature and engaging in behavior based upon these beliefs. Multiple perspectives of the universe are possible, Sarbin maintains. That is, there is more than one way of construing the world, and it is possible for a person to shift back and forth among the different perspectives. As in Cervantes' novel, a reader can create a new identity as a result of reading; hence, imaginative literature can function as a constructed environment for a person under certain psychological conditions that are discussed in the paper.

The second chapter illustrates forcefully the usefulness of the historio-linguistic analysis applied to well-known but ambiguous and elusive psychological concept, anxiety. In this chapter Sarbin asserts that the concept of anxiety is a mythical mental state, and urges that a new metaphor needs to be substituted for the old concept. According to the investigation reported in the chapter, the term did not originally indicate a mental state. Though initially used only in a metaphorical sense, the concept of anxiety was later transformed into a literal truth (i.e., myth).

A common theme cuts across the research reported in this section (and in several other papers). It is argued that many words were initially used in a hypothetical or metaphorical sense to denote certain events, but were transformed into reified entities over the course of time. The hypotheticalness, tentativeness or "as if" quality that existed originally seems later to fade away, and the terms take on a concrete reality of their own. Many psychological constructs appear to have been subjected to this transformation from metaphor-to-myth (or from "as if" to real), with an accretion of confusion having been collected along the way. Sarbin has taken pains, however, to attempt to look again (which, incidentally, is the meaning of the word research) at the original meaning and usage associated with terms that have come to be accepted uncritically by contemporary psychologists. Results of his research may stimulate us more effectively to challenge the old myths of the past in our science, and may lead to a more effective and humane psychology of the future.

11

THE QUIXOTIC PRINCIPLE:
A BELLETRISTIC APPROACH TO
THE PSYCHOLOGICAL STUDY OF
IMAGININGS AND BELIEVINGS[1]

I

Although it has become customary to "explain" literary productions with the technical vocabulary of psychology, especially psychoanalysis, I am turning the interpretative process around. I take a concept from belles lettres as a point of departure for illuminating the psychological concepts "imagining" and "believing."

Hypnosis and hallucination, two well-established problem areas, initially stimulated my interest in the psychology of imagining and believing. At first, I addressed a set of questions the answers to which would identify the sometimes difficult-to-explain behaviors associated with hypnosis. After nearly 40 years of study, I concluded in some recent papers (see, for example, Sarbin and Coe, 1972) that "believed-in imaginings" is the most felicitous concept to describe the content of the role of the hypnotized person. The phrase "believed-in imaginings" denotes that the actor responds to his imaginings as if they had the same warrant of credibility as perceptions constructed from the shared world of occurrences. When we take into account the effects of settings, instructions, experimenter bias, subject bias, etc., the remainder of the events traditionally labeled hypnosis is the subject's report and actions that convincingly communicate to his audience that he is responding to his imaginings as though they were credible.

This description is not unique to the domain of hypnosis. It applies with equal force to those events traditionally labeled "hallucination." The concept "believed-in imaginings" provides a way of dissolving some of the mystification of hallucination. If we begin from the theoretical assumption that imaginings are active constructions rather than passive happenings, then "believed-in imaginings" would be an appropriate term to denote those events which have been labeled "hallucination"--at least by Western medicine for the past century and a half (Sarbin and Juhasz, 1975).

Because of the penumbra of ambiguity surrounding the concepts of imagining and believing, it is necessary briefly to define the terms. Currently the most productive view is that imaginings are constructed, built up, created, in the same way as so-called impressions or perceptions (Paivio, 1971). In an earlier paper, Sarbin and Juhasz (1967) presented data and argument to support the notion that imaginings develop out of imitatings, that is, the copying or mimicking of behavior with models present. Imitatings may also be produced when models are withdrawn or absent: these imitatings are best identified as role-taking. Such role-taking, or, to use Piaget's language, deferred imitation, may be muted or attenuated. Imagining, then, is the short-hand label for identifying muted or attenuated role-taking.

Believing is a more complex and more controversial term. It may be the case, as Needham (1971) has argued, that the term has no empirical reference, that it is employed only as a speech act (Searle, 1969). To illustrate the complexities in employing the term "belief" Needham quotes, among others, Quintillian, who declared "I believe that which is impossible." Because it would take us too far afield to discuss Needham's argument, I shall propose the following working definition: to believe in one's imaginings is to conduct oneself as if the imaginings had the credibility that is given to constructions that have their antecedents in publicly observed ecological events. An alternative way of defining believing is that the actor assigns a high truth value to a particular proposition. It is not material whether the proposition is derived via induction, imagining, or authority. That is to say, "believed-in imaginings" may be regarded as having the same truth value as inductions derived from contact with material things, or they may be treated the same as declarations from a respected authority.

When applied to phenomena outside the technical vocabulary of psychology, the employment of the concept "believed-in imaginings" confers a form of validity on my explanation of hypnosis and hallucination. Authors, for example, have spoken of the "reality" of their fictional characters, i.e., although the characters were fictive, constructed, made-up, the authors assigned credibility to them sometimes to the same degree that they assigned credibility to non-imagined persons. Robert Louis Stevenson, Flaubert, Byron, Symonds, and Dickens are among the many writers who have been outspoken on this point. The criteria of credibility, of course, varied from one writer to another.

Pirandello provides an excellent point of departure. In a preface to his successful play, Six Characters in Search of an Author, he wrote as if his fictively constructed characters met the same criteria of credibility that he would have employed in testing empirical inductions. He says:

> I can only say that, without having made any effort to seek them out, I found before me, alive--you could touch them and even hear them breathe--the six characters now seen on the stage. And they stayed

there in my presence, each with his secret torment and all bound together by the one common origin and mutual entanglement of their affairs, while I had them enter the world of art, constructing from their persons, their passions, and their adventures, a novel, a drama, or at least a story.

Born alive, they wished to live.

He went on to say that at first he was not able to give an acceptable meaning to these fictive characters, and he tried to "put them away" without success. Then he continued:

But one doesn't give life to a character for nothing. Creatures of my spirit, these six were already living a life which was their own and not mine any more, a life which it was not in my power any more to deny them.

Thus it is that while I persisted in desiring to drive them out of my spirit, they, as if completely detached from every narrative support, characters from a novel miraculously emerging from the pages of the book that contained them, went on living on their own, choosing certain moments of the day to reappear before me in the solitude of my study and coming--now one, now the other, now two together--to tempt me, to propose that I present or describe this scene or that, to explain the effects that could be secured with them, the new interest which a certain unusual situation could provide, and so forth (1952, pp. 364-365).

Pirandello communicates to us that the imaginary characters had a life of their own. His description is not different from the imaginary characters in a so-called madman's pseudocommunity (Cameron, 1943, 1951). The reader is faced with a problem--a not uncommon one. Does Pirandello want us to read this paragraph as metaphor? He does not label the passage as metaphoric by saying "it seems," or "it was as if," etc. If the reader grants Pirandello the freedom to shift from one fictive perspective to another, the way we grant the young child the freedom to shift from his world of imaginary companions to the world of parents, dolls, and bicycles and back again to the world of imaginary companions, then it is not material whether we call the passage metaphoric. Perhaps Pirandello began with a metaphor but became so involved in his imaginings that the characters became credible.

Pirandello's comments point to the credibility of imaginings from the writer's point of view. Let us turn our attention now to the reader. The reading of literary works may produce and guide the construction of the reader's imaginings. Such imaginings may have such clarity, vividness, and life that they influence the covert conduct of the reader, for example, the arousal of anger upon reading of injustice or cruelty. More than influencing covert conduct, imaginings created through reading may have such credibility that they influence directly the overt conduct of the reader. The reader "believes" in the existence of the fictive characters and plot and engages in public conduct based on his beliefs. The best known example of action stimulated and guided by the absorptive reading of imaginative literature is, of course, Don Quixote.

II

Even a casual or second-hand acquaintance with Don Quixote makes clear that the reading of literary works can serve as an antecedent condition for the enactment of roles based on involvement in one's imaginings. Cervantes provides the paradigm case. He tells of a lonely 16th century Spanish gentleman, one Alonso Quesada, who becomes fascinated with the content of chivalry as the result of intensive and almost exclusive reading of the adventures of knights-errant and of the institutions of chivalry. Like many readers of knight-errantry, he constructs imaginings centered on the deeds of famous knights. In this respect, his conduct is like that of most readers. However, Cervantes' hero does more than turn his attention to such imaginings--he goes one step beyond and builds an identity for himself out of his created fictive world. He takes an appropriately knightly name, Don Quixote, and sets out to right wrongs, to rescue damsels in distress, to slay dragons, to foil wicked enchanters, and to engage in all the obligatory conduct of the discredited and ancient role of knight-errant.

It is instructive to note that the novel as an art form is usually dated from Cervantes. The novel perhaps better than other literary forms exemplifies the art of fiction. (Pertinent here is the etymology of fiction. Derived from fingere meaning "to make" or "to make up," both meanings are species of the same genus.) The novelist strings words together to convey his imaginings about ordinary people and events. To be successful, he must induce his reader to construct from the literary medium a set of imaginings that are credible--at least at the time of reading.

Professor Harry Levin (1970) has assembled scores of instances where novelists have employed the device of identity building from the reading of fiction. He has labeled the shaping of such an identity through reading the "Quixotic principle." In the typical case, a character builds a role for himself or herself as the result of involved reading. At first the role-taking is muted, then overt. Such role-taking directs the hero or heroine in his or her search for persons enacting reciprocal roles in appropriate settings. The search is undertaken in order to make good the claims of a contrived identity that has not yet been legitimated by members of the social community.

It is this shaping of an identity through reading that I would like to discuss in more detail as a basis for later outlining an extension of the theory of imagining. My ultimate objective is to construct a set of categories that can illuminate such diverse events as hypnosis, hallucination, imaginary companions, daydreams, in fact all conduct that is usually identified as counter-factual. Professor Levin applies the Quixotic principle exclusively to literary characters; after all, Don Quixote was a fictional creation whose adventures were stimulated by the reading of medieval romances. The principle is applicable to nonfictional characters and settings as well. I shall sketch a few instances where significant conduct reorganization could be traced to the reading of specific literary works. To focus on the Quixotic principle is not to deny that other literary forms are instrumental in identity shaping. To be sure, the reading of religious tracts, sermons, morality tales, fables, and guides to personal growth may influence conduct reorganization. However, the mediator between the reading and the action is not necessarily an imagined role. In these instances, the mediator is more likely to be in the form of a rule, precept, or moral law, rather than a constructed social role.

To illustrate my extension of the Quixotic principle, I note briefly the effects of Sir Walter Scott's novels on the cult of chivalry in the South, the effects of Goethe's Sorrows of Young Werther on the suicide rate in mid-nineteenth century Europe, and the effects of reading Hemingway upon the life and death style of Jack N., a former client. These illustrations by no means exhaust the historical, literary and clinical case material that gives body to my extension of the Quixotic principle.

The Quixotic principle may help to explain the phenomenon of nationalism in the Old South. Nationalism in the South is said to have rested on a tripod: cotton, slavery, and Southern romanticism. The latter included "the cult of chivalry as its most persistent manifestation and the idea of nationalism as its most ambitious impulse" (Osterweis, 1949, p. 216). The popularity of Scott's novels and poems in the United States, and especially in the South, is readily documented.

> The tale which had the greatest influence in stimulating the cult of chivalry was Ivanhoe... Wilfred of Ivanhoe, the beautiful Rowena, Richard the Lion-Hearted, the proud Normans, the churlish Saxons, Isaac of York and the appealing Rebecca, all became familiar figures to the antebellum Southerner. The tournament at Ashby-de-la-Zouche was to have its faithful reenactments in the colorful jousts staged by the Maryland, Virginia, Carolina and Louisiana gentry (Osterweis, 1949, p. 45).

A number of observers have pointed out that the planters of the South referred to themselves as "The Chivalry." It communicated the ambience of knighthood--gallantry, extravagant courtesy, and the importance of maintaining and defending one's "honor." Needless to say, the cult of chivalry would not have developed as it did in the absence of the particular set of social, economic and political conditions of the antebellum South. Scott's works were popular in the northern states, but the plantation system and the institution of slavery--the other legs of the tripod--were absent. Scott's novels undoubtedly provided guides to imaginal behavior of northern readers, but tales of chivalry were ill-designed to serve the aesthetic needs of a developing technological and industrial society.

The cult of chivalry brought entertainment into the plantations. The monotony of agrarian social life was diminished by the reading of romantic literature, by the exaggerated adoration of womanhood, by the cult of the military, by the emphasis on manners, and by flamboyant oratory. It provided a way of life that later proved to be the rallying point for Southern nationalism. The idea of a separate and independent Southern nation was one of the effects of the adoption of the chivalric way of life of the antebellum South. When the culture of the South was threatened by the abolition of slavery and the destruction of the plantations system, the themes of Sir Walter Scott's novels gave metaphysical support to the idea of a nation of "Southrons" (to use one of Scott's coined words.)

This brief statement is intended to illustrate the extension of the Quixotic principle into organized social roles. Scott portrayed fictional roles for his readers. To be sure, the roles were identified with such characters as the courageous Sir Wilfred and the gracious Lady Rowena. These fictions, however, were not mere literary adornments, they became guides to action, they were "believed-in." It is important to note that the men and women who enacted these roles were no mere dissemblers of Norman society. Conditions of antebellum plantation life were not the same as Norman England. But the novelist's constructed fictive roles provided a performance style, a prototype identity, a pattern of how to conduct oneself within the constraints of the concurrent political, economic, and technological conditions. Unlike Don Quixote whose knightly identity was not endorsed by the role enactments of significant others, the chivalric roles of the Southern planters were enacted against a backcloth of a social system that legitimated the chivalric role enactments. Those who held power believed in and supported the system that validated a person's identity as a Southern gentleman or lady. The established social system and the literature-inspired fictive community were not incongruent. Therefore, witnesses to the dramatic role performances of antebellum Southerners--unlike Don Quixote's very anxious relatives--did not raise questions of madness or hallucination.

In 1774 Goethe published The Sorrows of Young Werther--much of which was autobiographical--a story of unrequited love and overabundant sentimentality. It came at a time when death and dying, especially dying by one's own hand, had a romantic quality. There was something heroic, noble, and grand about dying, especially if one could write his own death scenario. Goethe's portrayal of young Werther was adopted as a guiding fiction by young men of fashion. Since unrequited love was not an uncommon event, the solution chosen by Werther became the solution for scores of romantics. Suicide rates appeared to have increased during the years following the publication of the novel. A biographer wrote: "There was a Werther epidemic: a Werther fever, a Werther fashion. . . Werther caricatures and Werther suicides" (Friedenthal, 1963, p. 128). The typical suicide was carried out in full Werther costume, blue tailcoat, yellow waistcoat and boots, and the pistol was aimed just above the eye.

The reading of the novel influenced the creation of imaginings in some of the readers. The readers became so deeply involved in their imaginings that they engaged in overt role performances. An analysis of the poet and critic, A. Alvarez, is consistent with my extension of the Quixote principle. He says:

> For the reading public, Werther was no longer a character in a novel, he was a model for living, an individual who set a whole style of feeling and despair. The rationalists of the previous generations had vindicated the act of suicide, they had helped change the laws and moderate the primitive churchly taboos, but it was Werther who made the act seem positively desirable to the young Romantics all over Europe (Alvarez, 1971, p. 209).

Hemingway's short story, The Short and Happy Life of Francis Macomber, served as the mediator for the conduct of a client with whom I worked some time ago. The setting of the short story is an African safari, the principle characters are Francis Macomber, his wife, and the white hunter. Macomber is represented as a weak, ineffectual, self-hating person. The story opens on a scene when Macomber has just demonstrated cowardice during the hunt. That night, his wife shares the hunter's tent rather than Macomber's.

The next day, some heated words are exchanged and Macomber reflects considerable strain, but the hunt continues. As if adopting a role of a person who had nothing to lose, Macomber acts fearlessly, almost without regard for his lifelong concern with safety. In this role, he is exultant. His happy life of a few minutes is cut short by a bullet from his wife's rifle--presumably she was aiming at a charging buffalo.

This tale apparently served the quixotic function for my client, Jack N. He was a graduate student in literature and had just begun a thorough study of Hemingway. He read everything that Hemingway had published, as well as most criticism. Jack appeared as an ineffectual, ungainly person, he had been shabbily treated by the power figures in his extended family and had a self identity as a failure. I noticed some change in his overt conduct during his Hemingway period. He appeared more dominant, wore clothes that might have come out of a lumberjack store; he announced that he would like to emulate Hemingway, become a war correspondent, a writer of short stories, and of adventure novels. The masculine image of Hemingway and the lifelong passive self image were obviously incongruent.

At one point in our discussion he said that Francis Macomber's change of role was a self-initiated decision following upon the insult to his manhood. It was during his ruminations about Hemingway as hero that he heard of the opportunity to become a lieutenant in the Marine Corps. After a short training period, he was commissioned and sent to Korea where he was assigned duties as a platoon leader. This job required making night patrols, capturing enemy soldiers, destroying enemy outposts, etc. He wrote me detailed letters of his adventures. The style was compact and very much like Hemingway. He was exultant and happy. But like his model, his happy life was a short one. After a month of highly rewarding action, he was killed while on night patrol.

Alfred Adler's conception of the guiding fiction is applicable equally to the adventures of Don Quixote, the exaggerated behavior of Southern ladies and gentlemen, the suicide of 18th century romantics, and the life and death style of Jack N. Influenced by Vaihinger's conception of "as if," a conception without which it is difficult to talk of imagination, metaphor, role taking, fiction and in fact any human activity, Adler emphasized the importance of the fictions that human beings construct to guide their lives. While he did not employ the vocabulary of role theory, it is clear that he regarded the imaginal life as a way of solving problems through creating a new identity.

It is instructive briefly to contrast Freud's views with Adler's later work. Freud saw fantasy as regressive, as the resultant of the bound inter-connections of psychic forces; Adler saw imaginings (and dreams) as progressive, as preparation for action. For Freud, imaginings were safety valves, ways of establishing equilibrium under the strain of loss or disappointment; for Adler, imaginings were rehearsals for action and guides to conduct.

II

The reference cases just described were selected from a larger collection drawn primarily from biographical and autobiographical sources. At this point I will assert without further documentation that the Quixotic principle has wide application. Some people do create new identities as a result of reading imaginative literature. For my present purposes it is immaterial whether the newly constructed identity--the composite of answers to the continuing question "Who am I?"--is consensually legitimated. Rather, I am interested in exploring how reading the printed page can have such profound personal and social effects.

Two complementary strategies of exploration are necessary: (a) the phenomenology of book reading, and (b) the discovery of empirical correlates. The following sketchy remarks are best interpreted as a prologue to the study of reading as an antecedent to identity formation.

Perhaps the most striking outcome of doing a phenomenological analysis of book-reading is the recognition that the book as a ponderable object disappears from the reader's cognitive matrix. Not only does the manufactured object of paper and print and binding vanish, but the words and sentences which are silently read are not "seen." In the same way that the reader is non-responsive to whether the typeface is light or bold, 8 point or 10 point, roman or bodoni, the reader becomes non-responsive to the book as a commonplace object. The act of involved reading, for you and for me no less than for Don Quixote, results in an involvement in the constructed effects of reading--the creation of imaginary people, fictive events, and fanciful landscapes. In the act of reading, a transfiguration of the reader occurs. The physical objects in the immediate surroundings disappear, including, as I said before, the book being read. These physical objects are replaced by imaginings, by the constructing and creating of a fictive theater, a pseudo-community, a created world. Sometimes the reader himself is an actor in the created world of occurrences, other times an observer. Using some personal metaphors, one phenomenological analyst, Georges Poulet (1969), put it this way:

> Reading, then, is the act in which the subjective principle which I call I, is modified in such a way that I no longer have the right, strictly speaking, to consider it as my I. I am on loan to another, and this other thinks, feels, suffers, and acts within me. The phenomenon appears in its most obvious . . . form in the sort of spell brought about by certain cheap kinds of reading, such as thrillers, of which I say "It gripped me." Now it is important to note that this possession of myself by another takes place not only on the level of objective thought, that is, with regard to images, sensations, and ideas which reading affords me, but also on the level of my very subjectivity. When I am absorbed in reading, a second self takes over, a self which thinks and feels for me. (p. 57)

This brief sample suggests a number of hypotheses that might be tested through employing a phenomenological perspective. What additional hypotheses should we entertain to account for the following observation written by a Cervantes scholar? He is writing of Don Quixote and Sancho Panza.

> I can hear their voices, see their gestures and faces. It is little enough to remark that this book is alive, evocative and suggestive . . . I have known Don Quixote and Sancho forever, and I will go on knowing them until I die . . . None of the people who have been my companions . . . have ever comforted me with words so full of kindness and humanity as these two have been (Cassou, 1948, p. 26).

Suffice it to say here that such self reports of the effects of book reading will direct us to hypotheses about the conditions under which readers move from the perspective of the commonplace to the perspective of constructed imaginings.

To complement the phenomenological approach, I looked for empirical observations in which book reading is a variable. Published studies are few indeed. Ronald Shor (1970) found that persons who had a history of book reading were more likely to be apt hypnotic subjects. Josephine Hilgard (1974) also reported a correlation between subjects' reports of involvement in imaginative reading and performance of the hypnotic role. Given the theory expounded in this essay, such findings are not unexpected. Like reading novels, enacting the hypnotic role involves, among other things, the ability to shift perspective from the commonplace world to a constructed world of the counter-factual.

It is unnecessary for me to assert that the Quixotic principle is not a universal phenomenon. In the first place, some cultures have no literature. Some persons in literate cultures do not read. As I said before I have been able to find very little direct evidence to suggest the correlates of the employment of the Quixotic principle. However, the belief that books can have profound effects on the overt conduct of readers appears to be part of the folk wisdom of the West. Marlowe's Faust, like Don Quixote, begins his adventures from a book-lined study. In the end, contrite over his misdeeds, he wishes he had never "read book." Book burnings and censorship attest to the strongly-held belief that readers may become contaminated. Of course the injunction against reading certain books may not be directed against the Quixotic principle as such, but concern with the principle might be contained in the ideological premises of the censors and book burners. One critic has suggested that there may even be a relation between certain kinds of effectiveness in literature and totalitarianism in politics. Yeats, in a time of actual civil violence, recognized this possibility when he wrote "We had fed the heart on fantasies/The heart's grown brutal from the fare" (p. 424). The period of living by imaginings, of course, is not limited to the mass reading of propagandistic literature. From the news reports of a recent mass murderer who was diagnosed as "paranoid schizophrenic" one might more accurately say that he was guilty of acting on his imaginings as if they had been legitimated and given credibility by an appropriate transcendental authority. (2)

When Don Quixote rode his horse upon the Manchegan plain in search of adventure, he brought to life a role which had reposed between the covers of books for four hundred years. This action set in motion two contrasting worlds: the commonplace world of early 17th century Spain and the created world of the book. Each world provided a perspective for the interpretation of the world of occurrences: Was a certain building to be instantiated as a 17th century inn or a medieval castle; was a certain young woman to be perceived as a village prostitute or a noble maid; was a certain metal object to be regarded as a barber's basin or as an enchanted helmet; were certain features of the landscape to be classified as awesome giants or as ordinary windmills? Each perspective has its own validity, and each is situated within the literary context. Yet the author has created the conditions for the reader and the critic to talk about the effects of fluctuating perspectives without constantly announcing that Don Quixote was fictional. Of course, on reflection we declare that Don Quixote is a made-up character, yet we ordinarily talk about him with the same vocabulary that we use to talk about historical persons. In reading the novel, we transcend the implicit frame placed around it. We give a warrant of credibility to the existence of Don Quixote. The warrant must come from the fact of involvement in the imaginings created in the act of reading Cervantes' prose. In short, when we speak of Don Quixote as if he were a historical figure, we have unwittingly slipped into the use of the Quixotic principle.

An anecdote appears in a biography of John Addington Symonds that is pertinent to the problem of establishing what events or conditions are warrants for belief. He was regarded as a highly imaginative child. He "saw," for example, in a neighboring basement a magician mixing ingredients in a large vessel. The magician became, he said, "a positive reality of his imagination." When he reported his experience to his family, he was scolded for telling lies. In recalling the event as an adult, he wrote, ". . . the magician (is no) less real to my memory than most people who surrounded me at that time" (Prescott, 1959, p. 202).

Expressions of skepticism and rejection are frequently heard when a person publicly reports his imaginings as if they were perceptions. If one is talking of an imagining, goes the usual argument, one cannot be talking about reality. And to be "in contact with reality" (to employ a phrase dear to psychiatrists) is the ultimate criterion of credibility. Such an argument can be maintained only if one takes a naive view of the abstract term "reality." Elsewhere (Sarbin, 1967c; 1972b) I have presented arguments based on the work of Morris R. Cohen (1931) and J. L. Austin (1962) that the word "reality" is an excluder word. It has no genuine negative, its meaning can only be derived from a knowledge of what it is that is meant to be excluded. That the word "real" carries too much semantic freight is apparent in the following questions: "Is that real grass or is it real astroturf?" a spectator asks at a football game. "Is that a real apple, or a real wax apple, a real plastic apple?" a visitor to an art gallery asks.

The problem in part is a linguistic one: the term reality is required to do jobs for which it was not intended. "Real" is the adjectival form of the Latin res (= things, objects). "Real" and "reality" were words constructed to talk about the universe of things and of thing character. Now the word is used to stand for all kinds of universes. In connection with discussions of reality, I am reminded of a story told by Stephen Nachmanovich Miller. It is the story of a disgruntled man who complained to Picasso that he disliked modern art because it was not a faithful representation of reality. Picasso asked him: "What does faithfully represent reality?" The man thought for a moment and then produced from his wallet a 2 x 2 photograph of his wife. "There," he exclaimed, "is a real picture. That's what my wife looks like." Picasso examined the photograph and said, "She's awfully small." To achieve understanding of believed-in imaginings it is imperative to abandon the protean word "reality." Instead, let us employ a term that is not yet loaded with excess baggage: viz, perspectives.

Don Quixote illustrates well the theme of multiple perspectives. The quixotic principle exemplifies William James' point that the mere fact of imagining something is its warrant of credibility unless countered by a contradictory belief. Believed-in imaginings, such as those of Don Quixote and the cases cited, can be understood in the context of the notion of multiple perspectives. A person can locate objects, people, and events in constructed universes other than the commonplace perspective of the material universe.

One cannot adequately account for human conduct without recognizing that persons behave from a variety of fictive perspectives; in short, the actions of human beings may follow from the actor's location of self in more than one perspective. Singer (1966), among others, has experimentally demonstrated that most people are continually shifting back and forth between different perspectives. A person who is driving a car may engage in a rich fantasy life. Thurber's portrayal of Walter Mitty nicely illustrates simultaneous performance in both the workaday world and in the world of fantasy.

A more complex situation arises when one views the "same scene" in several ways at once. In describing a sunrise, William Blake, the eighteenth-century poet and mystic, considered two perspectives and vividly expresses which perspective he prefers. "'What,' it will be questioned, 'when the sun rises, do you not see a round disk of fire somewhat like a guinea?' 'O, no, no, I see an innumerable company of the Heavenly host crying "Holy, Holy, Holy, is the Lord God Almighty."' I question not my corporeal or vegetative eye any more than I would question a window concerning a sight. I look through it and not with it" (1971, p. 617).

Similarly, an astronomer may view the same sunrise from the perspective of modern astronomy. At the same time, he can "see" Rosy Fingered Dawn preceding the Chariot of the Sun God. None of these perspectives is mutually exclusive, nor is any one more credible than any other; they refer to two different kinds of constructions. To be sure, some of the astronomer's observations may suffer from too much involvement in the poetic or mythic perspective. A poet, on the other hand, might be unnecessarily frustrated by too great an involvement in the perspective of astronomical science. It is not that the mythic perspective is less useful than the astronomical; both are useful. However, preoccupation with one ecology may impede certain but by no means all role performances. Furthermore, certain perspectives may be prescribed by certain societies at certain times. Unmodulated talk about participating in a fantasy world, for example, may in some circles be grounds for ostracism or degradation.

I am operating from the premise of constructivism that all perspectives are constructed or "made-up." (3) The perspective of the imaginer may lead to fictive events and the imaginer may try to communicate these fictive events to others. The problem of translating from one perspective to another emerges. The imaginer must go from a cognitive mode that is in part non-linguistic and non-social to the linguistic and social mode.

The translation from one perspective to another is facilitated by the use of figures of speech and action, such as similes and metaphors. To make sense of the inputs from sensory activities, the perceiver will use whatever linguistic tools are available. Consider a California sunrise in November. The sensory inputs are uncountable--hues, saturations, luminosities, forms, textures, and so on. To translate an infinitude of sensory experience into communicative acts, the actor may employ a variety of techniques, such as oil paints on canvas, Italian melodies, choreography, blank verse, or speech. When employing these communicative acts, the actor has considerable freedom in labeling them. If, for example, speech is employed, the actor may say "the sunrise is like a fireball," and we know that only similarity is intended. If he says "it is as if the sunrise is a flaming sphere," we can safely assume that he is taking another perspective and wants us to know that he is still "in touch" with the listener's perspective. The use of "as if" is intended to guarantee that the speaker and listener share the same perspective. If he says "it is a spouting blast furnace," the listener must construct from the context whether the speaker intends similarity or identity. If the listener concludes that the speaker intends identity, at that moment he concludes also that the speaker is operating from a noncommonplace, nonphysicalistic perspective.

Translation from imagining to speech involves shifting from one fictive perspective to another. The perspective of hues and luminosities is no more fictive than Blake's mystical perspective. At this point, it is instructive to remind ourselves of the "stimulus error" concept advocated by Titchener (1901). The stimulus error was defined as the "mistake" of seeing an ecological object qua object rather than as a set of discrete sensations. One who had been trained in the introspective methods of Wundt and Titchener would not "see" and report a table (if he did, he would be guilty of the "stimulus error"); rather he would utter a report something like "a brownish plane tilted about 15 degrees from the horizon, alternating striata of darker and lighter brown, increasingly luminous from top to bottom, surrounded by a homogeneous field of grey. . . ."

The problem of translating is nowhere better illustrated than in the perceptual constancies. Take the stock illustration of comparing a piece of white chalk and a chunk of anthracite coal. Illumination can be arranged in such a way that the coal reflects more light than the chalk. From the perspective of a physicist measuring reflected light energy, the coal is brighter. This leads to the inference that the coal is whiter, white being defined as greater brightness. From the perspective of the ordinary human observer, the chalk continues to be perceived as white and the coal as black. It would be a mistake to conclude from the perceptual constancy experiments that the perspective of the physicist is more or less fictive than the perspective of the ordinary perceiver. Neither is declared to be "out of touch with reality," although they approach the cognitive task from mutually contradictory perspectives. In the case of the perceptual constancies, departure from the physicalistic perspective is the ordinary approach and is taken as the measure of normalcy. Alternatively, not to commit the stimulus error would be seen by many observers as a sign of deviance. Take the hypothetical case: a psychiatrist, in conducting an examination, points to an orange on the table and says, "What is this?" The putative patient trained in the methods of Titchener replies: "alternating bands of brown and grey, bluish hues interposed in a luminescent sheen on which is superimposed an elliptical form, predominant hue varying from 580 to 660 millimicrons, with punctiform grey masses in a regular grid tightly packed around the edges of the irregular ellipse, et cetera, et cetera." Would the failure to commit the stimulus error lead to a diagnosis of "schizophrenia?" (Sarbin and Juhasz, 1975).

In the preceding paragraphs, I have tried to show how a constructivist posture makes it possible to entertain more than one fictive perspective, i.e., there is more than one way of construing the world. Such a posture facilitates our understanding of how literature can function as an environment, an environment in which we must locate ourselves in satisfying ways. The use of pejorative terms like hallucination is out of place in describing the products of cognitive work derived from perspectives different from our own. Let us return now to a few unanswered queries about the Quixotic principle.

IV

What are the conditions that influence the imaginer to break out of his covertly established frame and participate in a pseudocommunity? There is hardly a reader who cannot report the imaginal formation of a new identity in the manner of Walter Mitty. But the reader ordinarily maintains a partition between his enactment of social roles in community life and his silent and fanciful theatrical performances.

Two kinds of strategies may be employed to identify the conditions that influence a person to construct a new identity and then to enact roles appropriate to that identity. The first strategy is situational: a person suffers cognitive strain as a result of unsatisfying answers to the social identity question: who am I? The strain may be resolved, as Adler suggests, with the creation of a guiding fiction. As part of a community of fictive others, a person's newly formed fictive identity may be more satisfying; at least the fictive identity may make more sense, given one's metaphysical assumptions. Elsewhere I have shown the usefulness of the concept: degree of organismic involvement (Sarbin, 1956). Some roles are enacted with minimal involvement or engrossment, others are enacted with great intensity. The concept applies to imaginal roles as well as to publicly-enacted roles. The organismic involvement in any fictive identity may be so great that the covert fantasies of a Walter Mitty spill over into the overt acts of a Don Quixote.

The legitimation of one's contrived identity poses some interesting problems. The southern planters organized a social system that gave substance to the enactment of prototype roles drawn from Scott's novels. A social organization—the U.S. Marines—provided the community for role enactments appropriate to Jack N.'s new identity. Don Quixote, like many other people called mad or hallucinating, ratified his knightly identity through the fictive formation of reciprocal others, some of whom were enchanters and magicians. The actions of the latter were invoked by Quixote to make sense of the different interpretations of events arising from the commonplace perspective of Sancho Panza and the imagined perspective of chivalry.

In a word, one may find solutions to life's problems by adopting a fictive perspective other than the perspectives of everyday life. Making sense of inconsistencies, anomalies, and unexpected events in the alternative perspective is no different in principle from making sense of incongruities in the commonplace world of occurrences. For example, Don Quixote made sense of incongruities by invoking the concept "enchantment." Some theorists of hypnotism, to explain counterexpectational behavior, invoke the concept "trance."

The second strategy is biographical: some individuals may have had experiences that influenced the acquisition of skill in shifting from one perspective to another. What developmental condition could provide practice in shifting perspectives, practice in moving from one metaphysical posture to another? A quotation from R. L. Stevenson suggests one answer to the question. "Fiction," he said, "is to the grown man what play is to the child."

Play is the developmental concept most likely to provide clues to an understanding of the operation of the Quixotic principle. What I mean by "play" is the adoption of a perspective where activity is carried out as an end in itself, rather than as a means to some end as in instrumental behavior.

This is not the place to present a thoroughly articulated theory of play (Bateson, 1972; Miller, 1973). Let me call your attention only to the probable influence of play on the development of skill in shifting from one perspective to another. The child's first "playings," the open-ended, purposeless manipulation of toys, spoons, rattles, etc., are motoric. He plays with objects. With increasing maturity, he plays with other human beings, and then he acquires skill in muting that play. As I said earlier, he can acquire skill to imitate a model, even though the model is absent. The muting of this skill might be called symbolic play, or dramatic play. Unlike motoric play, it is not constrained by the properties of objects.

To say of any symbolic or motoric activity, "this is play," then, means that the player is engaging in performances that are congruent with a perspective that values activity for its own sake, not in the service of some near or remote end.

Ultimately, motoric play becomes the framework for games, for activities that usually involve props or other players; activities that are guided and constrained by rules. Dramatic or symbolic play is free of constraints imposed by props, other players and rules. A stick can be a horse, a fairy's wand, a conductor's baton, a magical instrument, or just a stick. With practice, the child can get along even without sticks and can construct any number of magical worlds.

Herron and Sutton-Smith (1971) have raised the question whether the ability to adopt the "as if" set in play is related to the ability to adopt constructs in conceptual tasks. They cite a correlational study that at least suggests an answer: "lower class children who exhibited an inability to categorize in representational terms were also impoverished in their play, showing a high frequency of motoric activity, minimal role playing, and block play of low elaboration."

The study of persons who in early childhood had created imaginary companions would help illuminate our problem. Imaginary companions in childhood readily fits my description of dramatic play; it is parallel to the Quixotic principle. The child builds, as it were, an exclusive pseudo-community from whatever experiential raw materials are available. The model for the companion may have appeared in a story read by parents, in the observation of another family with multiple children, and so on.

We have no hard data that tell us the conditions that encourage a child to prolong the motoric phase of play or to shorten it in favor of symbolic or dramatic play. We can frame two hypotheses relating conditions of family life to individual differences in preference for motoric or symbolic play: (1) number and spacing of siblings, and (2) whether or not parents value story-telling and story reading.

A review of the literature on imaginary companions in childhood suggests protracted loneliness is a condition of the lives of children who create imaginary companions. Absence of siblings who could serve as regular playmates appears as a frequent antecedent condition. Another antecedent condition is the form of the social milieu during the important period of language development: the milieu is adult-oriented. Taking the fictive perspective of dramatic play may have a synergic effect: children with imaginary companions are more likely to initiate playful activities and to create well-developed fantasy lives. In one study, highly creative adolescents, as assessed by art productions and writing, report a significantly greater number of imaginary companions in childhood than their non-creative peers (Manosevitz, Prentice, and Wilson, 1973).

Findings of this type give initial validity to the notion that some people acquire skill in adopting the perspective of play, the perspective that influences the creation of silent scenarios. Future research will test the plausible hypothesis that the development of dramatic skills in childhood is forerunner to the creation of auxiliary worlds and of new identities through reading of imaginative literature.

V

Rather than include a summary of my exposition of the Quixotic principle, of the utility of the concept "believed-in imaginings" and of some suggestions for studying the effects of reading on identity-formation, I shall conclude by quoting a stanza from Byron, a poet whose life and works illustrate most of the points made in the preceding pages. Biographers agree that Byron, to solve various problems of life, created an identity for himself: morose, gloomy, mysterious, romantic. Then he set forth to "live" the character, to enact roles appropriate to the imagined identity. When Byron composed the Childe Harold, he had only to describe (with appropriate poetic elaboration) an identity that he at first imagined, then enacted with a full supporting cast. The stanza fittingly epitomizes the implications of my essay:

Tis to create, and in creating live
A being more intense that we endow
With form our fancy, gaining as we give

The life we image, even as I do now.

Footnotes

1. This paper has not been published previously.
2. The reader may question my not including television, movies, and the theater as sources of the quixotic principle. That the performing arts provide an environment cannot be denied. However, it is a different environment from literature. In the reading of imaginative novels, the source of the reader's construction is print on paper. He creates characters and plots from printed words, each of which is surrounded by a penumbra of ambiguity. Each reader builds the characters from scratch. In short, the creation of identities from literature requires effort and involvement. In television, movies, and the theater, the director and the actors perform part of the cognitive work. A member of the audience "knows," for example, that he is witnessing Richard Burton-as-Hamlet, not Richard Burton and not Hamlet. To construct an identity from television, for example, involves imitation (as defined before) more than role-taking. This is not to minimize the social importance of television as a source of imitatings, given the preference for violence among sponsors, producers, and viewers.

Viewers sometimes become so involved in their imaginings created in the theater that they engage in quixotic actions. Like Don Quixote who destroyed Don Pedro's puppet show when he became so involved in the plight of the lovers being pursued by the Moors, a theater-goer may occasionally break out of the conventional frame that separates audience from players. Hollard (1968) reports that at the first Broadway run of Look Back in Anger, a woman in the audience rushed on stage to attack the villian with her umbrella. It is not uncommon for children attending Saturday matinees to break out of the theatrical frame and shout advice, warning or encouragement to the cinematic hero.

More closely related to literature as an imaginative environment is the now defunct "soap opera." These daytime serials demanded more cognitive work from the audience, and therefore more involvement, than the theater. More like story telling, the soap opera provided an environment for the creation of an identity that is not unlike the identities created in one's pseudocommunities. Hollard remarks: "During the heyday of the radio soap operas, ladies by the dozens would send baby presents and wedding gifts, ask or give advice, to the fictional heroes and heroines (p. 96-97)."

3. My good friend, Philip Hallie, has raised an important point. When I asserted that all perspectives are fictive, I unwittingly made an ontological argument. Although my intent was to employ a theory of knowledge, how "the world" is interpreted, constructed, "made up," I failed to offer a theory of "the world." It is not uncommon to slip from epistemology to ontology. My ontological assumption is clearly that "events occur." These events are like William James' description of the infant's world, "a big, buzzing, blooming confusion." The "confusion" is variously formed or deformed through the person's constructs. Much more needs to be said about this problem, such as the axiological contributions to ontological assertions, but this is not the place for a proper discussion of the issues.

12

ONTOLOGY RECAPITULATES PHILOLOGY: THE MYTHIC NATURE OF ANXIETY[1]

> "In the beginning was the Word..."
> John I:1

The reader will recognize in the title a play of words on the now discredited biogenetic principle--ontogeny recapitulates phylogeny. The intent of the sesquipedalian title is to dramatize through an ennobled slang the central thesis of this paper: a person's construction of what is real is guided to a great extent by the words available to him. This thesis bears a kinship to the Whorfian hypothesis that posits the shaping of a person's Weltanschauung through grammar, syntax, and other formal aspects of his language (Whorf, 1956). Not intended to be as general as Whorf's, the present thesis claims that attempts to fill gaps in knowledge (to answer cosmological questions) are facilitated by the use of metaphor and that under some conditions metaphors are illicitly transformed into literal truths or myths. Since myths require no independent empirical confirmation, cosmological uncertainties can be resolved by invoking a myth. Thus, ontology (the sequences of answers to questions about what is) is dependent upon philological, that is, etymological, developments (words available through metaphor and myth).

This paper extends and elaborates an argument presented a few years ago, that the official doctrine of anxiety may best be regarded as the reification of a metaphor (Sarbin, 1964). My point of departure was the fact that "anxiety" is a member of a class of mental state words in psychology, words that seem to lead lives of their own--their status uninfluenced by empirical events or by rational argument. For this reason, I turned to a historico-linguistic analysis.

In condensed form, I began the argument as follows: The word "anxiety" entered modern English as a variant of Middle English "anguish." The word came into use when the effects of the great religious revivals in Europe were carried to the common man in the towns and villages. Unlike the older ecclesiastical words that denoted the more ritualized aspects of formal religion, the new words were intended to present the inward and personal forms of faith. Devotion, duty, pity, comfort, conscience, purity, and salvation were among other words introduced during the thirteenth century coincidentally with the building of the great churches and monastic houses of medieval England (Smith, 1912).

These ecclesiastical words were the forerunners of the mental state words of which "anxiety" is a prime example. Intended to denote the activities of a shadowlike entity in a private, misty word, they are unlike terms standing for distal or proximal occurrences. Since words have a natural history, it is possible to reconstruct the development of mental state terms. The rule that seems to apply in most instances may be stated concisely as follows: The construction of words is motivated by metaphor. (2) The natural history of word formation appears to follow a course somewhat as follows: Words were coined in the first instance to denote distal (external) events, the recognition of and communication about these events being functional in the maintenance of a collectivity. When it became necessary to communicate about proximal (somatic) events, words were borrowed from the distal language system and employed to denote the proximal event. The borrowing was metaphorical: because of some partial similarity, some shared characteristic between the distal and proximal referents, a word from the distal idiom was employed for the proximal event. A current example is the phrase "butterfly in the stomach," based on the similarity between a rhythmic somaesthetic experience and the rhythmic fluttering of a butterfly. Some people use "flutter" and others "butterflies" as shorter descriptive terms for the same somatic event.

On the theory presented here, the word anguish should have denoted events in the distal or proximal ecology before it was borrowed to denote a religious (and later, a mentalistic) experience. As used in medieval times, the predecessor of "anxiety," "anguish," carried the meaning of suffering of the soul. But "anguish" was the anglicized version of the old French word "anguisse" which denoted a painful, choking sensation in the throat. Thus, we find a bodily, proximal referent for a term which was later borrowed to denote a state of mind. Since metaphor is achieved through composing an analogy, we might reconstruct the origins of "anguish" as follows: A choking sensation in the throat produced, let us say, by swallowing a fish bone is denoted by the term anguisse or anguish. The death of close kin, a misfortune, the recognition of sin, and similar events often lead to a similar proximal event--a lump in the throat. Here are two proximal events that share one property, namely, discomfort in the throat. To complete the analogy, their symbols are also shared; the term denoting one is employed to denote the other--ignoring the weighty fact that their antecedents are in different modalities, different idioms.

It remains to be demonstrated, however, that anguish became a term denoting a mental state rather than certain proximal events in the throat, following certain social and metaphysical developments. The context in which mental state is used is best expressed by the polarity "inside-outside." For an approach to the understanding of how the mental or psychical world was allocated to the inside, I suggest the following: Two classes of proximal inputs can be identified. The first occurs in a context of distal events. Thus, pain in a skinned knee occurs in the context of falling on a hard, abrasive sidewalk; a burning irritation in the eye occurs after clumsily walking into an open door, etc. The second class of proximal inputs occurs in the absence of recognizable distal events, such as toothaches, headaches, precordial pain, neuritis, gastritis, etc. Since the antecedents of the latter proximal inputs could not be located in the outside world by medieval man, the locus of the bodily perception was taken as the causal locus, that is, inside the body. Having little knowledge about nor interest in anatomy--medieval man knew in a dim way that there were some organs, tubes, fluids, and bones, and he knew there were empty spaces. So, under the authority of the preachers (and later the philosophers) he learned that an invisible, mysterious spirit resided in these otherwise empty spaces. On this kind of belief system, events for which there were no observed distal contexts could be attributed to the workings of this inner spiritual entity. So proximal events, such as lumps in the throat, which could not be causally related to happenings in the distal environment were causally related to occurrences inside the person. Certain of these occurrences later came to be identified as differentiated properties of the soul, or spirit, through the tour de force of employing dispositional terms that had become detached from their distal-proximal moorings.

II

A few remarks about dispositional terms are in order. Dispositional terms increase efficiency and convenience in a language in that they denote sequences of occurrences that cluster together. It is as if dispositional terms were a form of linguistic shorthand. When applied to distal events, this linguistic shorthand denotes a range of events, for example, "springlike" is intended to denote events dealing with weather, vegetation, rainfall, relative periods of light and dark, and so on. Such shorthand terms have also been invented or borrowed to communicate about human actions that occur together: common examples are industrious, kind, gracious, wicked, strong, and loyal. Note that the adjectival form of such words is employed to denote sequences or clusters of actions applicable to human beings. From the shorthand adjectival form, the dispositional or trait forms arose. Dispositional terms convey the notion that given such-and-such conditions, certain properties of a thing or person will be revealed.

The utility of dispositional terms is evident in describing important characteristics of persons, and, in a sense, forecasting human conduct under specifiable conditions. To identify a man as "honest" provides a current description and a forecast of that he will do under certain conditions. Further, in addition to this descriptive and forecasting function, where the referents are in the distal/proximal ecologies, dispositional terms make it possible to communicate about events with subsistent referents, that is, imaginary things and vague events that are not so reliably determined as ordinary distal events and commonly experienced proximal events. Among the subsistent referents for which such dispositional terms are borrowed are those created, constructed, or hypothesized to fill gaps in knowledge through the use of dispositional terms which denoted objects or characteristics that had no empirical reference, such as mental states, psyche, and mind, etc.

The etymological history of anxiety follows the sequence just outlined. Although originally coined to denote a somatic event, anguish came to be used as a dispositional term--a shorthand expression for a cluster of events, one of which was constriction of the throat. Unlike its earlier somatic usage, as a dispositional term it probably denoted associated antecedent and concurrent conditions, such as interruption, conflict, choice, or disappointment. Its use implied a catalog of interconnected events, each item of which was, in principle, knowable.

It now remains to show how the use of anguish as a dispositional term with empirical reference became converted to a mental state term. As I suggested before, on the near absolute authority of the clergy the ontological status of the soul was not doubted. Events for which there were no observed distal contexts could readily be attributed to the operations of the immortal soul.

This state of affairs paved the way for locating dispositions inside the person and calling them actions of the soul and, later, states of mind. If the cause of an event had no external locus, it must have an internal locus. If the causal event is stated in dispositional terms, then the dispositional referent must be located inside. The soul and in later years the mind, thus became the repository for reified dispositions, and in keeping with the assumed thing character of the soul, the dispositions were codified as substantives. Codified in this way, dispositions tend to be treated in the same way as other substantives, as having the same order of qualities as palpable objects. If nouns were names of things, and things had location, the problem became that of where to locate the referent for these nouns. The answer was the same as that for locating the cause of pain in the absence of distal contexts--inside. In this way, anguish--as well as joy, anger, hostility, and other dispositions--came to be located inside the previously hypothetically constructed mind. With increasing attention from scholastic writers, the substantives came to be regarded as names for differentiations of basic mind-stuff.

III

I have just described a four-stage linguistic process in which a construct is formed. The motivation to invent concepts, it may be asserted here, is to resolve uncertainty or ambiguity.

Given the strength of belief in theological entities and given questions about causality of human conduct, gaps in knowledge may readily be filled by postulating mental states. Anxiety was one of these mental states. In modern jargon, it was introduced as a hypothetical construct to account for behavioral outcomes that could not be satisfactorily explained with existing knowledge. In general, the hypothetical construct is first labeled so that its hypotheticalness, its metaphoric status, is apparent. For example, some obscure medieval churchman might have said, "It is as if there is a stuff that controls thinking (or minding)"; a seventeenth century mental philosopher, taking his cue from Aristotle, might have argued, "It is as if the mind is split, like Gaul, into three parts," Bleuler's achievement might have begun from an attempt to summarize his observations with, "It is as if the intellect is split from the will." Freud's writings show the use of metaphor in, among other things, noting the operations of a fictive censor. Anxiety as a mental state had its origins in the same way.

The history of psychology shows repeatedly that such metaphors or hypothetical constructs tend to become reified. The auxiliary grammatical device, the "as if," is dropped, and the deformed sentence renders the construction as literal truth. It is frequently the case that filling the gap in knowledge through the use of metaphor is satisfying only for a short time. For reasons still unknown there is a common human tendency to drop the metaphoric auxiliary terms. That is to say, when an explanation is given in the tentative mode through metaphor, the listener or reader short-circuits or unlabels the metaphor and reproduces the explanations as literal truth.

This common tendency was reflected in the now classic study reported by Carmichael, Hogan, and Walter (1932). The experimenter presented figures that could be described by two labels. For example, two adjacent circles were described by the experimenter under one condition as "this resembles a pair of glasses" and under another condition as "this resembles a dumbbell." When the subjects reproduced the figures, they dropped the "as if," the metaphoric modifier implicitly contained in the word "resembles," and drew pictures of glasses or dumbbells.

If we apply this model to more global aspects of cognition, we can posit a common tendency to transform metaphors to myths. (The word myth is here used to mean a literal statement, unsupported by empirical evidence, used as a guide to action.) As was stated before, a historical analysis of psychology (and other sciences as well) seems to show repeatedly how a thinker will note that two events have a common property and will construct a verbal analogy. In uttering it to himself or to his first audience, he will label the metaphor. But his audience will tend to drop the metaphoric qualifier, and in so doing, will create conditions for myth making.

To test the generality of this tendency for metaphor-to-myth transformation, I recently performed an exploratory experiment. I read to a class of 200 undergraduates short news releases of three recent developments in pharmacology and psychiatry. Each of the accounts contained metaphoric constructions of the form, "It was as if the volitional faculty was separated from the action faculty." Under conditions of recall and reproduction, immediate and remote, the frequency of metaphor-to-myth transformations was exceedingly high. There were 15 opportunities for each subject to make a metaphor-to-myth transformation. On the average, each protocol contained about 11 such transformations. (Some of the subjects appeared to be resistant to this general tendency, and I hope to find correlates to help account for the variation.) The point need not be further belabored. Human beings--including psychologists--construct their cosmological worlds, their explanatory systems, out of beliefs, some of whose origins are contained in illicit metaphor-to-myth transformations.

IV

Not all potential transformations are carried to their illogical conclusions; not all "as ifs" are deformed to "truths." In the experiment just mentioned, some conditions produced more transformations than others. The form of the label used to denote the metaphor was related to the proportion of metaphor-to-myth transformations. A common everyday English phrase, "the talking machine," provided the least number of transformations; a coined word, "Aerophine," that contained phonic and orthographic properties related to another metaphor produced an intermediate number, and a "scientific" sounding Latin word, "sinvoluntatia," returned by far the largest number of transformations.

This finding leads directly to the next point--the dimension of transparency as applied to the word anxiety. For the person who first employs a metaphor, the word embraces common characteristics of both the new and conventional referents. For him the metaphor is necessarily transparent. That is to say, the connection between the new term and the old is obvious. When that unknown medieval writer borrowed "anguisse," a term representing a proximal event--a choking sensation in the throat--to refer to a differentiated state of the soul, he did so with the knowledge that he was engaging in a metaphoric transformation. Needless to say, a writer cannot construct a metaphor unless the meaning of the new term is known to him, unless he can "see through" the transformation. Let me illustrate from a simple bilingual translation: a person who is fluent in English and Greek may in his own ratiocinations substitute "schizophrenia" for "divided soul" without intending to modify the reference. To him, the translation is transparent; that is, the stock of Greek roots and affixes are as semantically useful as the English equivalents. When the transformation is reproduced for another generation, the Greek word schizophrenia may become opaque if the users of the term are not bilingual. That is to say, if the Greek word is employed, the meanings attributed to it must be constructed afresh, through the use of dictionaries, etymological analysis, phonic analysis, or other cognitive work. Such cognitive effort is not required when the concrete referent is indicated by a word that is transparent, that can be automatically deciphered (Ullmann, 1962).

The dimension of transparency is a useful one in understanding the use and abuse of scientific terms. When the original metaphor maker used "anguisse," the transformation was transparent; that is, the label for a characteristic of choking and constriction was used to refer to a conjectured and constricted state of the soul. For later readers and writers whose language skills did not include ready access to Norman French idioms the metaphor became opaque. That is to say, unlike the stock of words that is acquired in childhood, where reference is automatic and relatively stable, opaque words do not have the immediate reference and are subject to unreliablilty and ambiguity of reference.

A review of the history and employment of the modern word anxiety reveals that it is an opaque word. That is to say, it is not acquired early in life--it is, if anything, a word for grown-ups. It does not, as it were, contain its own reference as does the word "worry." Thus reference must be supplied by the reader or listener. In the absence of glossaries and dictionaries, the reference must be supplied from the context, phonic properties, syntax, etc. An opaque word, then, is something like an inkblot--reference is read into it, and no two references are necessarily alike.

Parenthetically, I was surprised to learn that textbooks of psychology and psychiatry made no use of "anxiety" until the 1930s. After the translation of Freud's (1926) Hemmung, Symptom and Angst, the word became exceedingly popular among psychiatrists and psychologists. The first translation appeared under the title Inhibition, Symptom and Anxiety (1927), the second as The Problem of Anxiety (1936). It is important to note that Freud used a common German word "angst," a word that German-speaking children learn early in life. The translation to the opaque word anxiety introduced references probably not intended by Freud.

The lack of transparency of the word may in part account for the multiple and unstable reference. For the behavior scientist, such unstable reference creates a confusing picture, as witnessed by a perusal of textbooks, dictionaries, journal articles, and other sources. The inkblot nature of "anxiety" is further revealed by the multiplicity of referents. Some referents are expressed in terms of overt behavior such as tremor, coughing, stuttering, and twitching; some in terms of complex conduct such as avoidance, defense, and denial of stimulus inputs; some in terms of antecedent events such as aversive stimuli and memory of traumatic events; some in terms of heart rate, GSR, and respiratory rate; and some in terms that have only vague subsistent referents such as apprehensions, emotional states, states of mind, affects, and feelings. This collection of referents places great strain on the credibility of statements such as, "Everyone knows in a general way what is meant by anxiety." Such a state of affairs cannot meet the criterion for a scientific vocabulary recommended by Mandler and Kessen (1959), "that its words, from whatever source, must show a high consistency of usage from the user to user and from occasion to occasion (p. 45)."

The methods for inferring the presence of this hydra-headed term are similarly multiple. Some 120 different procedures for inferring the presence of "anxiety" were isolated by Cattell and Scheier (1961). Probably more than these are currently in use. Although the proliferation of methods in science is in part due to technological advances, the proliferation to the study of a single-named construct is facilitated by the lack of transparency in that construct, a lack that makes it all things to all men.

The mythic character of anxiety is indirectly supported in Levy's (1961) analysis of entries in Psychological Abstracts. Be made frequency counts of entries in which "anxiety" appeared in the title. A positively accelerated increase in the number of articles followed the introduction of the Taylor Manifest Anxiety (MA) scale (Taylor, 1953). The publication of a children's form of the MA in 1956 showed a similar spurt. No comcomitant increase was noted in publications dealing with related topics of drive and emotion.

Levy's (1961) conclusion is stated in terms of the docility of behavior scientists to techniques rather than problems. In the idiom of the present analysis, it would seem that psychologists welcomed the invention of a technique that could measure an entity whose ontological status was so unsatisfactory. The employment of a scientific tool bearing the name anxiety led to the illicit conclusion that anxiety had empirical reference after all. Hundreds of experiments have been done under the belief that the MA measured an elusive mental state, or psychic trait, or both.

In recent years, the recognition of the multiple reference for anxiety has led some writers to distinguish between "trait anxiety" and "state anxiety." The distinction probably resulted from the failure to find expected correlations between self-report measures and physiological measures, both of which supposedly reflected the presence of anxiety. As Levy (1961) has demonstrated, the introduction of the MA, constructed along conventional psychometric lines to measure Hullian drive, increased the interest in finding correlates of self-reports. The form of the scale, together with its face validity, easily led its users to treat scores in a fashion parallel to their treatment of scores for scales constructed by a similar method. Such scales are traditionally assigned names that represent traits or dispositions--organized and durable systems of response ready to be activated under appropriate stimulus conditions. Anxiety as a trait, however, has not fared well. In the first place, the MA correlates with psychiatric ratings of anxiety to the same extent as with measures that have little to do with conventional formulations of psychiatric disorder. Further, the scale appears to be negatively correlated with social desirability (Mukherjee, 1966). The semantic properties of trait anxiety, upon reflection, appear to be no different from other mental state terms. It is as if the mind could be differentiated into various substructures of a dispositional sort--not unlike the Gall-Spurzheim phrenological notion. In this sense, trait anxiety is not different from anxiety as a mental state.

The construction of the concept "state anxiety" undoubtedly followed from the age-old observation that under some conditions (sometimes called "emotional states") various physiological systems were activated. It is not easy to determine whether "state" in this usage is to be regarded as the same "state" as in state of grace, state of intoxication, state of health, state of repairs, state of being, etc. Because physiological systems normally activated by readily observed distal and proximal events, such as running and swimming and hyperventilation, are activated in the absence of such antecedent conditions, a state of mind was postulated as the causal agent. Under the older view of an organism partitioned into two domains, it was proper to ask questions of the sort that led Cannon (1929), for example, to write of the "bodily reactions" to pain, fear, anger, and related conditions. Without the dualistic mythology, a different set of questions could have been asked--for example, "What are the antecedent ecological conditions that bring about physiological changes?"; "Do physiological changes have effects on the efficiency of problem solving?"; etc.

The inference to be drawn from these observations is that the creation of the expressions "trait anxiety" and "state anxiety" has not been fruitful. The former term was coined because of psychometric similarities between anxiety scales and scales that purportedly measured other dispositions, the latter because of the historical associations between physiological arousal and antecedent conditions called emotional states.

V

Most of my remarks are applicable to many currently used concepts other than anxiety. Historico-linguistic analysis of other concepts would lead to similar conclusions: to wit, we are great mythmakers and myth users. However, being human and being subject to uncertainty in our efforts to understand the world about us, there are times when we must adopt beliefs so that we are not transfixed for lack of truth (Scheibe and Sarbin, 1965). The psychologist, no different from the man in the street, lacking truth and needing it to provide a course of action, makes it up. In so doing, he runs the risk of locking himself into a conceptual prison from which there is no escape save to explode the myth that he had constructed.

The implications of my remarks cannot be tossed off with a cavalier reference to trivial semantics, to hairsplitting, or to "I don't care what you call it." The labels we use contain implicit and explicit connotations; these connotations constrain implications for action in research, in practice, and in theory building. However, as long as the metaphor is labeled and recognized for its hypotheticalness, its "as if" quality, the use of the metaphor can be governed by openness, by tentativity, and by modulated commitment. When the metaphor turns myth, the system closes. The user of the concept becomes committed to a point of view and unwittingly assigns ontological status to the subsistent referent. Most important, having made up a "truth," he is now susceptible to the query--by self or others--"What is anxiety?" a query for which only unsatisfying verbal definitions can be offered.

The scientist follows the same cognitive plan as the man in the street whose gaps in knowledge are closed by similar operations. However, when the man in the street engages in mythmaking--the dropping of "as if" in favor of "is"--he may be labeled with the pejorative "superstitious" or "delusional" (Sarbin, 1967c; Scheibe and Sarbin, 1965).

Because the argument is extended and must of necessity proceed on parallel sets of tracks, let me recapitulate. Although anxiety is an infelicitous word, the thrust of my argument is not that we find a new word. No. The conclusion that follows from my argument is that mental states, including anxiety, are ontologically mythical. Substituting, let us say, "apprehension" for "anxiety" would change nothing if the referent were still a mythical mental state. The effect of continuing to rely on mental states as events intervening between antecedent variables and outcome variables is to continue the fruitless scholastic search for verbal answers to such questions as, "What is anxiety?" Popper (1963) has convincingly argued that such questions have no place in science; they lead nowhere but to more words in the hope of discovering the essence contained in the word. He stated:

> Every discipline, as long as it has used the Aristotelian method of definition, has remained arrested in a state of empty verbiage and barren scholasticism, and the degree to which the various sciences have been able to make any progress depended on the degree to which they have been able to get rid of this essentialist method...(p.9).

The antidote to the essentialist method is to ask questions of another type: what are the antecedent and concurrent conditions responsible for, let us say, efficiency in problem solving? Or for vocational choice? Or for avoidant behavior? Or for unconventional conduct? Such questions require no mental state terms in their answers. To be sure, metaphors will be useful in giving form to, and in communicating about, such answers. But as long as the metaphors are implicitly or explicitly labeled as such, the risk of transformation to myth is limited. Newton's advice is worth noting here: scientists should take their hypothetical constructs lightly. He also pointed to the imaginary nature of scientific fictions and the necessity for regarding them only as "queries" (Turner, 1961). (4)

The reader who has followed the argument to this point might say, "I agree that anxiety has become a mental state word. I further agree that mental states, since they have only vague verbal referents, stand in the way of developing a theory of conduct that would meet current logical and scientific requirements. But all this does not convince me that my experiences which I call anxiety are mythical. And if I am convinced of the reality of my experiences, then how is the anxious suffering to be accounted for?"

To explode a myth or to undress a metaphor is not to deny occurrences. The distal and proximal occurrences--for which any particular metaphor is a device for communication and for which the transformed metaphor is a unit of explanation--may be labeled and explained in an infinite number of ways. The kinds of explanations used by psychologists tend to be causal (Peters, 1958)--constructs inside the organism or mind that "cause" observed behavior. Such explanations are put together when the rule-following explanations fail to take into account all the observations. Anxiety is a prime example of the causal type. In view of its current semantic and ontological status, its employment has negative utility for a science of human conduct. When an investigator employs anxiety as a mental state term, he is constrained to look into the hypothetical mental apparatus for the causes, for example, of overriding moral questions raised by Luther and Kierkegaard and other persons assailed by doubt and suffering. The cognitive conduct of these doubters and sufferers can be more fruitfully regarded as efforts to deal with contradictory belief systems, with moral choice, and with uncertainty. Such an alternate formulation to anxiety has the effect of steering inquiry head-on into the antecedent and concurrent personal and social events and away from hypothetically constructed states of mind.

The foregoing remarks may be condensed into a single proposition, to wit: where (and how) we seek the antecedent conditions of conduct is influenced and guided by the metaphors we use. A mental state term, such as anxiety, when separated from its metaphorical roots, constrains its user to look "inside," to observe the workings of the mythical mind. Terms not associated with mental state doctrine are less likely to suggest such internal causal explorations. Rather, the objects of search and exploration are more likely to be the concurrent distal conditions, the beliefs held, and the values cherished. Admittedly, we need conceptual aids to understand the human condition in settings of doubt, of uncertainty, and of unconvincing answers to the persistent existential question: "What am I?" The feebleness and futility of anxiety constructs as aids to understanding are nowhere more apparent than in that occurrence when the Man on the cross cried out, "Father, why hast thou forsaken me?"

VI

It is unlikely that psychologists and philosophers will return anxiety to its earlier metaphorical status. For this reason, new metaphors must be introduced to denote the conduct, the occurrences, which were labeled anxiety, when anxiety enjoyed status as a metaphor. The dismissal of an old myth can occur only in the context of a new set of metaphors that have heuristic and pragmatic utility. Elsewhere (Sarbin, 1962) I have proposed "cognitive strain" as a new metaphor to denote the human condition that arises in connection with solving problems of choice, conflict, interference, interruption, overloading, etc. The components of the phrase are chosen to emphasize "knowing" and "effort"--the seeking of concepts and of supplementary inputs to help instantiate (make sense of) uninstantiable inputs (Sarbin, Taft, and Bailey, 1960). Hopefully, this metaphor, along with others, will help us form new knowledge useful in understanding human conduct. In this way we shall free ourselves from the bondage of mentalism and from reliance on mythical states such as anxiety.

Footnotes

1. Reprinted from American Psychologist, 1968, 23, 411-418.
2. The author recognizes that there are other motivations involved in word formation besides metaphor, for example, onomotopaeia (Ullmann, 1962).

PART VII
Metapsychology, Metaphysics and Metaphor

One cannot speak of psychology without the use of metaphors. Yet the particular metaphors that are chosen as the provisional language of psychology are not uniformly useful or appropriate. Because all metaphors are based on a partial resemblance between the thing to be described and the chosen metaphorical vehicle, metaphors can mislead as well as illuminate.

A good deal of Sarbin's work as a psychologist consists of the introduction of new metaphors for the explication of human conduct and experience. Role theory employs the language of the drama in conjunction with certain of the common "structural" metaphors employed by classical sociology. Contextualism as the preferred position is a product of a search for new "root metaphors" to guide the work of the psychologist. A "model of social identity" is but another metaphor for advancing our ability to conceptualize the human condition--it is not meant as a characterization of "the way things really are." "Mental illness" is a metaphor that has outlived its usefulness because the term carries implications for action and treatment which have been shown to be dysfunctional.

Metaphors are made, used, misused and, in time, acquire the status of myth. A good deal of the work that appears in this book is a product of Sarbin's attempts at "the demythification of psychology." Metaphors are flexible, provisional, useful in context, not fixed characterizations of the truth. It is serious work in psychology to go about disintegrating myths and simultaneously creating new metaphors.

It is not surprising that Sarbin has recently turned his attention directly to the topic of metaphor. The first essay concerns the use of metaphor in referring to human death. Sarbin surveys the metaphors in common use for describing the phenomenon of death and finds that the several metaphors have very different implications in terms of how death is understood. These implications for the understanding of death, in turn, produce consequences in what is considered to be appropriate conduct for the individual who is about to die or for the people around such a person. The consequences of metaphors for death, then, are shown to circle back to how life is lived.

The final essays are pure addresses to the topic of metaphor, which represents Sarbin's current work. Certainly the issues he addresses in these essays are absolutely fundamental -- they underlie science, psychology, and humane inquiry in general. Whitehead states, "The history of human thought in the past is a pitiful tale of self-satisfaction with a supposed adequacy of knowledge in respect to factors of human existence." Sarbin's two essays on metaphor, consistent with the body of his work, are attempts to defeat self-satisfaction about the adequacy of received knowledge. The spirit that animates this restless search for new vision is humane and even poetic. Science can afford nothing less.

13

METAPHORS OF DEATH IN SYSTEMS OF CONDUCT REORGANIZATION[1]

This paper is divided into four sections--each of the first three sections making separate arguments. First I sketch a general model of conduct reorganization, a model that identifies a set of occurrences that are prerequisite to drastic personality change. Central to this model is the concept "symbolic death" as employed in the theme "death" and "rebirth." However, symbolic "death" is not an unequivocal term. To help make sense of this language, I turn to an examination of metaphors of death.

The second section is a necessary preliminary to the discussion of metaphors of death. It is addressed to the need to improve clarity of analysis by distinguishing between "death" as an abstraction and "dying" as an act.

The third section concerns the theme, Death and Civilization, and discusses a fourfold classification of metaphors of death.

The fourth section makes use of conclusions from the other three. The resultant is intended to be a more clearly stated, and therefore a more useful, model for understanding "symbolic death" as a component in significant transformations of personal identity.

I

In order to talk about conduct reorganization, it is necessary to invoke the concept "self." This concept ordinarily presents no difficulties to humanists. The concept of self is troublesome only to those theorists who strive to be consistent with the implications of the mechanistic paradigm, a world view that has demonstrated its utility to scientists for the last two centuries. Rejecting mechanistic theories, however, does not imply a retrogression to mentalistic world views. Rather, the complexities of human conduct call for a heuristic model that locates man, not as a machine, but as an actor operating in complex contextual relations with various internal and external ecologies. Not unimportant in these contextual relations are the implicit and explicit labels used by persons to denote referents for the pronoun "I", such as in the sentences, "I am weak," "I am wholesome" "I am a pawn in the game of life," etc. The self, then, need not be viewed as a construct parallel to the overworked mentalistic conceptions of soul, mind, and psyche but rather as a linguistic response to one's actions performed in the multiple frameworks of daily life and imaginary dramas. Such a conception leads to the hypothesis that the degree to which the person incorporates such a label as "being saved" or "reborn" (with its attendant role behaviors) into his overall self-concept determines whether he can or cannot easily dispense with unwanted conduct and initiate actions that are consistent with a newly re-constituted self.

In the model to be presented, the effort to reform persons, to initiate drastic behavioral change, to re-organize long-held values, is seen in the context of the person as actor responding to inputs generated by proximal and distal conditions. It is my view that therapies directed toward drastic personal reorganization must be derived from the root-metaphor of contextualism--a root metaphor that encourages the change-agent to perceive the client as a cognizing, believing, imagining, doing creature rather than as a reservoir of habits or a passive object whose form is predestined by heavenly forces or by the failure of his parents to have read and understood the Oedipus myth.

Self-reconstitution processes was the label first used in a paper written in collaboration with Dr. Nathan Adler (see "Self-reconstitution processes", this volume). It is a convenient shorthand to organize the common features of a large number of systems of conduct reorganization. We were curious about the fact that some long-term felons, whose style of life, social status, prison background, apparent attitude, etc., falsify actuarial predictions and upon release from prison unexpectedly take up a new law-abiding life and become model citizens. For clues to such reformations, we reviewed our own cases--successes and failures--and also selected examples of religious, ethnological, and political systems of altering conduct and beliefs. In our essay we proposed (a) that all successful treatments aimed at conduct reorganization follow an identifiable sequence, and (b) that all such methods incorporate "nonrationalistic" components. The term "nonrationalistic" is an evaluative word suggesting that certain actions are not reasonable (more often, not polite or genteel) given our dedication to scientific models and to traditional logic. Since the middle of the nineteenth century, behavioral scientists in their devotion to the scientific method have consistently avoided or rejected models that included explicit nonrationalistic components such as fasting, flagellation, and other ceremonials. In so doing, they have systematically by-passed the wealth of behavior reorganization methodology most often presented in metaphors of religion, magic or ritual.

Until recently, the ideological tradition in psychological science has assumed the human being to be a passive organism; the therapist or other person endowed with power manipulated "ideas" and "sensations" in order to alter the "mind," which in turn would modify actions and habits. Conceptual analysis becomes frozen into circularity because of the conceptual partitioning of the subject from his social milieu and from his self-reflexive behavior. A review of contemporary psychological theories suggests that we have not entirely freed ourselves from this earlier emphasis on mental forms. (Most psycholiterary criticism depends upon mentalistic theories.)

To counter the gross limitation of earlier associationistic psychology, the construct of an active self is put forth. The image of a passive, stimulus-bound organism is neither plausible nor useful; instead contemporary theory employs the conception of an intrinsically active organism whose ongoing knowledge-seeking activity leads to broader and more structured resolutions of the world of occurrences. Freud's passive organism, waiting for the stirrings of tissue needs or the promptings of "anxiety" signals and only then looking for an external tranquilizer, is an obsolescent construct. The newer view of man as actor requires a metaphor that embraces the fact that he is an inveterate, ongoing decision maker, rehearsing (often silently) possible role behaviors on the basis of expectancies garnered from the environment. Such rehearsal involves not only generalized beliefs about the external world (e.g., "tolerating frustration requires strength") but also beliefs about the self (e.g., "I am strong"). To be an effective decision maker a person must assign meanings to self as object as well as to other persons and things. In addition, the human being as actor can construct abstractions about himself as well as about the regularities in the behavioral environment.

At this point, I shall identify some of the concepts that have been helpful in accounting for the outcomes of drastic personal change, variously identified as religious conversion, reconstitution of the self, transvaluation of social identity, and profound conduct reorganization. These concepts include the sources of information from which persons make decisions regarding action. Two categories are posited: (a) the proximal ecology which provides sensory input from posture, movement, somasthesis, and imaginings; and (b) the distal ecologies. Five distal ecologies are differentiated: the self maintenance ecology, the spatial-temporal ecology, the normative ecology, the social ecology, and the cosmological or transcendental ecology. A person warrants a course of action for himself by making sense of the data gleaned from these input sources; in other words, he tries to construct answers to persisting ecologically relevant questions such as, "What am I in relation to the self maintenance ecology?" "Where am I?", "Who am I", "What am I in relation to the abstraction 'justice,'" and so on, in terms of his concurrent organization of knowledge.

For our present purposes, it will suffice to concentrate on the source of inputs for constructing (1) a social identity, i.e., finding answers to the persisting question for establishing self in various imperfect social organizations, and (2) a cosmological or transcendental self, i.e., finding answers to contruct a self as abstraction in relation to other abstractions, such as fate, justice and death. Answers to the "Who am I" questions provide the basis for one's social identity. Answers to the "What am I?" questions, drawn from inputs generated both proximally and distally, represent the self as cosmological object--the subjective aspect of "thingness."

To recapitulate: significant conduct-reorganization occurs as the sequelae of events that lead to new or revised answers to ecological questions. The conditions for such changed answers are not recondite or mysterious; they occur as the result of efforts to change the conditions for location of self in the cosmological and the social ecologies. Efforts to change the subjective aspect of thingness (self as cosmological object) may include such knowable antecedent operations as altering body-image boundaries through motoric activity, drug intake, physical exercise, fasting, or breathing exercises. Efforts to alter social identity supports are achieved through degradation rituals, isolation, ostracism, humiliation, shame, or aversive social reinforcements.

From our review of selections of the world literature on conduct reorganization, Adler and I abstracted five common themes. (See "Self-reconstitution process," this volume.) The first and most conspicuous theme is that of death and rebirth. The symbolic death and rebirth of the self is a recurrent theme in all systems of conduct reorganization. (The other themes--control by a group, ritual, proprioception, and triggering--are of less direct relevance to the problem at hand and will not be discussed here.)

In symbolic death certain personal behaviors drop out of the convert's repertoire and are replaced by a new set of role behaviors and corresponding self-definitions. The death-rebirth theme in this context may be viewed as the dissolution of a self and the rebirth or formation of another. In the language of modern social psychology, the point of death occurs when the individual becomes a "nonperson." This transformation is brought about when the individual encounters events in which his claims to being a person are not ratified, when he is degraded, disparaged, and, as it were, "depersoned." To restore himself to personhood the individual must reorganize his beliefs in relation to his beliefs about cosmological abstractions or his beliefs about his social world.

The metaphoric use of the words dying, being reborn, and saved is well known in religious literature. Frequently employed in autobiographical and literary descriptions of conversions, the dual process is noted in such metaphors as "death and rebirth," "death and transfiguration," "once born and twice born," "the spiritual awakening," "degradation and renewal." In all the systems we reviewed the recurrent theme of symbolic death and rebirth is noted whether it takes the form of a ritualized dying ceremony, "surrendering" before one begins a new life, "hitting rock bottom," "renunciation" of worldly and bodily pleasures, penance, humiliation, or being forcibly degraded to a symbolic cipher. The specific operations by which this symbolic death is brought about, the point at which the death is reached, the rebirth phenomenon, and the group acceptance which follows are keys to understanding the conversion process.

Humiliation is one of those processes systematically employed in the death-rebirth transition. The point of death is reached when the humiliated individual becomes a "nonperson" and is treated by relevant others as not being able to meet minimal cultural expectations; he is perceived as not having the human requirements to perform actions to make good the occupancy of even the most undifferentiated, granted social roles, such as father, male, human being. The remote effects of organized humiliation is that the person begins to look upon the self as similar to, if not identical with, the moribund person.

The symbolic death process is characterized by a mounting of physiological arousal and cognitive strain. The converters or behavior changers place temporal, spatial, and contractual restrictions on the use of adaptive techniques for reducing the strains imposed by being treated as a nonperson. If he is to make sense of the confusion of inputs, the de-personed individual must change his beliefs. He must relocate himself in the social or cosmological ecologies. The practices may be viewed as an assault upon the individual's conception of self as a cosmological object or as a social identity. Stock answers to the questions who am I and what am I in relation to God, justice, humanity are no longer operative. Then the modification, reevaluation, or transformation of the convert's beliefs follow. Alternative, more congruent, and more readily classified views of self are made available by the change agent, therapist, or guide. The new self (after the rebirth) is tagged with labels carrying connotations of health, strength, virtue and nobility rather than illness, weakness, wickedness and helplessness.

The active induction of stress, of directed organismic involvement, is a central feature in all the systems reviewed. This is perhaps more easily recognized in radical techniques developed outside the genteel traditions of behavior science. The assault on the self is brought about in numerous ways: such as, the "meat-axe" and "hot-seat" therapy of some group procedures, the Synanon "haircut," the exhaustion, toxicity, and the sensory deprivation of "marathon" therapy, the controlled use of involved imaginings as in the exercises of Loyola.

Crucial to the process of inducing the convert to undergo a symbolic dying is a set of procedures designed for intense organismic involvement. The lack of organismic involvement is one of the factors that accounts for most failures in behavior change and psychotherapeutic efforts; often such failures are referred to as "intellectual insight without emotional involvement." The process of vividly imagining, of entertaining the counter-factual as if it were factual, and of assigning tokens of credibility to one's imaginings gives the convert a basis for hope and redemption. The greater the organismic involvement in the imagining, the greater the probability of the shift in self-conception, and the more probable the renunciation of the former self. Experienced practitioners can, through symbolic means, induce high involvement. Such practitioners may depend for source material on such works as Dante's Inferno. Others may borrow from St. Patrick and urge a forty-day fast.

The "self-reconstitution" model is appropriate for understanding drastic personal change. "Symbolic death" is the central concept. But "symbolic death" is an abstract phrase. For the modern practitioner of conduct reorganization, the term "symbolic death" must be made less ambiguous. Toward this goal I now turn to the semantics and pragmatics of the abstract noun "death."

II

Presently, I shall report on an informal study of the vocabulary of death. We need no reminder of the semantic confusions surrounding death. The confusion has been confounded by the overlapping meanings of "dying" and "death." The latter is, of course, a verb form and refers to a doing or a happening. To be sure, the act of dying is no unidimensional event--however, it is an action, and like other actions, can in principle be described in objective language.

When most dying was the result of fatal disease processes, the dying took place over time, and, besides being a psychological and biological event, it was an important social and moral event. Aries (1974) refers to the practice in the Middle Ages of the "nuntius mortis," a professional who announced to the moribund person that his time had come and that he should prepare to enact the role of the dying person, a role that specified certain actions with regard to setting his own worldly and spiritual affairs in order.

Contemporary students and commentators in thanatology in general condemn the practice of dying in ignorance. They are critical of the widespread employment of a defense maneuver that results in specific cases being treated as if they were immortal. Aries discusses the shift in practice from allowing the person to participate in his own dying to the present practice of concealing information from the moribund patient that he is about to die. This shift in practice has deprived a dying person of his own death, as it were, and accompanying this practice, the denial of mourning. "In the late Middle Ages and the Renaissance," he writes, "a man insisted on participating in his own death because he saw in it an exceptional moment--a moment that gave his individuality its definitive form. He was the master of his life to the extent that he was the master of his death. His death belonged to him, and to him alone . . . " (Aries, 1974, p. 5). Later, his dying and death were shared with the family. This sharing made it possible for the development of the present practice where the family participates in the conspiracy of silence about dying.

The involvement of the family and other potential mourners as significant actors in the death drama made it necessary to wait for certain signs to appear, signs that were perceived as the termination of life--usually the cessation of breathing. Our contemporary technological sophistication has complicated the assessment of dying: the mere cessation of breathing is not enough--electrical activity of the brain and mechanical activity of the heart must also be monitored. To be sure, the social role of the dying person has changed--it is becoming more and more common for the patient with terminal illness to enact his final social role surrounded by the paraphernalia of technology in hospitals or nursing homes--the oxygen tent or I-V preparation serving as a mute technological "nuntius mortis."

Where the dying occurs over a short period of time, as in bombings, airplane crashes, automobile collisions, television dramas, movies, and modern warfare, the victim may have no audience of relevant others to enact reciprocal roles. The subjective response to overwhelming violence to the body serves as the silent and rapidly-acting nuntius mortis.

Unlike many human actions that are reflexive, the diagnosis of the end of life cannot be performed by the actor. He can serve as coroner for others but not for himself. He cannot monitor respiratory or cardiac or brain-wave machines to determine when he has completed the act of dying. Others are charged with the task of declaring when the dying has been completed. If the abstract concept "death" refers to the state of affairs that follows the dying, then the meanings attributed to "death" will be influenced by the form of dying, and the physical, social and ritual conditions surrounding the determination of death.

This brief digression--which could be expanded to include additional kinds of dyings--is necessary as a backcloth for talking about the word "death." Unlike the word "dying" that stands for observable, concrete biological and social happenings and doings, the word "death" is an abstraction. Like other abstractions, "death" lends itself to multiple meanings. The metaphorical and etymological origins of "death" are lost in antiquity. "Death," if I may be permitted a slight impropriety, is a dead metaphor. It is used in many ways but always either explicitly or by implication contraposed to another abstraction, "life." I hasten to add that "life," too, is a dead metaphor.

"Death," unlike "dying," has no stable set of concrete referents. However, it is a word widely employed in daily conversation, in poetry, in technical discourse and even in some commercial announcements of mortuary entrepreneurs. The Thorndike-Lorge word count of 1931 rates "death" among those words appearing in print 500 times in one million words. This is the category of most frequently appearing words. The problem is how to determine whether death has a common core of meaning, and if not, whether the multiple meanings can be classified in any useful way.

Several procedures may be employed: one can carry out a social survey, and intrusively inquire of selected respondents about the meaning of the abstract word "death." The results, of course, might be colored by the respondent's frustration upon being asked to perform the work of a door-step metaphysician, if not a stand-up lexicographer. If able to overcome his surprise, the respondent might give a trite answer or a response based upon his expectation of what the inquiring reporter wanted. It is clearly not a method of choice for useful studies of the meaning of death and dying.

Another method of inquiry--taken from experimental social science--is the semantic differential procedure. Here our respondents would be asked to "locate the concept death" on arbitrarily constructed dimensions of meaning, such a good-bad, hot-cold, sweet-bitter, active-passive, and the like. The major utility of this method is that the concept "death" could be located in semantic space and compared with the location of other abstract words such as justice, liberty, or madness. However, the method would be silent in regard to a description of death that would be useful to humanists.

Having rejected these rigorous methods of social science, I sought a method carrying a humanistic accent. Appropriate would be analysis of poetry and the classification of the imagery invoked by selected poems. This has been convincingly accomplished by my colleague Prof. Arthur McGill. McGill constructed four classes of poetic images. My abbreviated vocabulary for these images are 1) death as a life-nourishing process, 2) death as status transformation, 3) death as sleep, and 4) death as destructuring. The analysis was carried out on selected poems of well-known published poets. It is possible that other classifications of imagery might have been derived had the analysis been carried out on the poems of little-known or unpublished poets.

The method of choice for me is the analysis of metaphors of death. Rather than the images of poets, the raw material for this analysis is the stock of words and phrases found in lexicographic sources. My major purpose is to present the analysis as a preliminary to establishing a set of meanings for symbolic death, although at the same time I hope to offer some clarification of the abstraction "death."

I can justify the choice of method by echoing J. L. Austin's (1970) defense of "linguistic phenomenology." Besides alerting us to the traps of language, and helping us separate words from events, especially recognizing the shaping power of words on events, Austin takes into account the "natural selection" processes in linguistic history.

> Our common stock of words emodies all the distinctions men have found worth marking, in the lifetimes of many generations: these surely are likely to be more numerous, more sound, since they have stood up to the long test of the survival of the fittest, and more subtle, at least in all ordinary and reasonable practical matters, than any that you I are likely to think up in our armchairs of an afternoon (Austin, 1970, p. 181).

Unlike the social science methods mentioned before, the observations and analysis of ordinary language would be an exemplar of "unobtrusive measures,"highly preferred by the practitioners of contemporary social psychology.

It can be demonstrated that words which were once explicitly used as lively metaphors become literalized or reified. As metaphors, they become lost, hidden, fossilized, opaque, and dead. Emerson's expression is often quoted:

> . . . language is the archives of history, and . . . a

sort of tomb of the muses. For, though the origin of
most of our words is forgotten, each word was at first
a stroke of genius, and obtained currency, because for
the moment it symbolized the world to the first
speaker and to the hearer. The etymologist finds the
deadest word to have been a brilliant picture.
Language is fossil poetry. (Emerson, 1841, p. 215).

More recently, Sparshott (1975) echoed: "A language is
nothing but a necropolis of dead metaphors" (p. 80).

In my analysis of a number of contemporary psychological
words, among them hallucination, imagination, schizophrenia,
mental illness, and anxiety, I have found it extremely useful to
seek out the metaphorical origins, to attempt to reverse the
historical process and to try to breathe metaphoric life into
dead metaphors, thus re-opening closed conceptual systems to new
interpretations. The method, in brief, is to locate the earlier
usages when a metaphor maker found it necessary to communicate
about some perplexing or esoteric event and was at a loss for
common words. The speaker would attempt to solve a problem in
communication by employing a word from one universe of discourse
to describe events (including other words) from another
universe.

Words arise in the context of people communicating to
others, or to themselves, where the currently stock word is
feebly inappropriate to convey a meaning proportional to the
complexity, strangeness, gravity, or ambiguity of the event to
be described. To know of a person's imagery for the abstract
noun "death," it is helpful to be acquainted with that person's
actual or vicarious encounters with dying persons or animals,
with the presence or absence of sacral features represented by
mysterious, perplexing rituals, and the acquisition of special
metaphors to speak of "death."

As I have already remarked, a special problem arises in the
use of abstract nouns. To set this problem in perspective, let
me use a non-abstract term as an illustrative device. The first
black smoke-belching locomotive espied by the Plains Indians was
metaphorically dubbed Iron Horse. They had had commerce with
iron in various forms and with horses as beasts of burden.
Another antecedent condition was the clear-cut necessity to be
able to communicate about a machine that might have untold power
in the continuing struggle between the Plains Indians and the
white encroachers. If the Plains Indians have continued to use
Iron Horse to denote locomotives, it is probably not a dead
metaphor--Iron Horse has not been literalized or given mythic
status.

In contrast, the construction of a metaphor for an abstract
word, rather than a concrete thing such as a locomotive, calls
for more subtle and usually less precise analysis. The
difficulty is immediately apparent when we consider the
cognitive and expressive problems of philosophers, jurists,
moralists, and others who try to answer questions with an
abstract word in the predicate, such as "What is virtue?" or
"What is justice?" Imagine a young child, asking the question
"What is death?" The linguistic observer would have to note the
context of the question--he would ask: "What events led to the

question?" He would note the emotional or dramatic ambience in which the question was asked. Not unlikely the child heard the word "death" spoken in the context of the sacred. If, say, a grandfather had died after a lingering illness, if religious practices were instituted--these events would be part of the child's cognitive matrix when the parent--now cast in the role of Emerson's poet--searches for a metaphor to answer the child's question. To use the simile "death is like sleep" may leave the child dissatisfied. The more sophisticated parent might compress the simile and still use a metaphoric marker and say "It is as if grandfather is asleep;" the curious child might inquire further and the parent now utters a statement: "Death is sleep." One is reminded here of C. S. Lewis's discussion of the master's metaphor and the pupil's metaphor. The master knows he is intending only a metaphor and not equivalence when he says "death is sleep." The pupil has a problem: since the contextual markers may be absent or obscure, "death is sleep" may be taken literally. The implications of this conclusion leads to other questions and answers, most often centered around sleep as a special state of being and further that sleep has a chronicity dimension--there are short naps, long sleeps, and eternal rests. A further question may arise: if the child perceives the sentence as expressing equivalence, then the terms may be reversed to: "sleep is death." The effects of this cognitive activity, incidentally, may have profound side effects on the child's sleeping habits.

The credibility of this metaphor turned myth depends on a number of supports. The first is the child's experience with the antecedent condition for the word "death," namely, the act of dying. Is the metaphor "death as sleep" credible if the antecedent act of dying was characterized by violence, attended by bombardment and chaos and confusion? Under these conditions, sleep might not be credible metaphor.

These illustrations are offered here to suggest that the construction of metaphors of death is influenced by the form or forms of dying observed by the questioner, by the presence or absence of surrounding sacred properties, and by the poetic facility of the person who constructs the master's metaphor.

It is important to remember that "death" as a word is normally contained in a sentence. Whether fully formed for public expression or inchoately formed for private rumination, the sentence is constructed within a context of other sentences, happenings and doings. For this reason, the study of the metaphors of death may not discount the part played by observations of the form of dying, the events between time, when the behavior of the person in question meets the criteria for "alive," and time, when the person meets the criteria for "dead."

A former client of mine, when he was five, asked an older companion about death. The companion--unable to find an appropriate verbal metaphor--employed a non-verbal figure. With the heel of his shoe, he crushed a small insect. "There," he said, "the bug is no more. No more. That's death." I might add that as an adult, the client made a practice of not walking under advertising signs, marquees, or other structures that might collapse and crush him like a bug.

III

Now to the study of metaphors of death, taken from dictionaries, thesauruses, and slang books. The contexts of the original usage are not always given, and, by the time words become sufficiently useful to find a place in dictionary, they may have become pupillary metaphors.

Metaphors of death may be constructed out of nearly every kind of human enterprise. Slang is more creative and more transparent than formal language and is rich in metaphors of death. The theater has contributed to our vocabulary in many ways, e.g., "take the last cue from life's stage" and "curtains," so has gambling (e.g., "throw sixes," "go to the races," "cash in your chips"); transportation (e.g., "pull in at the last terminal," "last station") and work (e.g., "payday," "punch your time card").

The present analyses of the metaphors of death are based on those words and phrases which had achieved a place in Roget's International Thesaurus.

A list of some eighty words and phrases roughly equivalent to "death" was assembled. Etymological study led to inferences about what concrete thing or operation provided the source of the metaphorical borrowing. The Oxford English Dictionary was the primary source for the etymologies. The following are illustrative of the analyses:

Demise: meaning to "send off," also "to send down"; a metaphor of death as travel, of going away or down.

Passing away: another metaphor of travel.

Release: comes from "relax," to resume a state of looseness, diffusion, disorganization. Suggested is the process of biological decay which follows the cessation of life.

The summons of death: The full image here is that of death as personified, demanding that the victim appear before him. The dying person is seen as going away unwillingly, even being pulled away by an external agent. "Summons" also has a legal sense and perhaps suggests imminent judgment for the dying person.

Be taken: This phrase suggests the metaphor of death as an event in which the person is pulled away from his earthly existence by an external agent, not necessarily personified.

Snuffed out: Used when a dying appears to be "easy" and "quick." Another metaphor is in the background: life as a fire or light. Death occurs when "the candle of life" is "quenched" or "extinguished." At its root is the equation of death with stopping, with utter cessation. Agency is not necessarily implied.

Certain regularities began to appear in these analyses. Without being unnecessarily Procrustean, four different "themes" or "root metaphors" appeared to account for all the terms.

(1) The transit metaphor. The word "death" is employed to suggest a journey away, down, across or (sometimes specified, sometime not) travels under his own agency (i.e., willingly), though sometimes with help. (Examples are "demise" and "passing away.") Implied is a destination for the journey.

(2) The destructuring metaphor. The word "death" is employed to connote "falling apart" or "breaking up." Death is disorganization, structure breaking into its constituent parts. "Death" destructures life. Violence as represented in modern films and TV news reports of guerilla warfare reflect this root metaphor.

(3) The instrumentality metaphor. The word "death" is employed to convey the notion of "being pulled away." Death is personified, treated as an external agent. The victim is seen as being without power to resist, having no choice. (Examples are "summons of death,"the grim reaper," " be taken.")

(4) The terminus metaphor. "Stopping" is the central meaning. Death is thought to be the "terminus," the event (as opposed to process), the point in time in which becoming is suspended. Stopping or cessation has submetaphors: "sleep," "quenching," perhaps even "falling." "Stopping" may or may not involve agency. (An example is "snuffed out." Another example is the child who cried "no more" on seeing a caterpillar stomped.)

This four-fold classification is not a simple one. Beyond the four basic concepts, one may discern a number of logical dimensions in the underlying "structure." Each root metaphor can be seen as a different combination of dimensions. The most general of these dimensions appear to be:

Consequent dimension: Death is thought to be followed by continuation, passage, survival (personal or impersonal) in an "afterlife" or by non-continuation, utter cessation, "nonbeing."

Evaluative expectancy dimension: People may see death as something to be feared; or to be faced with hope.

Agency dimension: This is actually two dimensions: death may entail agency or no agency; and if the former, then the agency may be external or internal.

Duration dimension: Death is a becoming, an ongoing process or bounded in time.

Point-of-view dimension: Death may be considered from the point of view of others, objectively, with reference to activity; or it may be imagined from the subjective viewpoint, phenomenologically, with reference to the experience of one's own death.

The complexity of classification is further demonstrated by the fact that each root metaphor of "death" draws most heavily on a typological arrangement of the various dimensions. For example, the root metaphor "transit" represents discriminations by using the first three dimensions: consequents, evaluative expectancy and agency. In this case, the metaphor is indifferent to the point-of-view and the duration dimensions.

Combinations of metaphors may occur. Traditional Christianity includes both transit (to Heaven) and instrumentality (being pulled to Hell, or to judgment) metaphors. It appears that no metaphor is completely adequate to do justice to the ambiguity, mystery, obscurity and complexity of the abstraction "death."

The four-fold model of course cannot necessarily be extended to other linguistic systems. The root metaphors of Eastern cultures may be constructed from different basic categories and the metaphors for death may connote a different set of structures.

IV

Now to return to symbolic death as the central feature in systems of conduct reorganization. Earlier I remarked that the ambiguity of the term "symbolic death" was a problem to the practitioner of self-reconstruction. If the four-fold metaphor analysis is valid, then it is reasonable to assume that the subject of the behavior change enterprise, whether he be called client, convert, or exercitant, has acquired at least one of the pupillary metaphors of death. When symbolic "death" is communicated either explicitly or through implication, then, the convert's metaphor and associated imaginings are activated.

Of special interest to the practitioners and theorists of conduct reorganization are the individual differences in response to the treatment. What would be the probable outcomes of self-reconstitution processes for persons with different interpretations of the abstract term "death"?

On examination, the "symbolic death" as employed in our model and "death" as an abstraction are not very different semantically. Both are abstractions. It is the context of usage that is different: "symbolic death" is communicated in a setting that warrants that dying of the biological sort is not required, whereas the abstraction "death" ordinarily presupposes antecedent biological dying. Communicated to the client is the distinction between the termination of life of the organic body, cessation of breathing, etc., and the death of a person. It is clear that the sacral surround of death has little connection with the mechanics of organic degeneration but is yet intimately connected to the recognition that a person, by definition an integral part of a system of persons, undergoes a status transformation.

In symbolic dying, the subject participates in a ritual that demands his constructing a set of imaginings, indeed the imaginings are so vivid, that the subject can respond to them in the same way that he responds to more common perceptual objects. The concept that carries this meaning is "believed-in imaginings."

For the person symbolically to die, then, demands his involved participation in an imaginary drama. If he is to "die," then, his imaginings must be related to his prior experiences with "dying" and with the related abstraction "death." The antecedent experiences for "dying," of course, are those first hand and vicarious experiences with persons or other animate beings who at one point in time were characterized as "living," and at another point in time as "dead."

A brief resume of a case history will help illustrate my argument. Henry Holmes, age 24, a veteran of the Korean war, was paralyzed from the hips down as the result of wounds suffered in combat. He was assigned to a veterans' hospital where the medical and nursing personnel effectively applied their skills. However, the paralysis was permanent and it was clear that Henry would remain a wheel chair invalid for the rest of his life. He was depressed and refused to participate in the recreational and occupational opportunities afforded amputees and other orthopedic patients. He was assigned to the psychological service for study and evaluation. The history was a telling one: Henry had been an outstanding athlete in school and an accomplished outdoorsman; he had worked as a woodsman in lumber camps. He was of brawny build, over six feet in height. A high school teacher had used the adjective "rugged" as a one word description of Henry.

The therapy, carried out by a young male psychiatric resident, was intended to lift the depression so Henry could participate in vocational retraining. For several months, no progress was reported. A new therapist was assigned, a woman social worker. For reasons unknown, during the first meeting, Henry who until now had been taciturn and nearly apathetic in demeaner, began to weep. Between sobs he cried, "I'm dead!" Then in a prolonged interview that lasted two or three hours, he communicated that the role of the vigorous outdoorsman was the only role he could imagine for himself. He had equated life with a style of living and death with any possible alternative.

The weeping persisted on and off for two or three days. At this point I participated in the therapy as a consultant. In the course of the interview I inquired about the prolonged weeping: he dried his tears, thought for a moment, and said softly and sadly, "I'm crying for my dead self."

For the same reason that grief work is a necessary condition for reestablishing equilibrium in the social group after a person's dying, so is it necessary for the symbolic death of the self. For Henry, the diacritical definition of self was strength and physical endurance. That self--that set of beliefs and images--could no longer be affirmed by action.

The energies of the therapeutic team were now directed to Henry's recognition that the self was dead, and that the act of dying had to be commemorated. With the aid of the therapist, a rebirth had to occur. The clinical notes were sketchy, and if one were to construct an inference about Henry's choice of metaphor for death, it would probably have been the destructuring metaphor. Having participated in hand-to-hand combat and witnessing "destructuring" of bodies at first hand undoubtedly played a part. Using directed imagery, the therapist began a program that emphasized death as a transit, calling on Henry's earlier religious training, and also on his having participated in various rites of passage. A clergyman was called in to give another perspective. The aim was to restructure Henry's belief system to make credible the metaphor of transit, of passing from one status to another. The details of Henry's rehabilitation are not germane to our present concern. I will say only that the social worker who continued as his therapist often spoke of being midwife at the birth of a new self.

Earlier, I said that self-reconstitution was a consequent of symbolic dying Further, in connection with the psychological methods for achieving the symbolic death, I referred to various degradation procedures that transvalue a man or a woman from a valued person to a non-person. A number of observations demonstrate that legal commitment procedures and the successive degradations that occur in the interest of management of mental hospital patients fit the description of symbolic death--especially where the assault is made on the identity of self as person in a world of reciprocally acting persons. Query: why the numerous failures in self-reconstitution when there is little question that a symbolic dying has occurred? From observations of hospital practice, it is clear that little effort is made deliberately to employ the symbolic dying as a step toward reconstitution. Whatever metaphors for symbolic death the patient might have employed earlier, the context of commitment and the practices of hospitalization emphasize the terminus metaphor. Such a pessimistic outcome may be thwarted, however, if a guide or therapist makes use of directed imaginings and makes credible the transit metaphor--that symbolic death is a necessary preparation for rebirth. There is abundant case material to support the hypothesis that significant personal reorganization can occur when conditions are established for the symbolic death of a self and for a rebirth or renewal.

The present metaphoric analysis has pragmatic implications for the therapist, director, shaman or other behavior change agent. The analysis provides a guide for making symbolic death credible. The self-reconstitution process deals with involved imaginings, and the therapist's job is to direct the imaginings so they are believed-in.

The imaginings will be more credible if the client's metaphor for "death" carries the potential for rebirth. Of the four root metaphors, the transit metaphor is most congruent with the theme of death-and-rebirth. The client who already perceives death as a passage from one status to another--all things being considered--is more likely to experience a rebirth than the client who perceives death through the metaphors of destructuring, terminus, or instrumentality. To the extent that the director or guide or therapist can dissolve the pupillary metaphors of the client and make them more like the transit metaphor, to that extent is the prognosis favorable for successful conduct reorganization. However, I am not sanguine about the ease of bringing dead metaphors back to life.

One might argue that theological metaphors and "irrational" ritual would be rejected by most sophisticated potential clients. Of course, this is an empirical question that can be examined by appropriate experiments. In the meantime, I would propose to the skeptic that he examine, for example, his own conduct when reading a novel, or viewing a play or a movie. If he becomes involved in his imaginings, he can hate the villain, weep upon the unfolding of the tragic destiny of the hero, and dry a tear of compassion when the alienated son and his long-suffering father are reunited in a deathbed scene. In short, all of us possess the psychological, i.e., imagining, skill for participating as clients in self-reconstitution.

It has been suggested that conduct reorganization based on symbolic death and rebirth metaphors might be ineffective because the historical epoch has passed when religious metaphors had the power to evoke conduct. Empirical tests may ratify this suggestion. However, it is not the religious content that is central, but the fact that involved imaginings are made believable. Scientists reared in the tough-minded traditions of the laboratory and in the use of "objective" vocabularies may reject out of hand my free use of the lexicon of religion and humanism. My justification is a simple one: The complexity of the process of drastic personal change demands a conceptual apparatus appropriate to the task--if the task calls for a vocabulary rejected by behavior science, then we have no choice but to return to the more congenial, if less rigorous, language of the humanists.

Footnote

1. This paper has not been published previously. It is based on a lecture given at the center of Humanities, Wesleyan University, on March 17, 1975.

14

THE ROOT METAPHOR OF METAPHORS: APPLICATION TO PSYCHOLOGICAL PROBLEMS[1]

> "To language, then--to language alone--it is that fictitious entities owe their existence, their impossible, yet indispensable existence."
> (Bentham)

The purpose of the present chapter is to extend my observations about the use of metaphor in psychological theory and practice. I shall make clear as I go along that the study of metaphor as a cognitive process, as well as a rhetorical act, is central to the vitality of contemporary psychology. A conclusion that will follow from the following argument is that increased attention to "poesis" may help psychology return to its place as one of the humanistic studies.

A review of the history of psychology would show that the topic of metaphor has been of peripheral interest to "practitioners of the normal science."[2] I use Kuhn's expression "normal science" to accent the claim that the overarching paradigm of twentieth century psychology--the mechanistic world view--cannot assimilate a topic central to the concern of humanistic scholarship.

I intend to show how certain topics in contemporary psychology can be illuminated through the application of the "root metaphor of metaphor." I have a two-fold task: (1) to stake out some approximate boundaries for metaphor, and (2) to demonstrate the application of metaphorical analysis to selected psychological problems, making use of a four-fold classification of metaphor. (A program for uncovering the psychology of metaphor will be discussed in the next chapter.)

Several years ago, in the course of developing some ideas about the origins of contemporary conceptions in psychology, I discovered the utility of the concept, metaphor. The results of my utilization of the concept are elaborated elsewhere. At this point, I need say only that the working conceptions of psychologists, like the working conceptions of other scientists, begin with metaphor. An event arouses the curiosity of a scientist (or layman); he has no literal term at hand to denote the event; he casts about for a way of talking about the perplexing event; the result of his casting about is a metaphor.

What is the function of metaphor? The theories that address this question may be roughly divided into two classes: those that stress ornamentation and those that stress semantic growth. The ornamentation view has been tied to the work of grammarians and rhetoricians. The metaphor is constructed not because a literal statement is unavailable, but rather to satisfy aesthetic criteria and to modify the effect on an audience. The metaphor substitutes for the literal expression, hence the frequently used label, substitution theory. It is important to note that this regards metaphor-making as a "choice" and not a "necessity" phenomenon.

In contrast to the ornamentation or substitution theories are those that stress growth in meaning. The origins of these theories are attributed to Hermogenes (c. 170 A.D.) (Chun, 1970; Stanford, 1936). Associated with the idea of metaphor as a means of semantic growth is the hypothesis that metaphor is a necessary feature of human communication. Literal language (which on reflection is little more than a lexicon of dead metaphors) is too feeble to convert the features of the constantly changing world of occurrences. Metaphor provides the only avenue for communicating novelty.

My approach to metaphor makes use of the writings of, among others, Black (1962), Wheelright (1962), Wittgenstein (1959), Whorf (1956), Richards (1936), Turbayne (1962), and Burke (1945, 1966). Clearly, I am on the side of those who break from the traditions of the grammarians and who look upon metaphor as a psychological process. The latter term does not mean that metaphor must be placed in a world of mysterious mental or psychic processes, but rather that metaphor is a human action. Constructing or interpreting a metaphor is something a person does. It requires work, effort, involvement.

Several technical metaphors have been advanced to help communicate about metaphor. Most common is the pair of words, tenor and vehicle, introduced by Richards (1936). Perhaps less opaque are the terms used by Black (1962), focus and frame. Downey (1929) wrote of principal and subsidiary terms. More recent writers employ continuous term and discontinuous term (Sapir and Crocker, 1977). "Literal" and "figurative" do the work for Perrine (1971).

While metaphors may be classified in many ways, e.g., as parts of speech, or in terms of content, the classification most useful to me is that suggested by Perrine. In addition to the literal-figurative dichotomy, he proposes a second dichotomy, expressed-implied. Conjoining the two dimensions yields four classes or types of metaphors.

Perrine's calling attention to implicit features of metaphor has broad application for the human sciences. As I shall point out presently, the fact that one or both terms may

	Literal	Figurative
Class I	Expressed	Expressed
Class II	Expressed	Implied
Class III	Implied	Expressed
Class IV	Implied	Implied

be unexpressed, but inferable from context, is central to a large number of human actions.

Metaphor may be employed as a model to enlarge our understanding of the actions of people. The following pages make use of Perrine's four-fold classification to promote a heuristic program. To emphasize that action is implicit in metaphor, I have made use of the popular word "encounter."

Metaphorical Encounters of the First Kind: Figurative and Literal Terms Are Both Expressed. Discussions of metaphor generally use Class I metaphors as illustrations. In the sentence, "The sky is an inverted bowl," "The sky" is the focus, the continuous term, the literal expression, "the inverted bowl" is the figurative. The speaker intends that the listener give a special geometric form to the amorphous "sky." In the fusion theory, the imagery called out by "sky" is contained in the imagery of "the bowl." Further, the possibility exists that features of the figurative term other than its spatial features may constrain the imagery of sky. For example, its ceramic properties (brittleness) may serve figurative functions, "the sky is breakable," being a potential, if unlikely, metaphor.

Nowhere is the employment of Class I metaphors more apparent than in the activities of scientists. Finding no literal terms to communicate about puzzling observations, the scientist (like Everyman) falls back upon metaphor. Sometimes the metaphors are extended, i.e., the scientist links chains of metaphors together to make use of imagery of great diversity, not unlike the work of poets and other imaginative writers. The basic formula is "A" is "B," usually derived from "A" is like "B." "A" is the observations, the thing or process to be communicated about, the literal term; "B" is the figurative term. When conjoined in a sentence, a metaphor emerges.

From the recognition that scientists cannot carry out their missions without metaphors, it follows that scientists who put their observations on paper are imaginative writers. Especially illuminating in this connection is the work of Stanley Edgar Hyman who applied the methods of literary criticism to the writings of Darwin, Marx, Frazer, and Freud. Darwin, for example, not only was a prolific metaphor maker, but was aware of the necessity for metaphor. Darwin wrote of the key term, "the struggle for existence" in the Origin of Species.

...I use this term in a large and metaphorical sense including dependence of one being on another, including (which is more important) not only the life of the animal, but success in leaving progeny. Two canine animals, in a time of death, may be truly said to struggle with each other which shall get food and life. But a plant on the edge of the desert is said to struggle for life against the drought, though more properly it should be said to be more dependent on the moisture. A plant which annually produces a thousand seeds, of which only one. . .comes to maturity, may be more truly said to struggle with the plants of the same and other kinds which already clothe the ground (Darwin, quoted by Hyman, 1966).

Hyman goes on to show with remarkable clarity that Darwin rather than his biological observations supplied a dramatic and tragic vision. Modern discussions of natural selection lack the dramatic quality of Darwin's metaphor—strewn writings. A modern textbook writer would avoid such expressions as "there is grandeur in this view of life," "the war of nature is not incessant."

Hyman writes: "The book's final paragraph achieves the ultimate transformation. It begins: 'It is interesting to contemplate a tangled bank, clothed with many plants of many kinds, with birds singing on the bushes, with various insects flitting about, and with worms crawling through the damp earth, and to reflect that these elaborately constructed forms, so different from each other, and dependent on each other in so complex a manner, have all been produced by laws acting around us.'"

"With the image of the tangled bank," Hyman continues, "so reminiscent of Shakespearean lyric, Darwin embraces all the rich complexity of life. The image of the great Chain of Life is ordered, hierarchic, and static, essentially medieval; the great Tree of Life is ordered, hierarchic, but dynamic and competitive, a Renaissance vision; but the great Tangled Bank of Life is disordered, democratic, and subtly interdependent as well as competitive, essentially a modern vision." (pp. 32-33)

I have included these excerpts from Darwin and from Hyman's interpretations as support for the argument that scientists begin their work with metaphor. And the metaphoric constructions are more than ornamental, more than substitutions for other available literal expressions, they are the stuff of which dramatic visions and action-provoking myths are made. They excite the listener to action. Note how imagery and imagination enter into Darwin's metaphors. Any reader of recent textbooks in biology would likely entertain the question: Why is the theory of evolution, such an abstract, prosaic, literal account? Where have the metaphors gone?

A partial answer to these questions is deferred until the next chapter. At this point I remind the reader that the natural history of vocabulary is from the poetic to the literal, from the concrete to the abstract, from lively images to static concepts. To demonstrate the abstract quality of contemporary terms employed by psychologists, I need only list the following: stimulus, response, reinforcement, emotion, drive, intelligence, association, hypnosis, hysteria, schizophrenia, attribution.

Were a historian to trace these common terms to their first use in the context of accounting for human conduct, he would perforce conclude that they were forged in an act of poesis. In the context of being repeatedly handed down from master to pupil as explanatory concepts rather than poetic metaphors, they became separated from their sustaining imagery. When a contemporary scholar employs "stimulus," it is not likely that he constructs an image of a small stick used as a goad. For "response," it is not likely that he forms images of one person answering another. For "drive," it is not likely that he generates a fancy of a drover "driving" a herd of cattle to pasture.

It is more likely that these terms are employed as parts of verbal or mathematical formulae, as units in conceptual schemata, as symbols in arrow-filled diagrams, etc. To recapitulate, metaphors of the first kind abound in all efforts to communicate about events for which the concurrent lexicon is inadequate. The scientific enterprise, constrained as it is by demands for objectivity, clarity, and precision, begins with poetic metaphors and ends with abstract concepts. As I shall argue in the next Chapter, the scientist may lose sight of the metaphorical origins of the abstraction, and re-interpret a poetic metaphor as literal truth, thereby preparing the ground for illicit reification and myth making.

Metaphorical Encounters of the Second Kind: The literal term is Expressed, the Figurative Term to be Inferred.(3) An especially striking example of Class II metaphor is contained in Victor Turner's account of Thomas Becket at the Council of Northampton in 1164. The story of Henry II and Becket has been told many times. The complex political, theological and personal cross-currents that led to the confrontation need not detain us. The relevant feature of Turner's analysis for our purposes is his premise that political action is ritual drama mediated by metaphors. One episode is of special interest.

Becket, upon entering the Castle, insisted on bearing the archiepiscopal cross, rather than follow the custom of having his official cross bearer perform the ceremonial task. Becket's bishops remonstrated because they saw this action as an overt metaphoric threat against the king, the ultimate result of which would be the impossibilty of a reconciliation between the two antagonists.

In the language of our present analysis, the archiespiscopal cross is the literal term, a part of the ceremonial structure. At one time, of course, the cross had been a live metaphor. Through time and repetition its metaphoric quality had been dimmed. (I am reminded of the once metaphoric but now literal effect of the American flag in courtrooms; and similarly, of the ceremonial singing of the National Anthem at National Football League games.)

Given the literal status of Becket's carrying the cross, what figurative term is to be inferred? In the context of Northampton, the figurative term was a composite: the protection from Henry's menacing barons and also the pageant that depicted Becket as the Lord carrying the Cross.

In the foregoing illustration, it is clear that metaphor need not be limited to written textual materials or verbal utterances. The speech act makes sense only in the context of other actions.

In contemporary political discourse, the use of Class II metaphors presents some interesting problems. That the politicians' adroit use of metaphor can influence the public is hardly in need of documentation.(4) Edelman (1967) has presented a balanced argument demonstrating the rhetorical power of political metaphors. "A politician more persuasively conveys a particular picture of reality when he simply assumes it in the terms he uses rather than asserting it explicitly" (p. 219). During the Viet Nam conflict, so-called hawks asserted that the American presence was a "defense of freedom" against communist aggression. In our vocabulary, this statement was intended as the literal term of a metaphor, the figurative term of which was to be inferred; to wit, that Americans were helping a valiant liberty-loving people who were shoulder-to-shoulder in their resistance to foreign aggression and invasion.

Ritualistic conduct of an idiosyncratic kind becomes subject to rational interpretation when seen as a Class II metaphor. Consider Lady Macbeth's handwashing compulsion. In the somnambulism scene, in the presence of the doctor and the gentlewoman, she is engaged in handwashing actions, and she exclaims "Out, damn'd spot! Out, I say!" (Act V, Line 38). It is clearly a literal statement; handwashing motions are literal actions. The figure is readily inferred from the context, Lady Macbeth's complicity in the assassination of the King. In the act of placing the bloodied daggers on the innocent grooms, she had soiled herself with blood. She had washed the blood from her hands on the night of the murder. In the context of her developing madness the efforts to rid herself of the imagined spot was an oblique way of cleansing herself of guilt.

In the foregoing paragraphs, I have suggested how metaphor is intimately involved in the political sphere and in the analysis of specific bits of deviant conduct of literary figures.

My final illustration of Class II metaphors attempts to show the utility of metaphoric analysis in the study of certain so-called psychiatric symptoms that emphasize ritualistic conduct. The idea has been suggested before that psychiatric symptoms are metaphors (e.g., Haley, 1971; Muncie, 1937). The illustration below makes use of the formulation that parts of the metaphor may be tacit.

When I was serving as a clinical psychologist, I conducted a psychological assessment of a 30—year-old man who could not speak. He could make vowel sounds, he could write messages, but he could not utter words or sentences. The dysphonia had begun seven years before. He had been assaulted and battered by four or five unknown assailants and left unconscious. Among the multiple traumata was a left hemisphere concussion. When he regained consciousness in the hospital, a few days later, he was unable to speak. The dysphonia was attributed to damage to the speech center of the brain.

The background of the case was pieced together from conversations with the client's wife and from written responses to my queries. He had been a police officer in a large western city for about a year. He had been induced by members of the crime commission to testify against his precinct captain who had been indicted on a number of felonies. He agreed reluctantly. A few days before the trial, he was going off duty at midnight when he was ambushed in the station parking lot.

The client and his wife were unable to offer clues to help in the identification of the assailants. I should mention that even without the client's testimony the police captain had been convicted and sentenced to a long term in the state prison.

Unable to continue as a police officer because of his speech disorder, the client took a job that demanded no vocal skills: operating a power lawn mower in the city parks department. It was in connection with his desire to prepare himself for more remunerative work that he was referred to me. He had consulted a counselor in the State Department of Rehabilitation who wanted a psychological assessment to help in decision-making. I saw him about four or five times and we established a warm relationship. My assessment, after reviewing his scores on standard tests and his responses in writing to a large number of questions, was that he was a man of better than average intellectual skills, good motor coordination, and otherwise quite unremarkable. His conduct and the absence of any obvious neurological impairment suggested no brain pathology.

Having completed the assessment I offered to try to help him regain his speech. I was working from the hypothesis that the dysphonia was not the result of cerebral injury, but was "psychological," i.e., was serving some covert purpose. In another language, the speech disorder was a doing, rather than a happening.

He agreed to be a subject for hypnotic therapy. He was too apprehensive, however, and after three efforts to guide his imaginings, this form of treatment was suspended. Instead, we decided on the use of intravenous sodium amytal as an aid to our efforts. A medical colleague joined me and the drug was administered. My plan was to try to learn what happened on the night of the assault, the identity of the assailants, and, most important, what purpose was being served by the dysphonia. The drug was administered slowly and had stopped at the point where the client was not quite asleep. I asked: "What happened on the night of January 14?" No reply. My medical colleague repeated the question. Still no response. More sodium amytal was administered. The question was repeated. Some phonation and gurgling from the client but no formed words. For about 30 minutes we persisted but without success. I was frustrated and disappointed, and, because of the monotonous repetitions of the single question, bored. I decided to discontinue the experiment. As if to mock my own repetitions of the question, in a sing-song voice, somewhat like an operatic recitativo I uttered what was to have been the final repetition. Immediately, the client sat up on the couch and without a moment's hesitation answered the question in detail. My medical colleague and I both continued asking questions in recitativo and the client gave full and clear responses in normal speech with suitable expressions of affect. The client continued to speak normally even after the effects of the amytal had dissipated. The details of his account are not germane to our present purposes, save that the assailants were police officers loyal to the captain, some of whom were still on the force.

I have tried a number of formulations to account for the development of the "symptom" and the sudden and dramatic change. None is as convincing to me as a metaphorical analysis.

When the client was ambushed, his fellow officers communicated both verbally and non-verbally that he was not to "sing." "Singing" was then, and is now, a slang term employed by the underworld and by the police to denote informing. "To sing" was originally a live metaphor for informing; through constant use it has become a literal term in the lexicon of the underworld and the police. Like any slang word, its vitality depends on novelty, a condition that no longer holds. The figurative term must be inferred—a complex image of informing, followed by negative evaluation of peers, accusation of disloyalty, and threats to survival. Under the conditions of extreme organismic involvement, the literal and the figurative terms, ordinarily held in tension through the use of an "as if" framework, had been isolated from each other. His focus of attention was clearly on heeding the admonition "don't sing," supported initially by the inarticulateness that followed the concussion. Taking "don't sing" literally (meaning "don't inform") had survival value.

To account for the sudden reversal of behavior, we must focus on the meaning he attributed to my singing. To my ordinary talk, he gave no response. Only when I sang in the ordinary literal sense did he "sing" in the figurative sense. I have already mentioned that we had established a warm and trusting relationship. It is probable that the client—who at the moment was a person who had a very inefficient (drugged) cerebral system—interpreted my singing as the vehicle for bringing back into metaphoric tension the equivalence of singing and informing.

This interpretation follows from a general theory of metaphor that I shall discuss later. In brief, I propose that metaphor is created when an utterance (or text) embraces a contradiction or paradox. Of special interest to psychologists are the various strategies for resolving or containing contradictions. One of these strategies is illustrated in the foregoing case summary: under conditions of great organismic involvement, the initial dysphonia resulted from the active denial of the tacit figurative term, "don't inform," and the concomitant dissolution of the metaphor. That such a formulation might illuminate those observations denoted by the opaque term "unconscious" has been hinted at by Szasz (1961), and by the French psychoanalyst, Jacques Lacan (in Ehrmann, 1970).

The foregoing examples of Class II metaphors have been presented to show the relevance of metaphoric interpretation to certain problems of a psychological nature: political influence and acts, ritual performances, and deviant conduct.

Metaphorical Encounters of the Third Kind: The Figurative Term   is Expressed, the Literal Term Must be Inferred.   Perrine gives a number of illustrations of Class III metaphors, pointing to a potential problem in interpretation, to wit, the utterance can easily be interpreted as literal. He uses a line from Romeo and Juliet:

"Night's candles are burned out."

The sentence makes good sense when interpreted literally: "candles that were lit to illuminate the dark hours are burned out." But in its context, the literal interpretation is inept. Romeo, looking toward the sky, says:

Look love, what envious streaks
Do lace the severing clouds in younder East
Night's candles are burnt out and Day
Stands tiptoe on the misty mountain tops.

The passage communicates the approach of dawn, "night's candles" are the dimming stars.

Included in Class III metaphors is the proverb. A figurative statement is uttered; the hearer must infer the literal component from the context. In one context a statement is literal, in another metaphorical.

Consider, in different contexts, the proverb "you can lead a horse to water, but you can't make him drink."

A rider dismounts and leads his horse to the water trough. The horse does not drink. A spectator says "you can lead a horse to water but you can't make him drink."

A college student writes to a friend: It took a great deal of effort and planning to persuade Frank to accompany us to the dance pavillion. In spite of his extreme shyness, we pushed him through the turnstile and guided him to one of the eager hostesses. Angrily, he turned and bolted out the door. You can lead a horse to water but you can't make him drink.

In the first context the statement is literal. In the second, the same statement is metaphoric. A third context would lead to an interpretation that is partly figurative and partly literal: John had never experimented with alcoholic beverages in any form, although drinking "booze" was a common practice in his fraternity house. One night he was persuaded to join his fraters at the local pub. A round of beers was ordered. John steadfastly refused to bring the glass to his lips. You can lead a horse to water but you can't make him drink.

Given that proverbs are interpretable only in context, it is a source of wonderment that they have been included in intelligence tests and in psychiatric examinations sans context. The inclusion of a proverb in a test of psychological functioning is based on a tenuous and probably unexamined assumption, namely, that the ability to treat a literal statement as metaphorical is independent of experience with specific proverbs.

The interpretation of proverbs has been a staple item in intelligence tests from the beginning of the mental testing movement (Terman, 1916). Proverbs have been used in psychiatric examinations at least since the 1930's. Benjamin (1944) reported on the use of proverbs as part of the mental status examination. A number of proverbs were listed in the mental examiner's handbook. The failure of a patient to break out of a literal set and interpret a proverb to the satisfaction of the examiner was taken as putative evidence of cognitive malfunction and a diagnosis of schizophrenia or organic brain disorder could be entertained. With the development of Goldstein's attributes of "abstract" and "concrete" (Goldstein and Scheerer, 1941), interpretations of proverbs could be conceptualized as abstract (i.e., efficient, "good" functioning) or concrete (i.e., inefficient, or "bad" functioning). Parenthetically, the attributes, "concrete" and "abstract," although characterized by an inherent vagueness and ambiguity, have been uncritically assimilated into psychiatric terminology as a pair of basic "givens."

In the 1950's Gorham (1956) employed a large number of proverbs to develop scoring norms, using the concrete-abstract dimension. Further, he developed a set of paper and pencil forms for ease of administration. The proverbs were graded according to difficulty; "Don't count your chickens before they are hatched," e.g., being easier to interpret, on the average, than e.g., "a new broom sweeps clean" or "a rolling stone gathers no moss."

Unlike anthropologists and students of belle lettres, mental health professionals who employ proverbs in the diagnostic examination have not been interested in developing ideas about the semiotic function of proverbs, nor the social conditions that would lead to an understanding of individual differences in interpreting proverbs. Psychiatric examiners, by and large, appear to operate from the assumption that knowledge of proverbs and the ability to interpret them is a universal attribute of mankind. Therefore, when a patient interprets the "rolling stones" proverb as "that's right, when a stone is rolling, it can't gather any moss," it is assumed that the patient's mental functioning is impaired. The corollary assumption is that all "normals" are able to offer a proper abstract interpretation.

In a folk culture where communication is mainly oral, proverbs and other metaphoric forms, such as riddle and aphorism, contain the folk wisdom. Values of the society are communicated in such easily remembered forms. But in cultures not exclusively oral, the employment of metaphoric bits of folk wisdom is likely to be minimal. Casual observation of urban middle-class citizens suggests that proverbs are seldom employed to convey values and wisdom to children. In one family I studied where the daughter "failed" a proverbs test, neither the father (Ph.D.) nor the mother (B.A.), could remember ever having used proverbs in talking to their children. Individual differences in interpreting proverbs are to be expected, then, and scores on a proverb test in part reflect one's prior experiences with proverbs.

In addition to differential contact with proverb-users, a second source of variability in interpreting proverbs may be identified: metaphoric skills. As indicated before, the task for the interpreter is to translate the metaphoric subject and metaphoric predicate into statements that contain general implications. It seems reasonable to posit that persons with linguistic competence would more likely discover and employ the translation formula: to find a cultural value, and convert it to a literal statement the subject and predicate of which are related by analogy to the metaphors of the proverb.

A third variable in the quality of interpretation of proverbs is the social context of testing. It is one thing to test a sample of students on a paper and pencil test for research purposes. It is another to test a patient in a clinical setting where the patient's future may be decided on the basis of answers to such questions as: "What does the following proverb mean?--It's an ill wind that blows nobody some good." In the research case, the subject has little to gain or lose in constructing meanings from such metaphorical sentences. He can afford to guess and to try out various formulae for transforming figurative to literal statements. In the clinical case, the patient has much to gain or lose. If the patient infers that improper interpretations could lead to negative consequences, e.g., more shock therapy, he might say, "I don't know." The psychiatric examiner may take this response as putative evidence that the patient does not have the "abstract attitude," and therefore in need of some (usually) chemical, surgical or electrical intervention.

I have suggested three variables to account for differences in performance on tests that call for the interpretation of proverbs. The first is exposure to the oral tradition. Persons reared in a folk culture will more likely have engaged in performances where proverbs are uttered. The second is the degree of strain imposed by the task. If the cost/reward ratio is high, as in the clinical examination, the patient's attention may be directed away from the cognitive work and the interpretation may be an "I don't know" or an apparently safe restatement of the proverb. The third variable is metaphoric skill. The particular form of skill may be called the readiness to use the as-if formulation, where the interpreter quickly recognizes that the terms of the proverb are metaphors, tht they are not to be taken literally, but must stand as an expression of some cultural value.

For the third source of variation, metaphorical skill, I present some data serendipitously derived from a study conducted in collaboration with John S. Watson (1967). We arranged various combinations of proverbs--ten to a sheet--and asked student volunteers to write interpretations.

Six of the proverbs on each sheet were taken from standard sources. They are from the pool of proverbs used by diagnosticians to assess cognitive functioning in psychiatric settings. The interpretations supplied by the students were scored according to established norms. The acceptable response for "barking dogs seldom bite" would be some variant of "people who make verbal threats seldom take action."

The remaining items on each sheet were "artificial" proverbs. Professor Watson and I put together items selected at random to form a nonsense statement that superficially resembled a proverb. The pool of "made-up" proverbs included, for example: "Wet hens lay small eggs;" "A long night makes a short day;" "Old nets catch small fish;" and "Mountain paths begin and end in the valley." As the reader can see, these nonsensical sentences are expressed in the rhetoric of proverbs, but have no intended metaphorical reference. (They were embedded in a list of standard proverbs, I should add.)

It is interesting to note in passing that ten percent of the 200 students were unable to interpret at least three of the standard proverbs according to published norms. If one subscribed to the view that literal (concrete) performance or non-performance is indicative of "schizophrenia," then these apparently well-functioning students would be candidates for professional intervention. A more parsimonious explanation is that these subjects had had no prior experience with the particular proverbs or were lacking in metaphorical skill.

Analysis of the interpretations of the made-up proverbs gave support to the hypothesis that metaphoric skill is a variable. Especially interesting were the subjects' interpretations of the "nonsense" of artificial proverbs; about half the subjects constructed at least one interpretation that could be classified as meaningful in that it represented some folk wisdom, some readily understood value. The inference is warranted that these subjects had acquired the rule for transposition: to wit, find an abstract value where the metaphoric subject and predicate of the proverb serve as concrete examplars for a literal proposition. Here are examples: For the artificial proverb "Wet hens lay small eggs," one student wrote, "One's productivity is reduced under conditions of emotional arousal (wet hens are mad!)." For the proverb, "Mountain roads begin and end in the valley," one student wrote, "between the beginning and the end of life, one must constantly struggle."

Like any other skill, there are individual differences in the quality of metaphoric decoding. To be sure, age is a correlate. One would also expect covariation with tests that tap other verbal problem-solving skills. Pollio and associates (1977) employed a large battery of verbal problem-solving tasks in an effort to discover correlates of the figurative ability. They concluded that figurative ability is an important component of verbal problem solving.

The foregoing illustrations of metaphorical encounters of the third kind underscore the constructive aspect of metaphorical thinking. When appropriate context is not provided for apparently anomalous or irrelevant sentences, the hearer will supply one from memory or construct one de novo. The implications for psychological theory and practice are obvious.

Metaphoric Encounters of the Fourth Kind: Neither the Figurative Nor the Literal Term is Expressed. The fourth class of metaphors requires more cognitive work from the hearer. Perrine gives several poetic examples, among them, the Biblical sentence, "Let us eat and drink, for tomorrow we shall die." The verb "shall die" expresses the literal component. "The supressed literal term is a lifetime and its figurative equivalent is one day. The general meaning is that life is very short" (Perrine, 1971). Neither the literal nor the figurative appear directly in the quotation--both must be inferred.

Another illustration offered by Perrine is Jacques' famous

speech in As You Like It: "All the world's a stage and the men and women merely players. They have their exits and their entrances . . . ." The speech is a series of metaphors of Class I and Class III. The several metaphors imply a general statement in which the suppressed literal term is "Life" and the suppressed figurative term is "theater." Shakespeare, in this place and elsewhere, is poetically conveying his dramatistic world view: life is theater. A play by a 19th century Russian playwright may be an extended, unexpressed metaphor for "life is futile."

Like the other classes of metaphor, Class IV is applicable to actions other than the writing or reading of poetry. It is my plan to show how hypnotism can be understood as a metaphoric encounter of the fourth kind. The conduct of both hypnotizer and subject, including their speech acts, follows from the mutual intentions of both parties. This co-intention is contained in a large metaphor the figurative and the literal components of which must be inferred.

Elsewhere I have reviewed the history of theories of hypnosis (Sarbin and Coe, 1972). Suffice it to say that most theories have been guided by the world view of mechanism. A modern alternate to theories generated by mechanistic postulates is role theory, guided by metaphors drawn from the theater. This approach, in brief, looks upon the actions of the subject as a dramatic performance. Not ignored in this formulation are the actions of the hypnotist. Each interactant is engaged in a role performance, the quality of the performance being related to some identifiable contextual constraints, e.g., prior knowledge of the role, cognitive and motoric skills. (For a more extended account see Sarbin and Coe, 1972.)

With this brief background I turn to my task: to show that a certain form of counter-expectational conduct (hypnosis) is an instance of Class IV metaphors. The defining criterion of metaphors of the fourth kind, to repeat, is the hidden, tacit, implicit, masked character of both the literal and figurative terms.

Let us begin by noting that the hypnotist talks to the subject. Although the hypnotist's talk appears to initiate the sequence of interactions, in actuality, the beginnings of the interactional segment are to be found in preliminary communications that lead to the person's stated or implied agreement to become a subject, client, or patient.

The style of the hypnotist's utterance may differ from his ordinary utterances in several ways. Changes in tempo are common: the hypnotist speaks more slowly than usual. Most hypnotists reduce their usual variations in pitch to a monotone. Words and phrases are repeated, incomplete sentences are expressed. The subject is confronted with the problem of making sense of these stylistic variations. The content includes a number of counter-factual statements, such as, "your arm is getting heavy," "you are floating," "you are becoming drowsy." Attending to these counter-factual statements along with his observation that the hypnotist talks in strange ways, the subject might covertly ask "what is the meaning of the hypnotist's communication?" The answer might be "Nonsense. My arms are not increasing in weight," in which case the subject and the hypnotist have no basis for continuing the interaction. An alternate answer to the question might be: "Since the hypnotist is dramatizing his talk to me, and is telling me things that I know are contrary-to-fact, maybe he is inviting me to play a game of let's-pretend-my-arms-are-heavy and also to pretend that it is serious business and not mere pretense. "By uttering these contrary-to-fact statements, he is casting me in a role for a theatrical enterprise." Such a hypothesis would follow from instantiating the counter-factual utterances as metaphors. "He wants me to perform as if my arms are heavy."

Within the context as pre-defined by both interactants the counter-factual statements of the hypnotist metaphorically serve the same function as the stage director's more literal instruction: "Sir Alec, you play the role of Lawrence." Children at play cast each other in roles also in literal language: one child agrees to enact the role of Dr. Welby and his playmate pretends to be the sick patient.

It is important to underscore the observation that both the hypnotist and the subject proceed by indirection. The induction recital is an extended metaphor, i.e., the various sentences contain metaphors of the other three classes. The overall metaphor is of the fourth type, and could be approximated thus: "This interaction between you and me is a miniature drama." Both participants enact their roles, neither describing the action as theater, neither expressing overtly the literal and the figurative terms.

The hidden metaphor in hypnosis is a special case of the Class IV metaphor already discussed: "Life is theater" employed in Shakespeare's "All the world's a stage. . ."

In recent years, the concept "hidden observer" has appeared as a descriptive category in hypnosis experiments. The instructions appear to be literal. A closer look suggests a metaphor of the fourth kind. The instructions include the following:

"When I place my hand on your shoulder, I shall be able to talk to a hidden part of you that knows things are going on in your body, things that are unknown to the part of you to which I am talking. . .
"

It would be more parsimonious to consider the instructions as metaphorical stage directions. I have already noted the dramatistic ambience in the hypnotic interaction. The stage directions metaphorically instruct the subject to shift his orientation from that of agent to that of spectator. The instruction to engage in the monodrama is not literal, it is an unexpressed metaphor: "You can be both actor and audience, performer and spectator."

Summary

When I began this chapter, the goal was to return a humanistic emphasis to psychology. Eschewing models derived from the mechanistic sciences, I sought inspiration and guidance from belles lettres. The belletristic orientation directed me to enlarge my views about poesis and to explore the world of metaphor. Although not a stranger to metaphor, I discovered a large number of problems of interest to psychologists the explication of which might be facilitated through the employment of metaphorical analysis. These problems were identified in terms of a fourfold classification developed by Perrine (1971). His recognition of the fact that one or both terms of a metaphorical expression can be tacit has numerous implications for the analysis of human conduct.

The foregoing application of a fourfold classification of metaphor is intended as heuristic. Special illustrations were selected to accent the suggestion that persisting psychological problems may be illuminated through metaphoric analysis. If we accept the claim that extended communication cannot occur without metaphor, and the associated claim that human action cannot be divorced from communication, then it behooves us to explore metaphoric analysis in depth. In the following chapter, I assemble some thoughts on the psychology of metaphor.

Footnotes
1. This paper has not been published previously. A portion of it was read to members and guests of the Center for the Humanities, Wesleyan University, April 26, 1978. I am grateful to the editors of this volume for suggesting that I bring together my ideas on metaphor, which are represented by this chapter and the following one. The present papers must differ from their expectations in that I found myself being pulled deeper and deeper into previously unexplored regions. For suggestions offered me at various stages of inquiry, I am grateful to a number of colleagues and friends, among them, Dr. Kitaek Chun, Professor Joseph B. Juhasz, Professor Henry Nash Smith, Professor Philip Hallie, Professor Marvin Rosenberg, Professor Joseph Silverman, Profesor Milton E. Andersen, Professor Stephen Friedman, and not least, the editors of this collection, Professors Vernon L. Allen and Karl E. Scheibe. I am grateful also to Jesue Salazar who served as my personal librarian with efficiency and good humor.
2. I am not unmindful of the work reported by Downey (1929), Werner (1948), Osgood (1961), Pollio (1977) and Ortony (1975) among others. Despite their fruitful efforts, a review of standard texts in psychology shows that little of this work has filtered into the "normal science."
3. It may not be necessary to caution the reader that it is impossible in all cases to maintain a clear-cut distinction between the literal and the figurative, the focus and the frame. Empson (1953) has suggested that as the number of possible meanings for metaphoric expressions increases, it becomes increasingly difficult to identify which serves as the literal and which as the figurative.
4. Ashcraft (1977) has written a cogent argument demonstrating the direction of political theory as a result of adopting economic metaphors". . .insofar as this language is used metaphorically as a means of establishing the nature and

purpose of political theory. . .it performs an ideological function similar to that Marx attributed to classical political economy, namely, presenting as a general or self-understood definition of political theory a type of political thinking, in which the fundamental characteristics of the existing socioeconomic system are uncritically assumed as given features of human existence" (pg. 316-317).

15

A PREFACE TO A PSYCHOLOGICAL
THEORY OF METAPHOR

As Grice (1975) has so well argued, conversations are governed by implicit rules. These rules are acquired in the course of socialization and enculturation. They serve to make communication optimal and to serve the needs of the participants, given that the purposes of speaker and hearer are complementary. Grice has formalized a set of maxims that function as rules in the governance of ordinary conversation, called the Cooperative Principle. Briefly stated, the interactants in a conversation tend to observe four maxims: Quantity, Quality, Relations, and Manner.

The maxim of quantity directs the participants to say what needs to be said, neither more nor less. The maxim of quality directs the speakers to utter true statements and to utter no statements that are believed to be untrue. The maxim of relation directs the speakers to be relevant. The maxim of manner directs the interactants to avoid obscurity and ambiguity.

Our interest in The Cooperative Principle is activated under conditions when the Principle is violated, when one or another speaker emits an utterance that violates the maxims of Quantity, Quality, Relations or Manner. For example, the violation of the maxim of Quantity is noted by the Queen in Hamlet when she remarks about The Player Queen, "the lady doth protest too much, methinks."

It is the non-observance of the maxims of the Cooperative Principle that gives rise to anomalies of communication. A problem is created for the hearer (or reader) when the maxims are not observed: to wit, how to make sense of an apparently anomalous utterance.(1)

The violation of any rule of conduct, especially an implicit rule, creates the conditions for the discontinuity of reciprocal conduct, for breakdown in cooperative action, for disharmony and embarassment. In short, rule violation imposes strain on the listener (or reader), and, reflexively, on the speaker. The strain is identifiable--it occurs in the domain of "knowing." When I hear the utterance "man is a wolf," I hear it against the definitions that I have already acquired about humans and about wolves. My first reaction is one of puzzlement, perplexity, and disbelief. I shall call this condition "kennetic strain" or "strain-in-knowing." It is induced by conditions that violate the Cooperative Principle. Thus any word, phrase, sentence, or action that is anomalous, that does not fit the concurrent context creates kennetic strain.(2) When the hearer's effort to make sense of an utterance is frustrated, kennetic strain occurs. It is as if he asks himself the question: "What is it?" and can construct no satisfactory answer.

To maintain the Cooperative Principle, the apparently non-instantiable, the anomalous, the incongruent, the not fitting input must be dealt with. If, for example, the discontinuous term or action can be regarded as an instance of the class "proverbs," the class "jokes," or the class "riddles," then the hearer can place a frame around the utterance or action and continue the conversation, or interpret the sentence or action in the light of the additional imagery or information provided by the proverb, joke, or riddle.

One theory holds that the principle condition for metaphor is that the figurative term be semantically anomalous (Kinsth, 1972). Ortony, Reynolds, and Arter (1978) have argued convincingly that semantically anomalous utterances aré instantiable as nonsense unless the written or spoken context provides a frame for making sense of the utterance. They suggest that metaphor be conceptualized as a speech act that is contextually or pragmatically anomalous and that the tension generated by the perception of the anomaly be resolvable. The order of events would be: (1) the utterance; (2) the attempt to make sense of the utterance as literal; (3) the creation of tension when the literal meaning results in nonsense or paradox; (4) the elimination of the tension through reinterpreting the anomalous term as figurative, i.e., metaphor.

A sticky problem is contained in this sequence of events. The implicit definitions employed by the hearer in assigning a contextually anomalous utterance to the class "metaphor" are hardly ever made public. It is probable that a hearer's criteria for metaphor (and for nonsense) may vary with contextual features such as degree of involvement, fatigue, risk attached to violating the maxim of quality that utterances be true, etc.

A clue to the hearer's criteria of metaphor may be gleaned from the definitional efforts of linguistic scholars: metaphor is a word or phrase from one domain of discourse applied to an event in another domain. Turbayne's (1962) term "sort crossing" is an apt description. On analysis, the definition contains an essential ambiguity--what are the boundaries to any particular domain?

The concept of domain or universe of discourse cannot be defined in any a priori deterministic way. "That man is a pygmy" contains two terms from the same domain if the speaker and hearer are engaged in a conversation about African anthropology. The same terms are from different domains if the context leads the hearer to interpret "pygmy" as an epithet for meager moral attainments.

The domain-of-discourse definition leads to the inference that the meaning to the hearer is the same as the intention of the metaphor-maker. This inference makes metaphor interpretation a passive process, essentially contained in the structure of language. I want to suggest that the hearer must work to make sense of a speech act, no less than when he is confronted with any bit of conduct that is at first noninstantiable. The hearer must engage in actions, to be sure, actions that are ordinarily covert. These actions are probably of two kinds: (1) searching for a class into which the anomalous act may be instantiated; is it a joke, a pun, a maxim, a proverb, a metonymy, a personalization, a synechdoche, an irony, a metaphor, or is it nonsense? (2) searching of the context for clues that may narrow the possible number of classes.

I propose to turn the traditional model around. Instead of the formulation that metaphor occurs with the relief of tension created by the use of a word in an alien domain, I suggest that we begin with the concept of kennetic strain as the essential ingredient of metaphor. In the most obvious case, the conditions that produce strain are those that pose a contradiction of two propositions. The classic example of contradiction is the type of metaphor known as the oxymoron, where the figurative term implies or expresses a contradiction to the implication of the literal term. Some examples are: "mute evidence," "cornerless box," "eloquent silence," "fragile toughness," "God-fearing atheist," "unconscious sensation," "bachelor's wife," "honest quack."

Although some analysts of metaphor, notably Campbell (1975), argue that oxymoron is quintessential to metaphor, I would counter with the assertion that it is kennetic strain and the actions that follow upon experiencing kennetic strain that are at the center of metaphor and other tropes. Out and out contradictions, as in oxymoron, most certainly induce the experience of kennetic strain, but so do other incongruities, contrarieties, ambiguities, anomalies, and paradoxes.

The Resolution of Kennetic Strain

Now it remains to propose the manner in which kennetic strain is resolved. Note that I use the term "resolved" rather than eliminated. I do not hold that human beings organize their lives to reduce strain to zero. Rather, they seek optimal degrees of strain or tension. Individual differences in what is optimum are to be expected.

By now, it should be clear to the reader that participation in a speech act is predicated upon rules of conversation (and reading is similarly predicated on the observation of certain rules or writing, editing, printing, book-binding, etc.). A violation of these rules, especially the rule of quality--that the speaker utter true statements and suppress false ones--is the condition for kennetic strain. Thus, the hearer is set to treat the utterances of the speaker as literal. If the literal interpretation contradicts the implicature of the context, then the hearer casts about for ways of resolving the strain. In the following paragraphs, I identify three classes of resolution of kennetic strain. In the first, the credo resolution, the anomalous term or event is treated as an assertion and assigned a token of credibility. In the second, the figural resolution, the anomalous term or event is interpreted as metaphorical. The hearer applies a criterion different from the credibility criterion: to wit, aptness. Given the context, does the metaphor create something novel?

In the third class of resolutions, the transfigural, kennetic strain is contained not by employing credibility or aptness criteria disjunctively as in the other resolutions, but both criteria conjunctively. To achieve this cognitive resolution, the hearer must enlarge his metaphysical networks. That is to say, the hearer must create a belief system that tolerates apparent paradox, that permits an utterance or other act to be instantiated as both literal (It is) and figurative (It is as if). The three classes of resolutions are elaborated below.

The Credo Resolution. Unless the context provides specific information that the speaker's utterances are not to be taken seriously, literally, or at face value, the hearer is ready to respond to an utterance as literal. To the utterance "Jefferson was a giant," the hearer can respond by affirmation (if the hearer assigns credibility to the concept of giants) and continue the conversation on the predication that Jefferson's bodily measurements approached those of giants. In such a case, "Jefferson was a giant" would produce no more kennetic strain than if the utterance had been "Jefferson was a statesman." The acceptance of the statement as literal is an example of the speaker's metaphor becoming the hearer's truth. Such a literalization or reification ordinarily occurs over time; through repetition, the once lively metaphor fades and dies. But the literalization can occur instantly as well. Consider the case where the speaker intends a remark as a jest (metaphor) and the hearer misses the intent and takes the remark literally (assigns a token of credibility, as in "that assertion is untrue").

The credo resolution (Latin: I believe) to kennetic strain is to literalize a potentially metaphorical speech act. Although I could cite many examples from the recorded utterances of so-called psychotic persons, it is more informative to examine the use of this type of resolution in the context of religious practice and in the work of scientists.

Of special interest are the kennetic acts involved in assigning credibility to a speech act involving the sacred. It is a truism that all societies confer sacred properties upon certain objects. A handful of clay is shaped, baked and glazed into a facsimile of a human figure. A medicine man, shaman, priest or other respected person declares that the transformed clay is sacred; he confers upon it the status of a religious object with numinous powers. His declaration might be translated as "this object is a god." If the hearer interprets the sentence literally, he ignores the object's usual instantiation as a bit of clay. This is the condition of idolatry (Berggren 1966). In the vocabulary employed in other papers, a transformation of metaphor to myth has taken place. The statue is not instantiated as a metaphor, an icon, a presumed likeness, but as believably sacred.

In this form of resolution, kennetic strain is reduced, perhaps to zero. An utterance in the context of the supernatural is assigned the same credibility as a mundane object that is subject to empirical checks (e.g., "This is a sheet of paper."). Under the special conditions of the religious context--invoking the sentiment of awe--the hearer may not entertain the hypothesis that the utterance violates the maxim of quality (truth telling) and is false or nonsense. This action serves as a barrier to entertaining the possibility that the utterance is a metaphor, that an "as if" is implied.

The acceptance of the authoritative utterance or the assigning of credibility to one's transcendental construction frees the person from the strain that is generated by contradiction. The concept of tension-binding is helpful at this point: The ability to bind tension, to tolerate paradox and inconsistency is an achievement of human beings. It varies among individuals and reflects differential contexts. Unbinding of tension is a prominent outcome of the credo resolution, unlike the outcomes of the other two classes of kennetic strain resolution. The figural and transfigural forms of resolution contain rather than reduce the tension created by such contradiction.

The readiness to transform a metaphor to a credible entity is not confined exclusively to persons engaged in conferring sacred properties on mundane objects. The tendency to deal with kennetic strain by means of the credo resolution is widespread. It is observed in the historical development of scientific concepts. I have argued in a number of papers that, in the history of psychology, such terms as anxiety, schizophrenia, hallucination, hypnosis, and mental illness, among others, began their careers as metaphors. They were actively working metaphors, they stimulated imagery in the listener or reader. They carried implicit or explicit tokens of hypotheticalness. They are now "retired" metaphors (Brown, 1965) and are treated as literal by contemporary users. In sentences, they function as abstract terms. These faded, bleached and colorless metaphors have given way to literal meanings that imply things. Upon being literalized, these figurative terms were assigned to the world of material objects, altering the course of scientific observation and experiment. Minding became mind, anxious feelings became anxiety, perplexing conduct became mental illness, schizophrenia became a disease entity, and so on.

Because the shift from figurative to literal contained directions for action, I employed the descriptive expression, metaphor-to-myth transformation. I located this conception in the context of scientific work. A synopsis of the science scenario would follow these lines: an event occurs that excites the observer's interest. If he or she has no literal term at hand to describe or classify the event, the scientist relies on metaphor. The casting of the experience is not whimsical but follows from embedding the experience in a context, the strands of which include the observer's stock of words, skill in employing words, ambient events, personal style, and intentions. The observed event and the metaphor chosen will have a ground of resemblance and--not to be neglected--non-resemblance. When first uttered by the scientist, the resemblance may be marked by such expressions as "like," "as," or "as if." Such markers, when used in scientific descriptions, provide a warrant for tentativity and for hypotheticalness. The markers enjoin the reader or hearer to supply the qualifying clause "It is as if" to statements of the type "A is a B." "(It is as if) the sense organ sends a message to the brain." In the typical case, the marker is dropped and the metaphorical quality must be inferred from the context. As I pointed out in the preceding chapter, the hearer (or reader) when confronted with a context-free sentence, may experience difficulty in discrimination between the figurative and the literal.

In another place, I have traced the origins of the now literal "mental illness" to its metaphorical beginnings. One of the historical strands is traced to Teresa of Avila, who said of some nuns who were exhibiting unusual conduct: "It is as if they are sick (como enfermas)." To spare the suffering women from the excesses of the Inquisitors, she likened their conduct to illness. It was not long until the "as if" marker was dropped. "They are sick" is a sentence that can be interpreted literally or figuratively. Soon after the coinage of this figure of speech, the metaphor faded and the literal quality took over. Thus, perplexing conduct (later called conversion reactions or histrionic neurosis) was assigned to the imagery of sickness, and by extension to the province of medicine and to the prevailing paradigms of physicians. Thus, a figure of speech, uttered out of compassion, ultimately became, in the hands of practitioners of the mechanistic world view, a myth.

Since myth is a belief system that becomes a guide to the day-to-day work of the scientist, it is important to keep the record straight and to know when the objects of one's attention is a historical event or a reified metaphor. My employment of the term "myth," then, is intended to connote an improper, or at best, a premature literalization of a metaphor cast for ostensibly scientific purposes. Turbayne (1962) has convincingly demonstrated how scientists not only use metaphors, but can be used by metaphors, thus setting the stage for myth-making. I am aware that my usage of "myth" is a particularistic one. I foresee no mischief if my readers will employ the same definition: a reified or hypostasized entity.

About ten years ago, Kitaek Chun and I embarked on a series of studies designed to identify some of the conditions that promoted the fossilization or effacement of metaphors. The studies were carried out under the guidance of the metaphor-to-myth hypothesis. The conclusions drawn from these studies point to the ready availability of the credo resolution. The studies are reported more fully elsewhere (Chun, 1970; Chun and Sarbin, 1970; Sarbin, 1968a).

We had earlier constructed the hypothesis that the metaphor-to-myth transformation (i.e., the credo resolution) is facilitated by the inclusion of opaque terms. It is clear that an English-speaking scientist has the option of labeling a concept or event with terms made up of Greco-Latin roots and affixes or terms from the everyday English lexicon. If he elects the first option, he runs the risk of his report being opaque to all but classical scholars because of the lack of immediate, pragmatic referents that might activate imagery. If he elects the option of employing a transparent metaphor--a familiar term that stimulates specific imagery--then the hearer is more likely to maintain the "as if" set and not engage in reification.

C. S. Lewis (1939) has written a delightful paper that helps clarify the transparency-opacity variable. He made use of the pregnant distinction: the master's metaphor and the pupil's metaphor. The master (read teacher, priest, guru, shaman, or other respected person), in trying to communicate some novel, strange, or perplexing experience, will cast about in search of a figurative term. The metaphor uttered will, or course, reflect his skill in imagining, his style of imagery, the purposes of the communication, the relevant audience, and other contextual features. The particular utterance is not the only one that might have been chosen by the master. He could have selected from a broad spectrum of metaphors. In any case, to the master, the metaphor is transparent.

For the pupil, the metaphor is not freely chosen. It comes under the cloak of authority. There is a necessity about the particular metaphor that was not intended by the master. Although the metaphor may be clearly marked by the context, the "as if" quality may be less noticeable than the predication. After all, the pupil is not likely to come to the interaction with the same imagery as the master. As a result, the master's transparent metaphor may reach the pupil's ears as an opaque word. In the absence of shared imagery, the interpreter can instantiate an opaque metaphor only by guessing, by interpreting on the basis of phonic inputs, or by referring to a dictionary. The problem of the pupil is magnified when the master employs a technical vocabulary, transparent to him, but not so transparent to the pupil.

Lewis' distinction may be applied with profit to the history of the concept schizophrenia. That schizophrenia is "a fact of life" can be deduced from a casual reading of nearly any textbook or journal in psychiatry or psychology, from the news releases of government health care agencies, and from the mass media generally. Yet there is no determinate criteria to establish whether a person is afflicted with the so-called disease. A review of the literature (Sarbin and Mancuso, 1980) turns up not even one psychological, neurological, chemical or other test that differentiates "schizophrenics" from "non-schizophrenics" in any consistent or reliable way. A metaphoric analysis may help explain the tenacity of the concept in spite of its weak ontological status.

Shortly after the turn of the century, Eugen Bleuler (1911) reported his observations on the patients that were brought to his clinic in Zurich. He noted that, unlike "normal" people, these patients were characterized by a lack of unity in their overt conduct, emotions, and intellectual reflections. The lack of unity had earlier been diagnosed as dementia praecox, but Bleuler noted that one need not be a juvenile to be nominated for patienthood.

Among the background conditions for Bleuler's seeking a metaphor to express his findings were the following: (1) the traditional view that a mind exists in parallel or in interaction with a body; (2) the mind, like the body, has parts or organs--the traditional tri-partite division was taken for granted--the intellect, the will, the affects; (3) the assumed resemblance between observable organ systems that operate in disorganized ways in sickness, and non-observable minds whose postulated internal connections could become disrupted, (4) the belief that the mind's parts, ordinarily functioning in harmony, could become dissociated one from the other. Bleuler applied the imagery distilled from these suppositions to the disturbed and disturbing people who were brought to his clinic. He concluded that the patients' perplexing conduct was a reflection of the improper working of the parts of the mind, i.e., the parts were isolated from each other, not working together.

At this point, he had to identify his discovery. Being a physician, and accustomed to the use of Greek as the language of medicine, he constructed a metaphor from Greek roots: schizo = split, cut, separated + phrenia = mind (from an earlier transformation that located the seat of the soul in the diaphragm). Schizophrenia was the master's metaphor. It was transparent to him, it reflected the imagery that was called out by his model of the mind.

The pupillary metaphor had to work backward from the Greek. If the pupil had experience with the Greek language, he might construe the master's metaphoric intentions. If he failed to construct the same imagery as the master, then he could do no more than construct meanings from the sound of the term ("sounds like a disease") or assimilate it to neurological or other doctrine.

"Schizophrenia" was a poetic creation, the language of medicine being employed to give public form to Bleuler's construals. In short order, the pupillary metaphor was transformed. In the absence of the poet's sustaining imagery, and in the context of turn-of-the-century theories of disease, schizophrenia lost its "as if" character. It became literalized and reified to disease. The social and political implications of this transformation from metaphor (a way of talking) to myth (constraints on action) are noted elsewhere (Sarbin, 1968a).

I have intentionally joined idolatry and the metaphor to myth transformation to illustrate the readiness of humans to adopt, under some conditions, the credo resolution. Interlacing the settings for idolatry and for scientific reporting, the transparency of metaphor must indeed be an important factor in the adoption of the credo alternative. It is unlikely that the idolator in the earlier illustration would employ the credo resolution if his informant pointed to the ceramic icon in human form and said, "this is one of your pet rabbits" rather than "this is a god." The counter-factual utterance would more likely lead the hearer to assign the utterance to the category of nonsense.

To recapitulate: I have discussed at least two factors that contribute to the credo resolution. One is the repetition of a metaphor over time, the effect being the reduction in power to generate imagery. The other is the employment of terms that in the beginning have little imagery-generating power for the hearer or reader, e.g., esoteric, dispositional, abstract, and unfamiliar words. Whether or not a person will adopt the credo resolution is not predictable out of context. Relevant contexts include the authority and purposes of the speaker and the skills and needs of the hearer.

The Figural Resolution. Virtually everything that has been said or written about models and metaphors is relevant to an understanding of the figural resolution. To collate, even to review the various approaches to metaphor, is beyond the scope of this essay. Instead, I intend to focus on those features of metaphorical action that are relevant to fashioning a psychological statement. I perceive my task as organizing some notions about how persons bind the tension, contain the paradox, or resolve the contradiction when they take part in metaphorical action. I have already posited that an utterance out of context or the performance of other actions that are not fitting to an ongoing drama produces strain-in-knowing, a condition that sets in motion a series of actions. I have adopted the label "figural" because it fits so well my conception of this form of resolution of kennetic strain. The etymology of the verb to figure provides a clue to its application in the present setting. It is derived from the Latin fingere: to make, to fashion, to form, to mould. To use metaphors, then, is an active process, in which both the speaker and the hearer form meanings. In so doing, they modify the corpus of meanings already contained in the literal term.

Let us refer again to Grice's maxims for optimal conversation. When a speaker violates a maxim, the hearer is placed in a condition of kennetic strain. He expects that the speaker will observe the maxims of quantity, quality, relation, and manner. How to make sense of a statement that is alien to the context? Consider Shelley's remark in A Defence of Poetry: "a poet is a nightingale, who sits in darkness and sings to cheer its own solitude with sweet sounds" (Shelley, 1821). Shelley's intention was to tell the world about poets and poetry. When we locate this sentence in the ambience of Grice's cooperative principle, the maxim of quality is not observed, for the imagery called out by "poet" and that called out by "nightingale" are not the same. Ordinarily poets and nightingales are not in the same semantic space. Because we want to take Shelley seriously we must modify the maxim of quality and transcend the potential interpretation "nonsense." Only if we, as hearers (or readers) "figure" the content can we assign meaning to the utterance. Having read Shelley's Defence, my imaginings when I see, hear or say the word poet, now include the lonely nightingale sitting on a bough, pouring out his heart to soothe the pangs of loneliness. By adopting the figural stance, I have resolved the momentary strain imposed by the implicature of the statement that poets are birds.

Like other artisans, the wordsmith brings a set of skills to his task. Central is the skill in using the "as if " formula. With this formula he can silently translate "the poet is a nightingale" to "It is as if the poet is a nightingale." The use of "as if" presupposes prior experience in "seeing as" (Wittgenstein, 1959) "let's pretend" (Ryle, 1949), "living in various degrees of hypotheticalness" (Sarbin and Juhasz, 1970), "deferred imitation" (Piaget, 1971), "Play" (Huizinga, 1955), "fictions" (Bentham, 1959), and so on.

"As if," a phrase made popular by Vaihinger (1924), is a shorthand term for taking-into-account the fictive character of an utterance. In noting that the context of the utterance helps to establish the "as if" set, I remind the reader that contextual markers may be subtle, such as change in tonal inflection, or open, as in introductory phrases or clauses, such as "Solve the riddle . . .," "Have you heard this joke?," "Let's pretend that . . . ." The mise-en-scene also provides both subtle and explicit cues. That work is involved in maintaining the tension of the metaphor is suggested by an analysis of the "as if" formula.

Vaihinger suggests that the if, or conditional, clause states something unreal, untrue, counterfactual, fictive. The person must maintain the fiction, at the same time considering the independent clause. Between the as and if, grammatically speaking, lies a whole sentence that must be held in attention, so to speak.

The maintenance of this assumptive behavior is possible only if the person has developed the skill of binding the tension created by the problem of doing two things simultaneously. To figure a metaphorical statement, then, involves the "as if" skill, alluded to earlier. In the credo resolution, the strain is reduced or eliminated by giving ontological status to the figural act. The idolator and the scientist resolve their respective paradoxes by conferring existence on the imagings contained in the metaphorical act. The verbal formula would be "it is." In the figural resolution, the kennetic strain is handled by containment, by binding the tension. The conclusion to the metaphorical act is semantic growth, an outcome of resolving the strain by declaring not "it is" but "it is as if."

In "figuring" the metaphor, the hearer or reader does not take literally the statement A is B; he simply entertains simultaneously the imagery of the literal term A and the imagery of the figurative term B. Additional work is required to attach appropriate imagery stimulated by B to the imagery of A. What makes one imaging appropriate and not another? The word artisan, simultaneously working with the imagings of both A and B must take into account--as I have already noted--the ongoing context in all its complexity. When the poet provides the hearer cues to his own semantic connections between the literal and the figurative and when the fashionings of the poet meet the aesthetic or pragmatic needs of the hearer or reader, then, we are likely to point to the aptness of the metaphor.

To say more about aptness as a criterion for metaphor requires a further contrast with the credibility criterion. The kennetic strain attendant upon an utterance or text that violates the cooperative principle can be resolved, in principle, by the credo resolution or by the figural resolution.

What are the conditions that influence the choice of resolution? Or alternately, what is the context that leads the hearer or reader to select one strategy over the other?

I have already pointed to the idolator and the scientist who are guided by the credo resolution. To say "I believe" suggests a scenario in which the person is seeking the truth. Given the social context and perhaps an existential crisis that fosters the need for certainty, the verbal formula, as I said before, may be stated as "It is." The posture of the interactant is to discover the truth, or, as Wheelwright (1962) has suggested, to determine What Is. The setting, the personal purposes, etc., of the hearer direct him to place the event under scrutiny in an ontological system.

By contrast, the figural strategy is employed not in seeking the truth, but in seeking a truth. Something useful, aesthetic, or clarifying is accomplished under the guidance of the "as if" posture. An imagining, activated by the metaphorical act, is reorganized with the help of the as-if formula. The person who reads a poem, enjoys the theater, or participates in the ceremonials of social life, acts from a posture similar to that of the child engaged in play. Few instances of the employment of the as if set are as telling as the child who treats things and events as if they are different from their ordinary meanings. The play, as Huizinga takes pains to tell us, is not taken lightly. It is serious, and the participants in the play must engage in conduct that preserves the aptness of the chosen metaphor. Huizinga (in Homo Ludens, 1955) captures the idea of involvement in the metaphorical act in the following description: "...play is not 'ordinary' or 'real' life... The contrast between play and seriousness is always fluid... Play turns to seriousness and seriousness to play. Play may rise to heights of beauty and sublimity that leave seriousness far beneath."

Not only does the metaphor of play--with all its seriousness--illuminate the figural process, it also reminds us of the significance of figural (creative, constructive) actions as a central component of the human condition. It is in employing metaphors that we transcend our animal heritage and our mechanical organization. A world without metaphors would be a world of "routine-bound morons, flotsam and jetsam in a fact-bound existence, lacking spontaneity of behavior, sensitivity, imagination, 'the personal touch'. . . what is not verbally odd is void of disclosure power; but words can be found in using which the universe and ourselves come alive together in a cosmic disclosure" (Ramsey, 1964, p. 46).

The Transfigural Resolution. But there is more to a psychological theory of metaphor. I have presented the credo and figural resolutions to strain-in-knowing as a disjunction. For example, the ether was introduced into physical science as early as the 17th century. In the 19th century, the ether (an as-if notion) was assigned total credibility. Lord Kelvin, among other great scientists, held that "nothing was so certain in physics as the reality of the luminiferous ether" (Matson, 1964). He was but one of legions of scientists who opted for the credo resolution. These same scientists could have responded to the counterfactual, or at least non-empirical, statement as a metaphor. When a priest assures a penitant that the holy water at Lourdes has curative powers, the penitant, as believer, is ready to act on that assertion. Another person, equally pious, could regard the water as a metaphor for holiness, and as a reminder of the values imbedded in the Christian religion.

The wide-spread acceptance of the logical axiom of non-contradiction--that something cannot be both A and not A--has been instrumental in setting up credo and figure as disjunctive ways of resolving kennetic strain.

The distinction between figural and transfigural is not always easy to make. In both we are dealing with metaphoric action. In the figural, we have suppressed the credo strategy so that our interpretation will not carry mythic qualities. In the transfigural, the metaphorical action is fused with believings.

Wheelwright's (1962) analysis of metaphor provides a basis for the distinction between figural and transfigural. He argued that metaphor has two components: epiphor and diaphor. "The role of epiphor is to hint significance, the role of diaphor is to create presence. Serious metaphor demands both." I can see correspondence between epiphor and the figural resolution, and between diaphor and the transfigural resolution. A recent sociological analysis has the title "Night as frontier" (Melbin, 1978). The content makes clear that the author regards night in urban areas as having similar properties as the frontier of the West and as being a frontier for the carrying out of social and political action. Epiphor and diaphor are both involved.

To make the transfigural resolution more concrete, I offer a few examples. The reader is reminded that the context of the present discussion is an utterance or performance that violates normative expectations, thus activating strain-in-knowing.

A Northwest Indian selects a tree from the forest, and fells it. In due time, he trims and cures the trunk and brings to his work space a log. After months of patient carving, painting, and finishing, he presents to his kinfolk, his gods and his ancestors a completed totem pole. In the course of the manufacture and presentation of the artifact, certain rituals have been performed, the aim of which was to confer noumenal properties on the transformed log. Query: Does the artisan classify the artifact as a carved and painted log or as a sacred object? If there were a fire, the artisan would strive to move the artifact to a safe place, suggesting that he would instantiate the artifact as a piece of combustible wood; he also engages in worship practices before the totem pole and declares that the artifact has sacred powers.

The carved and painted log is intended to remind the observer of the totemic animal--as such it is a metaphor. And it is believed to be more than a cylindrical piece of wood: it has mythic properties. Can it be both? If the axiom of non-contradiction is suspended, then the answer is yes. In short, the criterion of credibility and the criterion if aptness--ordinarily disparate concepts--are employable when certain metaphysical assumptions are set aside.

The kennetic strain is contained when the believer constructs a context in which the disjunction is transformed

into a conjunction. Such a feat is not likely to be accomplished save under special existential conditions, as when a
person is confronted with the necessity of locating himself with
reference to such abstractions as god, ancestors, spirits,
nation, death, etc.

I use this example to accent the conditions under which the
transfigural solution is attempted. The artisan "knows" from his
personal experience that the totem pole is a length of timber.
He "knows" from his cultural heritage that the totem has special
powers. How can he transform the metaphorical to the mythic when
he was the artisan responsible for fashioning the iconic
metaphor? What operations must be performed to tolerate the
paradox contained in the pairing of "it is" and "it is as if"?

Before attempting to explicate this knotty problem, I would
like to cite some additional reference cases of kennetic strain
that are resolvable through the actor's alterations of his
metaphysical assumptions.

In his later years, Jung (1970) directed his attention to
the alchemists, the predecessors of modern physical science. The
pertinent question was: did the alchemists believe that they
could transform base material into gold? The same problem, in
modern dress, is addressed to the Christian worshipper. Does he
believe that a magical incantation turns flour-and-water wafers
into the body of Christ?

As a beginning, Jung points to the "riddle" of what the
alchemists meant by the substances that they manipulated.

What, for instance, is the meaning of 'sal
spirituale?' The only possible answer seems to be
this: chemical matter was so completely unknown to
them that it instantly became a carrier for
projections. A state of participation mystique, or
unconscious identity, arose between them and the
chemical substance, which caused this substance to
behave, at any rate in part, like an unconscious
content. Of this relationship the alchemists had a dim
presentiment--enough anyway to enable them to make
statements which can only be understood as
psychological (1970, Pg. 249-250).

A substance used by the alchemists, table salt (NaCl), was
perceived as having properties of diverse kinds: as common salt
for seasoning food, as mythological entity, and as psychological
experience. Unlike the modern conception of salt, the salt of
the alchemists was more complex; it was perceived at the
intersection of two dimensions, inwardness-outwardness and
spirit-matter. To perceive salt as a psychological projection,
as a spiritual entity, and as a material substance was for Jung,
a signal achievement, not a mark of pathology. Such
participation was neither "primitive" nor "regressive." It was
natural to human beings whose openness to paradox and
contradiction had not been suppressed by conventional western
metaphysics and epistemology.

Berggren (1966) has written a significant paper "From Myth
to Metaphor" in which he grapples with the problem of
alternating resolutions. He employs the sacrament of the
Eucharist as a reference case. Although he employs a different

vocabulary, he is concerned with the cognitive problems associated with the transfigural resolution. If the communicant interprets literally the priest's problematic statement "This (wafer and wine) is the body and blood of Christ" (the credo resolution), then he is in an untenable situation, given the moral and legal sanctions on cannibalism. If he interprets the statement as a poetic metaphor (the figural resolution), then the force of the ritual is weakened. The potency of the ritual depends upon the accommodation of the paradox. The tension is bound through the use of simultaneous (or alternating) resolutions.The figural directs the communicant to the ethical principles associated with Christian doctrine, the credo directs the worshipper to his involvement in the life and death of Christ.

The totem pole artisan, the alchemist, and the communicant are reference cases where the disjunctive approach to anomalous sentences gives way to the conjunctive.

I do not want to convey the idea that the transfigural resolution is an oddity. The theater affords an opportunity to modify one's mundane metaphysics. When we become actively involved as the spectators in a drama, we lay aside our reliance on the conventional here-and-now. We have no difficulty in transporting ourselves through time and space to share in the lives of Hamlet or Lear. If the performance is convincing, we find ourselves responding via the credo resolution; when we reflect on the performance, we take the figural posture. The strain of entertaining the persistently counterfactual is thus contained.

"Perspective" is a felicitous term to denote the postulate system from which one constructs his world. A moment's reflection leads to the conclusion that human beings actively construct their worlds from a variety of interpenetrating epistemological perspectives. Most people continually shift back and forth between perspectives, as Singer (1966) has demonstrated in his work on fantasy. The solitary driver of an automobile on Interstate 80 may engage in a rich imaginal life: he operates the car from the psysicalistic time-and-space perspective; his fantasy life requires a perspective without time and space. Thurber's short story of Walter Mitty (1940) nicely illustrates role-performances in the mundane world and in the exciting world of the imagination.

In previous pages, I have asserted that utterances, other than literal expressions, contain contradiction and paradox. The tradition in psychology is to regard paradox as a noxious state of affairs and that human beings dispose of these unpleasant stimuli through various cognitive manoeuvres. Paradox--given our habitual thought patterns--is bad. This value orientation is reflected in the avoidant behavior of psychologists. As Brooks (1948) has remarked, "The scientist requires a language purged of paradox." Juhasz (1976) has made clear that "paradox" has not been indexed in Psychological Abstracts nor in standard textbooks. He argued that psychologists by and large tend to ignore the fact that contradiction and paradox characterizes much of human conduct. The working assumption of modern psychology is that in due course all human behavior will be accounted for by unequivocal rule. In the context of the present paper, contradictory communications would be resolved by the application of the disjunctive model: "it is" or "it is as if."

It would take us too far afield to explore the hypothesis-creating function of paradox. When a person confronts a paradox, he experiences kennetic strain. In the course of resolving the strain, he may entertain numerous hypotheses, some of which may become grist for the psychologist's or philospher's mill. But the transfigural strategy, as already noted, tends to be rejected by traditional scientists.

The so-called hallucinator, whether in the mental hospital or in the psychological laboratory, exemplifies paradoxical conduct. The scientific observer of the "hallucinating" patient or subject takes with him an epistemology based on the axiom of non-contradiction. As a result he cannot share the experience of the "hallucinator" who--for various reasons--has transcended the axiom of non-contradiction. Paradoxical statements of the "hallucinator" are labelled madness.

And yet, in our daily lives, we live with paradox. We not only act "as," but also "as if." We not only enact our social roles as fathers, teachers, and linebackers but also as if we are fathers, teachers and linebackers.

I bring to a close these paragraphs in which I have tried to describe the transfigural strategy for resolving strain in knowing. A propos is a quotation from G. K. Chesterton's On the Ethics of Elfland (1908). In a droll manner, he reminds us that at one time in our lives each of us had little difficulty in cultivating an epistemology that accepted paradox.

> My first and last philosophy, that which I believe with unbroken certainty, I learnt in the nursery. I generally learnt it from a nurse; that is, from the solemn and star-appointed priestess at once of democracy and tradition. The things I believed most then, the things I believe most now, are things called fairy tales. They seem to me to be the entirely reasonable things . . . Fairyland is nothing but the sunny country of commom sense . . . I knew the magic beanstalk before I had tasted beans! I was sure of the Man in the Moon before I was certain of the Moon. This was at one with all popular tradition. Modern minor poets are naturalists, and talk about the bush or the brook; but the singers of the old epics and fables were supernaturalists, and talked about the gods of brook and bush . . . old nurses do not tell children about the grass, but about the fairies that dance on the grass, and the old greeks could not see the trees for the dryads . . . I am not concerned with any of the separate statutes of elfland, but with the whole spirit of its law, which I learnt before I could speak, and shall retain when I cannot write. I am concerned with a certain way of looking at life, which was created in me by the fairy tales, but has since been meekly ratified by the mere facts. (1908, pp. 73-74)

Recapitulation

This essay has given me an opportunity to provide a guide to understanding metaphor as a semiotic process. Not contained in that abstraction called "language," the process of uttering and interpreting metaphor can best be regarded as a kennetic action. (I have just discovered why I prefer "kennetic" to "cognitive." The Anglo-Saxon root and the phonetic features are more "active" than the more scientific-sounding, Latin "cognitive.")

I have identified three strategies for resolving the kennetic strain that arises when a reader or hearer is confronted with an anomalous statement. The first strategy is to apply one's criteria for credibility. The second strategy is to apply one's criteria for aptness. Credibility and aptness are ordinarily seen as disjunctive strategies. The third strategy transcends the disjunction and applies both the criteria for credibility and the criteria for aptness. To achieve such transcendence, the interpreter must enlarge his epistemological framework.

Much more needs to be said further to clarify the issues raised here. I have said enough for now. I close this essay with a quotation excerpted from T. S. Eliot's East Coker that conveys my sense of incompleteness in my own "raid on the inarticulate."

So here I am, in the middle way, having had 20 years--
Twenty years largely wasted, entre deux guerres,
Trying to learn to use words, and every attempt is
A wholly new start and a different kind of failure
Because one has only learnt to get the better of words
For the thing one no longer has to say, or the way in
which One is no longer disposed to say it. And so each
venture
Is a new beginning, a raid on the inarticultate
With shabby equipment always deteriorating . . .
(1945)

Footnotes

1. Grice's maxims do not exhaust the rules for cooperative communication. Professor Philip Hallie has pointed out to me that most if not all examples of the workings of The Cooperative Principle are in the indicative mood. To be sure, children learn the indicative before the more complex subjunctive and conditional moods. And for most purposes, the indicative is sufficient for adequate communication.

   When a speaker utters a sentence in the conditional, for example, and the hearer's set is for the indicative, kennetic strain is a likely outcome. The hearer must then search the context in order to assign meaning to the anomalous sentence. The context, needless to say, will include actions of all sorts, not only speech acts.

I believe that psychologists interested in the acquisition of speech skills would find it rewarding to explore how a person learns to assign an appropriate meaning to subjunctive, conditional, and imperative utterances.

2. I prefer the more Anglo-Saxon "kennetic strain" to the Latin "cognitive strain, a phrase I have used in earlier work. The former is potentially a more transparent term and it has not become associated with existing theories of conduct. The feature I want to accent is that knowing is an action which can be disrupted by the introduction of incongruous, anomalous, or contradictory knowings.

REFERENCES

Aarne, A., & Thompson S. The types of the folktale (2nd ed., rev.). Helsinki: Suomalainen Tiedeakatemia, 1964.

Adler, N. The Antinomian personality. Psychiatry, 1968, 31, 325-338.

Aldington, R. A book of "characters." London: George Routledge and Sons, 1924.

Allen, A. H. B. The self in psychology. London: Kegan Paul, Trench, Trubner & Co., 1935.

Allport, G. W. Personality: A psychological interpretation. New York: Holt, 1937.

Allport, G. W., & Postman, L. J. Psychology of rumor. New York: Holt, Rinehart and Winston, 1948.

Alvarez, A. The savage God. New York: Random House, 1971.

American Psychiatric Association. Diagnostic and statistical manual of mental disorders. Washington, D. C.: American Psychiatric Association, 1958, 1968.

Angyal, A. Neurosis and treatment: A holistic theory (E. Hanfmann and R. M. Jones, Eds.). New York: Wiley, 1965.

Archer, W. Masks or faces? New York: Longmans, Green & Co., 1889.

Argyle, M. Research project on social skills. Progress Report, Oxford University Institute of Experimental Psychology, 1964.

Aries, P. Death inside out. The Hastings Center Studies, 2, No. 2 (May 1974), 3-18.

Arnold, M. B. On the mechanism of suggestion and hypnosis. Journal of Abnormal and Social Psychology, 1946, 41, 107- 128.

Ashcraft, R. Economic metaphors, behavioralism, and political theory: Some observations on the ideological uses of language. Western Political Quarterly, 1977, 30, 313-328.

Austin, J.L. Sense and sensibilia. Oxford: Clarendon Press, 1962.

Austin, J. L. A plea for excuses. In J. O. Urmson & G. J. Warnock (Eds.), Philosophical papers by the late J. L. Austin (2nd edition). New York: Oxford University Press, 1970. Pp. 123-152.

Axline, V. Play therapy. Boston: Houghton-Mifflin, 1947.

Bach, G. Young children's play fantasies. Psychological Monographs, 1945, 59, No. 2.

Barber, T. X. Physiological effects of "hypnotic suggestions": A critical review of recent research (1960-64). Psychological Bulletin, 1965, 4, 201-222.

Barber, T. X. Hypnosis: A scientific approach. New York: Van Nostrand-Reinhold, 1969.

Barber, T. X. Spanos, N. P., & Chaves, J. F. Hypnotism, imagination and human potentialities. New York: Pergamon, 1974.

Barker, R. G., & Wright, F. W. One boy's day. New York: Harper, 1951.

Bateson, G. Steps to an ecology of mind. New York: Ballantine Books, 1972.

Benedict, R. Anthropology and the abnormal. Journal of Genetic Psychology, 1934, 10, 59-82.

Benjamin, J. D. A method for distinguishing and evaluating formal thinking disorders in schizophrenia. In J. S. Kasanin (Ed.), Language and Thought in Schizophrenia. Berkeley: University of California Press, 1944.

Benne, K, & Sheats, P. Functional roles of group members. Journal of Social Issues, 1948, 4, 41-47.

Berggren, D. From myth to metaphor. Monist, 1966, 50, 530-552.

Berlin, I. Vico and Herder: Two studies in the history of ideas. London: Hogarth Press, 1976.

Berne, E. Games people play: The psychology of human relationships. New York: Random House, 1964.

Birdwhistell, R. L. Kinesics and context: Essays on body motion communication. Philadelphia: University of Pennsylvania Press, 1970.

Black, M. Models and metaphors. Ithaca: Cornell University Press, 1962.

Blake, W. Complete writings. London: Oxford University Press, 1971.

Bogardus, E. S. Sociotypes vs. stereotypes. Sociology and Social Research, 1949, 34, 286-291.

Boring, E. G. A note on the origin of the word psychology. Journal of the History of the Behavioral Sciences, 1966, 2, 145-147.

Braginsky, B. M., & Braginsky, D. D. Mainstream psychology: A critique. New York: Holt, Rinehart and Winston, 1974.

Brenman, M., & Gill, M. M. Hypno-therapy. New York: International Universities Press, 1947.

Brooks, C. The Language of paradox. In M. Schorer (Ed.), Criticism: The foundations of modern literary judgment. New York: Harcourt-Brace, 1948.

Brown, R. Metaphorical assertions. Philosophical Studies, 1965, 16, 6-8.

Bugenthal, J. F. T., & Zelen, S. L. Investigations into the "self-concept": I. The W-A-Y technique. Journal of Personality, 1950, 18, 483-498.

Burke, K. A grammar of motives. Englewood Cliffs, N. J.: Prentice-Hall, 1945.

Burke, K. Language as symbolic action. Berkeley: University of California Press, 1966.

Cameron, N. A. The paranoid pseudo-community. American Journal of Sociology, 1943, 49, 32-38.

Cameron, N. The psychology of behavior disorders. Boston: Houghton-Mifflin, 1947.

Campbell, P. N. Metaphor and linguistic theory. Quarterly Journal of Speech, 1975, 61, 1-12.

Cannon, W. B. Bodily changes in pain, hunger, fear, and rage (2nd ed.). Boston: Branford, 1929.

Carmichael, L., Hogan, H. P., & Walter, A. A. An experimental study of the effect of language on the reproduction of visually perceived form. Journal of Experimental Psychology, 1932, 15, 73-86.

Cassirer, E. The myth of the state. New haven: Yale University Press, 1946.

Cassou, J. An introduction to Cervantes. In A. Flores & M. J. Benardete, Cervantes across the centuries. New York: Dryden Press, 1948.

Cattell, R. B., & Scheier, I. H. The meaning and measurement of neuroticism and anxiety. New York: Ronald Press, 1961.

Chesterton, G. K. Orthodoxy. London: The Bodley Head, 1908.

Chun, K. A psychological study of myth-making: A 3-factor theory of metaphor to myth transformation. Unpublished doctoral dissertation, University of California, Berkeley, 1970.

Chun, K., & Sarbin, T. R. An empirical study of "metaphor to myth transformation." Philosophical Psychologist, 1970, 4, 16-20.

Coe, W. C., & Sarbin, T. R. An experimental demonstration of hypnosis as role enactment. Journal of Abnormal Psychology, 1966, 71, 400-416.

Cohen, M. R. Reason and nature, an essay on the meaning of scientific method. New York: Harcourt Brace, 1931.

Colby, B. N. Cultural patterns in narrative. In J. C. Mancuso (Ed.), Readings for a cognitive theory of personality. New York: Holt, Rinehart and Winston, 1970. Pp. 557-571.

Corn-Becker, F., Welch, L., & Fisichelli, V. Conditioning factors underlying hypnosis. Journal of Abnormal and Social Psychology, 1949, 44, 212-222.

Crawley, E. The mystic rose (rev. T. Besterman). Vol. 2. London: Methuen, 1902.

Cronbach, L. J. The two disciplines of scientific psychology. American Psychologist, 1957, 12, 671-684.

Cronbach, L. J. Beyond the two disciplines of scientific psychology. American Psychologist, 1975, 30, 116-127.

Cumming, J., & Cumming, E. Ego and milieu. New York: Atherton Press, 1962.

Davitz, J. R. The communication of emotional meaning. New York: McGraw-Hill, 1964.

DePorte, M. V. Nightmares and hobbyhorses. San Marino, Calif.: The Huntington Library, 1974.

Dershowitz, A. M. The law of dangerousness: Some fictions about predictions. Journal of Legal Education, 1970, 23, 24-47.

Dershowitz, A. M. Preventive confinement: A suggested framework for constitutional analysis. Texas Law Review, 1973, 51, 1277-1324.

Dewey, J. How We Think. New York: Heath, 1910.

Devereaux, G. Social and cultural implications of incest among the Mohave. Psychoanalytic Quarterly, 1939, 8, 510-533.

Dorcus, R., Bretnall, A. K., & Case, H. W. Control experiments and their relation to theories of hypnosis. Journal of General Psychology, 1941, 24, 217-221.

Downey, J. E. Creative imagination. London: Kegan Paul, Trench and Trubner, 1929.

Edelman, M. Myths, metaphors, and political conformity. Psychiatry, 1967, 30, 217-228.

Eliot, T. S. Four quartets. London: Faber, 1945.

Emerson, R. W. Essays, first and second series (E. Rhys, Ed.). New York: Everyman's Library, 1906.

Empson, W. Seven types of ambiguity (rev. ed.). London: Chatto and Windus, 1953.

Eysenck, H. J. Suggestibility and hysteria. Journal of Neurological Psychiatry, 1943, 6, 22-31.

Eysenck, H. J., & Furneaux, W. D. Primary and secondary suggestibility. Journal of Experimental Psychology, 1945, 35, 485-503.

Flugel, J. C. Man, morals, and society. New York: International Universities Press, 1944.

Ford, C. S. Smoke from their fires: The life of a Kwakiutl chief. New Haven: Yale University Press, 1941.

Freud, S. Hemmung, symtom and angst. Leilpzig, Vienna, and Zurich: Internationaler Psychoanalytischer Verlag, 1926.

Friedenthal, R. Goethe: His life and times. London: Weidenfeld and Nicolson, 1963.

Friedlander, J. W., & Sarbin, T. R. The depth of hypnosis. Journal of Abnormal and Social Psychology, 1938, 33, 453-475.

Furneaux, W. D. Prediction of susceptibility to hypnosis. Journal of Personality, 1946, 14, 281-294.

Gergen, K. J. Social psychology as history. Journal of Personality and Social Psychology, 1973, 26, 309-320.

Goffman, E. The presentation of self in everyday life. Garden City, New York: Doubleday, 1959.

Goffman, E. Asylums. Chicago: Aldine, 1961.(a)

Goffman, E. Encounters: Two studies in the sociology of interaction. Indianapolis: Bobbs-Merrill, 1961. (b)

Goffman, E. Frame analysis. New York: Harper & Row, 1974.

Goldstein, K. The organism. New York: American Book Co., 1939.

Goldstein, K., & Scheerer, M. Abstract and concrete behavior: An experimental study with special tests. Psychological Monographs, 1941, 33 (2).

Gorham, D. R. A proverbs test for clinical and experimental use. Psychological Reports, 1956, Monograph Supplement 1.

Gough, H. G. Clinical versus statistical prediction in psychology. In L. Postman (Ed.), Psychology in the making. New York: Knopf, 1962.

Green, G. The day dream. London: University of London Press, 1923.

Grice, H. P. Logic and conversation. In P. Coe and L. Morgan (Eds.), Syntax and semantics (Vol. 3): Speech Acts. New York: Academic Press, 1975.

Haley, J. Communication and therapy: Blocking metaphors. American Journal of Psychotherapy, 1971, 25, 214-220.

Hartley, E. L., Rosenbaum, M., & Schwartz, S. Children's

perceptions of ethnic group membership. Journal of Psychology, 1948, 26, 387-398.

Herron, R. E., & Sutton-Smith, B. Child's play. New York: Wiley, 1971.

Hilgard, E. A. Hypnotic susceptibility. Stanford: Stanford University Press, 1965.

Hilgard, J. R. Personality and hypnosis: A study of imaginative involvement. Chicago: University of chicago Press, 1970.

Hilgard, J. R. Imaginative involvement: Some characteristics of the highly hypnotizable and the nonhypnotizable. International Journal of Clinical and Experimental Hypnosis, 1974, 22, 138-156.

Hollard, N. H. The dynamics of the literary response. New York: Oxford University Press, 1968.

Hollingshead, A. B., & Redlich, R. C. Social class and mental illness. New York: Wiley, 1958.

Huizinga, J. Homo ludens. Boston: Beacon Press, 1955.

Hull, C. L. Hypnosis and suggestibility. New York: Appleton-Century, 1933.

Hunter, R. A., & MacAlpine, J. Three hundred years of psychiatry. New York: Oxford University Press, 1963.

Hyman, S. E. The tangled bank: Darwin, Marx, Frazer and Freud as imaginative writers. New York: Grosset and Dunlap, 1966.

Ichheiser, G. Misunderstandings in human relations--a study in false social perception. American Journal of Sociology, 1949, 55, Part 2.

Jacobson, E. Progressive relaxation (rev. edit). Chicago: University of Chicago Press, 1938.

James, W. Varieties of religious experience. New York: Random House, 1902.

Janet, P. Major symptoms of hysteria. New York: Macmillan, 1907.

Jebb, R. C. The Characters of Theophrastus. (J. E. Sandys, Ed.). London: Macmillan, 1909.

Jenkins, J. J. Remember that old theory of memory? Well, forget it! American Psychologist, 1974, 29, 785-795.

Juhasz, J. B. Psychology of paradox and vice versa. Psychological Reports, 1976, 39, 911-914.

Jung, C. G. The collected works of C. G. Jung, Vol. 14: mysterium conjunctions. (Translated by R.F.C. Hull). Princeton: Princeton University Psress, 1970.

Kahn, R. L., Wolfe, D. M., Quinn, R. P., Snoek, J. D., & Rosenthal, R. A. Organizational stress: Studies in role conflict and ambiguity. New York: Wiley, 1964.

Kantor, J. R. An outline of social psychology. Chicago: Follett, 1929.

Kety, S. S. From rationalization to reason. American Journal of Psychiatry, 1974, 131, 957-963.

Kintsch, W. Structure of semantic memory. In E. Tulving and W. Donalson (Eds.), Organization of memory. New York: Academic Press, 1972.

Klapp, O. E. Heroes, villians and fools. Englewood Cliffs, N. J.: Prentice-Hall, 1962.

Kleinmutz, B. Clinical information processing by computer. New York: Holt, Rinehart and Winston, 1969.

Kubie, L. S., & Margolin, S. The process of hypnotism and the nature of the hypnotic state. American Journal of Psychiatry, 1944, 100, 611-622.

Kuhn, T. S. The structure of scientific revolutions. Chicago: University of Chicago Press, 1962.

Laird, J. D., & Bethel, M. World hypotheses as psychological variables. Unpublished manuscript. Clark University, Worcester, Mass., 1976.

Langer, J., Werner, M., & Wapner, S. Apparent speed of walking under conditions of danger. Journal of General Psychology, 1965, 73, 291-298.

Lee, S. Social class bias in the diagnosis of mental illness. Ann Arbor, Michigan: University microfilms, 1968.

Levin, H. The Quixotic principle. In M. W. Bloomfield (Ed.), Harvard English Studies 1, the interpretation of narrative: Theory and practice. Cambridge: Harvard University Press, 1970.

Levy, L. H. Anxiety and behavior scientists' behavior. American Psychologist, 1961, 16, 66-68.

Levi-Strauss, C. Structural anthropology (Jacobson, C. and Schoepf, B.G., trans.). New York: Basic Books, 1963.

Lewin, K. A dynamic theory of personality. New York:McGraw-Hill, 1935.

Lewis, C. S. Bluspels and Flalansferes. In Rehabilitations and other essays. London: Oxford University Press, 1939.

Lewis, J. H., & Sarbin, T. R. Studies in psychosomatics: The influence of hypnotic stimulation on gastric hunger contractions. Psychosomatic Medicine, 1943, 5, 125-131.

Lincoln, C. E. The black muslims in America. Boston: Beacon Press, 1961.

Linton, R. The study of man: An introduction. New York: Appleton-Century, 1936.

Linton, R. The cultural background of personality. London: Routledge & Kegan Paul, 1947.

London, P., Hart, J. T., & Leibovitz, M. P. EEG alpha rythms and susceptibility to hypnosis. Nature, 1968, 29, 71-22.

Lundholm, H. An experimental study of functional anesthesias as induced by suggestion in hypnosis. Journal of Abnormal Social Psychology, 1928, 23, 337-355.

Lyman, S. M., & Scott, M.B. The drama of social reality. New York: Oxford, 1975.

Mancuso, J., & Sarbin, T. R. A paradigmatic analysis of psychological issues at the interface of jurisprudence and moral conduct. In T. Lickona (Ed.), Man and morality. New York: Holt, Rinehart and Winston, 1977.

Mandler, G., & Kessen, W. The language of psychology. New York: Wiley, 1959.

Manosevitz, M., Prentice, N. M., & Wilson, F. Individual and family correlates of imaginary companions in preschool children. Developmental Psychology, 1973, 8, 72-79.

Matson, F. W. The broken image. New York: Brazillier, 1964.

McNeill, J.T. A history of the cure of souls. New York: Harper and Row, 1951.

Mead, G. H. Mind, self and society (C. W. Morris, Ed.). Chicago: University of Chicago Press, 1934.

Meehl, P. E. Clinical versus statistical predictions. Minneapolis: University of Minnesota Press, 1954.

Melbin, M. Night as frontier. American Sociological Review, 1978, 43, 3-22.

Merton, R. K. The role set. British Journal of Sociology, 1957, 8, 106-120.

Messinger, S. L., Sampson, H., & Towne, R. D. Life as theater: Some notes on the dramaturgic apprach to social reality. Sociometry, 1962, 25, 98-110.

Miller, S. Ends, means and galumphing: Some leitmotifs of play. American Anthropologist, 1973, 75, 87-98.

Moreno, J. L. Role tests and role diagrams of children. In Psychodrama, Vol. 1. New York: Beacon House, 1946.

Mukherjee, B. N. "Social desirability" and "anxiety" variables in three measures of anxiety. British Journal of Social and Clinical Psychology, 1966, 5, 310-312.

Muncie, W. The psychopathology of metaphor. Archives of Neurology and Psychiatry, 1937, 37, 769-804.

Murphy, G. Personality: A biosocial approach to origins and structure. New York: Harper and Row, 1947.

Needham, R. Belief, language and experience. Oxford: Blackwell, 1972.

Nunnally, J. C. Popular conceptions of mental health. New York: Holt, Rinehart and Winston, 1961.

Orne, M. T. The nature of hypnosis: Artifact and essence. Journal of Abnormal and Social Psychology, 1959, 58, 277-299.

Orne, M. T. On the social psychology of the psychological experiment: With particular reference to demand characteristics and their implications. American Psychologist, 1962, 17, 776-783.

Ortony, A. Why metaphors are necessary and not just nice. Educational Theory, 1975, 25, 45-53.

Ortony, A., Reynolds, R. E., & Arter, J. A. Metaphor: theoretical and empirical research. Psychological Bulletin, 1978, 85, 919-943.

Osgood, E., Suci, G. J., & Tannebaum, P. H. The measurement of meaning. Urbana: University of Illinois, 1957.

Osterweis, R. G. Romanticism and nationalism in the old south. New Haven: Yale University Press, 1949.

Paivio, A. Imagery and verbal processes. New York: Holt, Rinehart and Winston, 1971.

Park, R. E., & Miller, H. A. Old world traits transplanted. New York: Harper, 1921.

Partridge, E. A dictionary of the underworld, British and American. London: Routledge & Kegan Paul, 1950.

Paterson, T. T. Management theory. London: Business Publications, 1966.

Pattie, F. A. The production of blisters by hypnotic suggestions: A review. Journal of Abnormal and Social Psychology, 1941, 36, 62-72.

Pear, T. H. Personality, appearance and speech. London: Allen and Unwin, 1957.

Pepper, S. C. World hypotheses. Berkeley: University of California Press, 1942.

Perrine, L. Four forms of metaphor. College English, 1971, 33, 125-138.

Peters, R. S. The concept of motivation. London: Routledge and Kegan Paul, 1958.

Phillips, D. L. Rejection as a consequence of seeking help for mental disorders. American Sociological Review, 1963, 28, 963-972.

Piaget, J. The construction of reality in the child. (M. Cook, Trans.). New York: Basic Books, 1954.

Pirandello, L. Naked masks. (E. Bentley, Ed.). New York: E. P. Dutton and Company, 1952.

Platt, A. M., & Diamond, B. L. The origins and development of the "wild beast" concept of mental illness and its relation to theories of criminal responsiblity. Journal of the History of the Behavioral Sciences, 1965, 1, 355-367.

Pollio, H. R., Barlow, J. M., Fine, H. J., & Pollio, M. R. Psychology and the poetics of growth. Hillsdale, New Jersey: Laurence Erlbaum Associates, 1977.

Polti, G. The thirty-six dramatic situations (L. Ray, Trans.). Boston: Writer, Inc., 1916.

Popper, K. R. The open society and its enemies (4th ed.). Princeton, N.J.: Princeton University Press, 1963.

Poulet, G. Phenomenology or reading. New Literary History, 1969, 1, 53-68.

Prescott, F. C. The poetic mind. New York: Macmillan, 1922. (Cornell University Press, 1959).

Propp, V. Morphology of the folktale (2nd ed.). Austin: University of Texas Press, 1968.

Ramsey, J. T. Models and mystery. London: Oxford University Press, 1964.

Richards, I. A. The philosophy of rhetoric. London: Oxford University Press, 1936.

Riegel, K. F. (Ed.). The development of dialectical operations. Basel: Karger, 1975.

Rivers, W. H. R. Medicine, magic and religion. New York: Harcourt, Brace, 1924.

Rosenhan, D. L. On being sane in insane places. Science, 1973, 180, 250-258.

Rosenow, C. Meaningful behavior in hypnosis. American Journal of Psychology, 1928, 40, 205-235.

Rosenzweig, S., & Sarason, S. An experimental study of the triadic hypothesis: Reaction to frustration, ego-defense, and hypnotizability. Character and Personality, 1942, 11, 1-19.

Rotenberg, M. The Protestant ethic against the spirit of psychiatry: The other side of Weber's thesis. British Journal of Sociology, 1975, 26, 52-65.

Rotenberg, M., & Sarbin, T.R. Impact of differentially significant others on role involvement: An experiment with prison social types. Journal of Abnormal Psychology, 1972, 77, 97-107.

Rothman, D. S. The discovery of the asylum. Boston: Little, Brown and Co., 1971.

Ryle, G. The concept of mind. New York: Barnes and Noble, 1949. (London: Hutchinson's University Library, 1949.)

Sapir, J. D., & Crocker, J. C. (Eds.). The social uses of metaphor: Essays on the anthropology of rhetoric. Philadelphia: University of Pennsylvania Press, 1977.

Sarbin, T. R. The concept of role-taking. Sociometry, 1943, 6, 273-284.

Sarbin, T. R. Contributions to role-taking theory: I. Hypnotic behavior. Psychological Review, 1950, 57, 255-270. (a)

Sarbin, T. R. Mental age changes in experimental regression. Journal of Personality, 1950, 19, 221-228. (b)

Sarbin, T. R. Contributions to role-taking theory: III. A preface to a psychological analysis of the self. Psycho- logical Reveiw, 1952, 59, 11-22.

Sarbin, T. R. Role theory. In G. Lindzey (Ed.), Handbook of social psychology. Cambridge, Mass.: Addison-Wesley, 1954. Pp. 223-258.

Sarbin, T. R. Physiological effects of hypnotic stimulation. In R. M. Dorcus (Ed.), Hypnosis and its therapeutic applications. New York: McGraw-Hill, 1956.

Sarbin, T.R. A new model of the behavior disorders. Tijdschiftvoor Psychologie, 1962, 10, 325-341.

Sarbin, T. R. Anxiety: The reification of a metaphor. Archives of General Psychiatry, 1964, 10, 630-638. (a)

Sarbin, T. R. A role-theoretical interpretation of psychological change. In P. Worchel & D. Byrne (Eds.), Psychological change. New York: Wiley, 1964. Pp. 176-219. (b)

Sarbin, T. R. On the futility of the proposition that some people be labeled mentally ill. Journal of Consulting Psychology, 1967, 31, 447-453. (a)

Sarbin, T. R. The dangerous individual: An outcome of social identity transformation. British Journal of Criminology, 1967, 10, 355-366. (b)

Sarbin, T. R. The concept of hallucination. Journal of Personality, 1967, 35, 359-380. (c)

Sarbin, T. R. Ontology recapitulates philology: The mythic nature of anxiety. American Psychologist, 1968, 23, 411-418. (a)

Sarbin, T. R. On the distinction between social roles and social types, with special reference to the hippie. American Journal of Psychiatry, 1968, 125, 1024-31. (b)

Sarbin, T. R. The transformation of social identity: A new metaphor for the helping professions. In L. Roberts, N. Greenfield, & M. Miller (Eds.), Comprehensive mental health: The challange of evaluation. Madison: University of Wisconsin Press,

1968. Pp. 97–124. (c)

Sarbin, T. R. A study of collegiate folk types. Unpublished manuscript, University of California, Berkeley, 1968. (d)

Sarbin, T. R. Imagining as muted role-taking: A historico-linguistic analysis. In P. Sheehan (Ed.), The function and nature of imagery. New York: Academic Press, 1972. Pp. 333–354. (a)

Sarbin, T. R. Schizophrenia: From metaphor to myth. Psychology Today, 1972, 6, 18–27. (b)

Sarbin, T. R. Ideological constraints on the science of deviant conduct. Keynote address, Fifth Annual Meeting of the American Association for the Abolition of Involuntary Mental Hospitalization, New York City, April 14, 1974.

Sarbin, T. R. Contextualism: A world view for modern psychology. In A. W. Landfield (Ed.), Nebraska symposium on motivation. Lincoln: University of Nebraska Press, 1977.

Sarbin, T. R., & Allen, V. L. Role theory. In G. Lindzey & E. Aronson (Eds.), Handbook of social psychology (Vol. 1). Reading, Mass.: Addison-Wesley, 1968. Pp. 488–567.

Sarbin, T. R., & Andersen, M. L. Base-rate expectancies and perceptual alterations in hypnosis. British Jounal of Social and Clinical Psychology, 1963, 2, 112–121.

Sarbin, T. R. & Andersen, M. L. Role-theoretical analysis of hypnotic behavior. In J. E. Gordon (Ed.), Handbook of clinical and experimental hypnosis. New York: McMillan, 1967. Pp. 319–344.

Sarbin, T. R., & Bailey, D. E. The immediacy postulate in the light of modern cognitive theory. In K. R. Hammond (Ed.), Psychology of Egon Brunswik. New York: Holt, Rinehart and Winston, 1966.

Sarbin, T. R., & Coe, W. C. Hypnosis: The social psychology of influence communication. New York: Holt, Rinehart and Winston, 1972.

Sarbin, T.R., & Evanson, S. Role skills in hypnosis. Unpublished manuscript, University of California, Santa Cruz, 1976.

Sarbin, T. R., & Hardyck, C. Contributions to role-taking theory: Conformance in role-perception as a personality variable. Journal of Consulting Psychology, 1955, 19, 109–111.

Sarbin, T. R., & Jones, D. S. An experimental analysis of role behavior. Journal of Abnormal and Social Psychology, 1956, 51, 236–241.

Sarbin, T. R., & Juhasz, J. B. On the "false alarm" metaphor in psychophysics. Psychological Record, 1966, 16, 323–327.

Sarbin, T. R., & Juhasz, J. B. The historical background of the concept of hallucination. Journal of the History of the Behavioral Sciences, 1967, 3, 339–358.

Sarbin, T. R., & Juhasz, J. B. Toward a theory of imagination. Journal of Personality, 1970, 38, 52–76.

Sarbin, T. R., & Juhasz, J. B. The social context of hallucinatons. In R. K. Siegel & L. J. West (Eds.), Hallucinations: Behavior, experience, and theory. New York: Wiley-Biomedical, 1975. Pp. 241-256.

Sarbin, T. R., Juhasz, J. B., & Todd, P. The social psychology of "hallucinations." Psychological Record, 1971, 21, 87-93.

Sarbin, T. R., & Lim, D. T. Contributions to role theory X: Some evidence in support of the role taking hypnosis. Journal of Clinical and Experimental Hypnosis, 1963, 2, 98-103.

Sarbin, T.R., & Madow. L. Predicting the depth of hypnosis by means of the Rorschach test. American Journal of Orthopsychiatry, 1942, 12, 268-270.

Sarbin, T.R., & Mancuso, J.C. Failure of a moral enterprise: Attitudes of the public toward mental illness. Journal of Consulting and Clinical Psychology, 1970, 35, 159-173.

Sarbin, T.R., & Mancuso, J.C. Schizophrenia: Medical diagnosis or moral verdict? New York: Pergamon, 1980.

Sarbin, T.R., & Miller, J.E. Demonism revisited: The XYY chromosomal anomaly. Issues in Criminology, 1970, 6, 195- 208.

Sarbin, T.R., & Nucci, L.P. Self-reconstitution process: A proposal for reorganizing the conduct of confirmed smokers. Journal of Abnormal Psychology, 1973, 81, 182-195.

Sarbin, T. R., & Rosenberg, B. G. Contributions to role-taking theory: IV. A method for the qualitative analysis of the self. Journal of Social Psychology, 1955, 42, 171-81.

Sarbin, T. R., & Scheibe, K. E. The transvaluation of social identity. In C. J. Bellone (Ed.), The normative dimension in public administration. New York: Marcel Dekker, 1978.

Sarbin T. R., & Stein, K. B. Self-role theory and antisocial conduct. Progress Report, National Institute of Mental Health, 1967.

Sarbin, T. R., Taft, R., & Bailey, D. E. Clinical inference and cognitive theory. New York: Holt, Rinehart and Winston, 1960.

Sarbin, T. R., & Watson, J. S. On the use of proverbs in psychodiagnosis. Unpublished manuscript, University of California, Berkeley, 1967.

Scheff, T. J. Being mentally ill: A sociological theory. Chicago: Aldine, 1966.

Scheibe, K. E., & Sarbin, T. R. Towards a theoretical conceptualization of superstition. British Journal for the Philosophy of Science, 1965, 62, 143-158.

Schrag, C. Social types in a prison community. M.A. thesis, University of Washington, Seattle, 1944.

Schultz, J. Das Autogene Training (Konzentrierte Selbstentspannung). Leipsig, 1932.

Searle, J. R. Speech acts: An essay in the philosophy of language. London: Cambridge University Press, 1969.

Shaw, G. B. Pygmalion. In Complete plays with prefaces.

Vol. 1. New York: Dodd, Mead, 1963. Pp. 191-295.

Shelley, P. B. A defence of poetry (1821). In J. H. Smith, & E. W. Parks (Eds.), The Great Critics (3rd edition.) >LM=15 New York: Norton, 1951.

Shor, R. E. The three-factor theory of hypnosis as applied to the book-reading fantasy and to the concept of suggestion. International Journal of Clinical and Experi- mental Hypnosis, 1970, 18, 89-98.

Siegler, M., & Osmund, H. Aesculpaian authority. The Hasting Center Studies, 1973, 1, 41-52.

Singer, J. L. Daydreaming. New York: Random House, 1966.

Skolnick, J. H. Justice without trial: Law enforcement in a democratic society. New York: Wiley, 1966.

Smith, L. P. The English language. New York: Holt, 1912.

Sparshott, F. E. "As," The limits of metaphor. New Literary History, 1974, 6, 75-94.

Spiegel, J. P., & Machoka, P. Messages of the body. New York: The Free Press, 1974.

Splitzer, R. L., & Wilson, P. T. Nosology and the official psychiatric nomenclature. In A. Freedman & H. Kaplan (Eds.). Comprehensivse textbook of psychiatry. New York: Williams and Wilkins, 1975.

Stanford, W. B. Greek metaphor: Studies in theory and practice. Oxford: Basil Blackwell, 1936.

Stein, K. B. Perceptual defense and perceptual sensitization under neutral and involved conditions. Journal of Personality, 1953, 21, 467-478.

Strong, S. Social types in a minority group: Formulation of a method. American Journal of Sociology, 1943, 48, 563-73.

Strong, S. Negro-white relations as reflected in social types. American Journal of Sociology, 1944, 49, 23-29.

Sykes, G. M. The society of captives. Princeton: Princeton University Press, 1958.

Szasz, T. S. The myth of mental illness. New York: Hoeber-Harper, 1961.

Szasz, T. S. The manufacture of madness. New York: Harper and Row, 1970.

Talayesva, D. C. Sun chief: The autobiography of a Hopi Indian (L. W. Simmons, Ed.). New Haven: Yale University Press, 1947.

Taylor, J. A. A personality scale of manifest anxiety. Journal of Abnormal and Social Psychology, 1953, 48, 285-290.

Terman, L. M. The measurement of intelligence. Boston: Houghton-Mifflin, 1916.

Thompson, S. The folktale. New York: Holt, Rinehart and Winston, 1946.

Thurber, J. G. The secret life of Walter Mitty. In Fables of our time. New York: Harper, 1940.

Titchener, E. B. Experimental psychology (Vol. I.). New York: Macmillan, 1901.

Tryon, R. C. Predicting individual differences by cluster analysis: Holzinger abilities and MMPI personality attributes. Multivariate Behavioral Research, 1967, 2, 325-348.

Turbayne, C. The myth of metaphor. New Haven: Yale University Press, 1962.

Turner, R. H. Role-taking: process versus conformity. In A. M. Rose (Ed.). Human behavior and social processes. Boston, Houghton Mifflin, 1962. Pp. 20-40.

Turner, V. Dramas, fields, and metaphors. Ithaca, N.Y.: Cornell Unviersity Press, 1974.

Turner, W. S. A re-examination of the two kinds of scientific conjecture. Psychological Record, 1961, 11, 279-298.

Ulett, G. A., Aklpinar, S., & Itil, T. M. Hypnosis: Physiological pharmacological reality. American Journal of Psychiatry, 1972, 128, 799-805.

Ullmann, S. Semantics: An introduction to the science of meaning. Oxford: Blackwell, 1962.

Vaihinger, H. The philosophy of "as-if." London: Kegan-Paul, Trench and Trubner, 1924.

Varendonck, J. The psychology of day dreams. London: George Allen & Unwin, 1921.

Vartanian, A. La Metrie's l'homme machine: A study in the origins of an idea. Princeton: Princeton University Press, 1960.

Ward, C. H., Besck, A. T., Mendleson, M., Mock, J. E., & Erbaugh, J. K. The psychiatric nomenclature: Reasons for diagnostic disagreement, Archives of General Psychiatry, 1962, 7, 198-205.

Welch, L. A behavioristic explanation of the mechanism of suggestion and hypnosis. Journal of Abnormal and Social Psychology, 1947, 42, 359-364.

Werner, H. Comparative psychology of mental development (2nd Ed.). Chicago: Follet, 1948.

Wheelwright, P. E. Metaphor and reality. Bloomington: Indiana University Press, 1962.

White, H. The forms of wildness: Archeology of an idea. In E. Dudley and M. E. Novak (Eds.), The wild man within. Pittsburgh: University of Pittsburgh Press, 1972.

White, H. Interpretation in history. New Literary History, 1972-1973, 4, 281-314.

White, R. M. A preface to the theory of hypnotism. Journal of Abnormal and Social Psychology, 1941, 36, 477-505.

White, R. M., & Shevach, S. Hypnosis and the concept of dissociation. Journal of Abnormal and Social Psychology, 1937, 42, 309-328.

Whorf, B. L. Language, thought and reality: Selected writings. (J. B. Carroll, Ed.) Cambridge, Massachusets: Technology Press of MIT, 1956.

Windelband, W. An introduction to philosophy. London: T. Fisher-Unwin, 1921.

Wirth, L. The ghetto. Chicago: University of Chicago Press, 1928.

Witkin, H. A., Dyk, R. B., Paterson, H. F., Goodenough, D. R., & Karp, S. A. Psychological differentiation. New York: John Wiley, 1962.

Wittgenstein, L. The blue and brown books. Oxford: Basil Blackwell, 1959.

Young, P. C. Hypnotic regression--fact or artifact? Journal of Abnormal and Social Psychology, 1940, 35, 273-278.

Ziegler, F. J., Imboden, J. B., & Rodgers, D. A. Contemporary conversion reactions: III. Diagnostic considerations. Journal of the American Medical Association, 1963, 186, 307-311.

AUTHOR INDEX

Aarne, A., 23
Addison, J., 165
Adler, A., 176, 182
Adler, N., 11, 67, 130,
    202, 204
Akpiner, S., 89
Allen, A.H.B., 76
Allen, V. L., 21, 57, 59,
    99, 103, 231
Allport, G. W., 18, 53, 61
Alverez, A., 175
Anaximander, 17
Andersen, M. L., 8, 49, 54,
    231
Angyral, A., 126
Archer, W., 41, 76
Argyle, M., 52
Aries, P., 206
Aristotle, 17, 191
Arnold, M. B., 83-84
Aronson, E., 57
Arter, J. A., 234
Ashcraft, R., 231
Auden, W. H., 34
Austin, J. L., 179, 208
Axline, V., 80
Bach, G., 80
Bailey, D. E., 3, 7, 10, 47,
    65, 198
Barber, T. X., 8, 28, 49, 94
Barker, R. G., 40
Barrymore, J., 77
Bateson, G., 183
Beck, A. T., 152
Becket, T. A., 221
Bellone, C. J., 112
Benedict, R., 79-80
Benjamin, J. D., 225
Benne, K., 40
Bentham, J., 217, 242
Berggren, D., 236, 245
Berkeley, G., 18
Berne, E., 24-25
Bethel, M., 33
Binet, A., 8

Birdwhistell, R. L., 92
Black, M., 218
Blake, W., 180-181
Bleuler, E., 191, 239-240
Bogardus, E. S., 63
Boring, E. G., 143
Bradley, F. H., 19
Braginsky, B., 154
Braginsky, D., 154
Braid, J., 8, 89
Brenman, M., 73
Bretnall, A. K., 75, 80
Brooks, C., 246
Brown, R., 237
Brunswik, E., 5
Bugenthal, J. F. T., 54
Burgess, E., 4
Burke, E., 218
Burke, K., 34
Burton, R., 185
Byron, Lord, 170, 184
Calvin, J., 120, 162
Cameron, N. A., 55, 80, 171
Campbell, P. N., 235
Cannon, W. B., 195
Carmichael, L., 191
Case, H. W., 75, 80
Cassirer, E., 102
Cassou, J., 177
Cattell, R. B., 194
Cervantes, Miguel de, 167,
    172, 177
Charcot, J. M., 8, 28, 89
Chaucer, G., 64, 142
Chesterton, G. K., 247
Chun, K., 16, 218, 231, 238
Cicero, 120
Coe, W. C., 52, 91, 93, 96,
    169, 229
Cohen, M. R., 179
Colby, B. N., 34
Corn-Becker, F., 74
Crawley, E., 43
Crocker, J. C., 218
Cromwell, O., 164

SUBJECT INDEX

Aesculapean authority,
162-164
Alchemy, 245
Alcoholics Anonymous, 130
American Association for the
Abolition of Involuntary
Hospitalization, 164
American Psychiatric
Association, 152
Antinomian character, 67
Anxiety, 167, 187-198, 209
Anxiety, etymology of,
187-190
Anxiety, trait vs. state,
194-195
Art, modern, 179
"As if" test, 7
As you like it, 228-229
Believing, 169-170
Belletristic psychology,
167-198
Bewitchment, 44
Black Muslim sect, 124
Catholic church, 139
Charisma, of physicians, 163
Chivalry, 173-174
Clinical-statistical
prediction, 7
Cognitive strain, 10, 129-130,
197, 205
Cognitive theory, 10
Cognitive process, use of
metaphor as, 217
Communicating, 233-234
Conduct reorganization,
in religion, 119-121
death-rebirth metaphor,
120-123, 128
and social identity
theory, 122-123
basic themes in, 123-131
systems of, 112-130,
148, 201-216
Constancy, perceptual, 181
Contextualism, 13, 14, 18,
19, 25-30, 32, 33,
199
and hallucinations, 29,
30

and hypnosis, 27-29
and schizophrenia, 26,
27
Conversation, cooperative
principle in, 233-234,
248
Conversion, trigger for,
112-130
Council of Northampton, 221
Criminals, rehabilitation
of, 202
Danger, 113
Dangerous classes, 162
Dangerous individuals, 114,
117
perception by others, 117
Daydreams, 172
Death, 199-200
Death, metaphors of, 201-206
Death metaphors,
classification of,
212-213
Death-rebirth, 123-126, 157
Death, symbolic, 204-205,
213-215
Degradation, 106, 145-147, 215
Delinquency, juvenile, 9
Deviant conduct, 133, 149-165
Diagnosis, 161-164, 227-228
Diagnosis, biases in, 153-156
Diagnosis, reliability of,
152-153, 158
Diagnosis, validity of,
153-154
Diagnostic and Statistical
Manual, 152
Disease concept, history of,
136-143
Dispositional terms, 189-190
Don Quixote, 172-179, 182,
185
Dramaturgical model, 20, 21,
37, 38, 90-92
Dramaturgy, 147
Dying person, role of,
206-207
Dysphonia, case of, 223-224
Ecologies, proximal, 203
distal, 203-205